D1233151

The IDEA MAGAZINE FOR TEACHERS.
MAILBOX.

The Education Center®

2008–2009 YEARBOOK

The Education Center, Inc.
Greensboro, North Carolina

The Mailbox® 2008–2009 Grades 2–3 Yearbook

Managing Editor: *The Mailbox* Magazine: Jennifer Bragg

Editorial Team: Becky S. Andrews, Diane Badden, Kimberley Bruck, Karen A. Brudnak, Chris Curry, Sarah Foreman, Margaret Freed (COVER ARTIST), Tazmen Hansen, Marsha Heim, Lori Z. Henry, Kitty Lowrance, Jennifer Nunn, Mark Rainey, Greg D. Rieves, Hope Rodgers, Eliseo De Jesus Santos II, Rebecca Saunders, Krystle Short Jones, Hope Taylor Spencer, Rachael Traylor, Sharon M. Tresino, Zane Williard

ISBN10 1-56234-923-6
ISBN13 978-156234-923-3
ISSN 1088-5544

The Education Center, Inc.
P.O. Box 9753
Greensboro, NC 27429-0753

Contents

Departments

Language Arts Units

ARTS & CRAFTS

Arts & Crafts

Pencil Pals

Excite students about journal writing with this simple craft! Provide each student with a new, sharpened pencil and three different-colored 12-inch pipe cleaners. To make a pencil pal, a student holds the pipe cleaners at the base of his pencil's eraser and tightly wraps the pipe cleaners around the pencil. He pokes his pencil point into a foam ball; then he removes the pencil. The student gently twists the foam ball onto his pencil's eraser. Then he uses decorative items—such as wiggle eyes, small pom-poms, and feathers—to complete his fancy pencil topper. Invite the student to use his specially designed pencil each time he writes in his journal.

Clever Book Caddies

Recycled cereal boxes make a great place to store students' reading books! Cut the narrow side of a medium-size cereal box at an angle as shown. To make a book holder, a child covers the box with paper and glues a library pocket on one side. The student personalizes the book holder with stickers, magazine pictures, and drawings. Then she stores books for silent reading in the holder. She keeps an index card in the pocket to record the book titles and the number of pages she read.

adapted from an idea by Melanie Guido, St. Francis-St. Stephens School Geneva, NY

I'll always be your Lovebug!

I made this bookmark especially for you Because of all the nice things you say and do.
Happy Grandparents Day!

Buggy Bookmarks

Celebrate National Grandparents Day with this cute keepsake.

Materials for each student:
copy of one of the patterns on page 15
two 4" x 4" squares of colorful tissue paper
jumbo craft stick
6" pipe cleaner
medium-size pom-pom
extra small pom-pom
2 wiggle eyes
fine-tip marker
glue

Steps:
1. Cut two hearts (wings) from the tissue paper and glue them to the top of the craft stick.
2. To make the body, bend the pipe cleaner into a U shape and place the medium pom-pom in the cradle of the pipe cleaner. Crisscross the pipe cleaner's ends and twist them together at the center. Bend the tips to look like antennae.
3. Glue the body on the craft stick between the wings. Then glue on the eyes and the small pom-pom (nose).
4. Write a personal greeting at the bottom of the craft stick.
5. Cut out, fold, and glue the bookmark pocket; then insert the bookmark.

Dad made homemade pumpkin pie.
I said I'd give it a try.
Who knew it would make me cry?
It was salty and quite dry!

Emilio

Revealing a Rhyme

To begin, a child writes a short seasonal poem. He uses a white crayon to carefully copy his poem onto a sheet of white construction paper. Next, he uses a wide brush to paint over the paper with watercolor paints, watching as his words appear. To finish the project, the student trims the paper into a seasonal shape and then glues it onto a sheet of black paper.

adapted from an idea by Marian Chertos
West Michigan Academy of Environmental Science
Walker, MI

"Puzzle-tively" Pleasing Trees

This project not only looks good but will also inspire colorful fall writing! First, students paint mismatched puzzle pieces in seasonal colors. While a child waits for the paint to dry, she trims a piece of brown paper into a tree shape and then glues it onto a sheet of light blue paper. Then the child glues her painted puzzle pieces onto the branches of her tree. The child refers to her art project as she completes a copy of the graphic organizer on page 16; then she uses the details from her organizer to write a paragraph titled "Fall Is a Colorful Season."

Monstrously Sweet Treat Holder

Here's a craft that's more sweet than scary!

Materials for one project:
paper half circle
scrap paper
pipe cleaner
crayons
stapler
hole puncher

Steps:
1. Draw a monster's face in the middle of the half circle. Then add hair around the curved edge.
2. Curl the paper into a cone shape and staple it in place.
3. Trim a piece of scrap paper to make a tag. Write a greeting on the tag; punch a hole in it.
4. Punch a hole on each side of the cone. Thread a pipe cleaner through the holes on the cone and the tag. Twist the ends to hold the pipe cleaner in place.

Mae Purrenhage, St. Ann School, Cadillac, MI

Refrigerator Snowpal

Here's a cool way to remind parents about special school events or inclement weather information. Guide each student to make a magnet as described below. Then write important date reminders or school closing information on a copy of an information card (page 17). Finally, have each student use his snowpal magnet to post a copy of his information card at home.

Materials for each student:
jumbo craft stick
1" felt or foam square
1½" piece of pipe cleaner
orange felt scrap
ribbon
3 buttons
piece of self-adhesive magnetic tape
white paint
paintbrush
fine-tip black marker
glue
scissors

Save the Dates

Dec. 18— Holiday concert
       7 PM, school auditorium

Dec. 23— Winter break begins.

Jan. 5— Winter break ends.

Jan. 16— Snowflake Social
       7 PM, school gym

Jan. 19— Read-a-Thon begins.

Steps:
1. Paint one side of the jumbo craft stick white and then set it aside to dry.
2. When the paint is dry, glue the felt or foam square (hat) to the top of the stick and the piece of pipe cleaner (brim) below the square.
3. Trim from orange felt a small triangle for the nose and glue it on the stick. Then use the marker to draw the snowpal's eyes and mouth.
4. Cut a length of ribbon and tie it around the craft stick.
5. Glue on the buttons and place magnetic tape on the back of the snowpal.

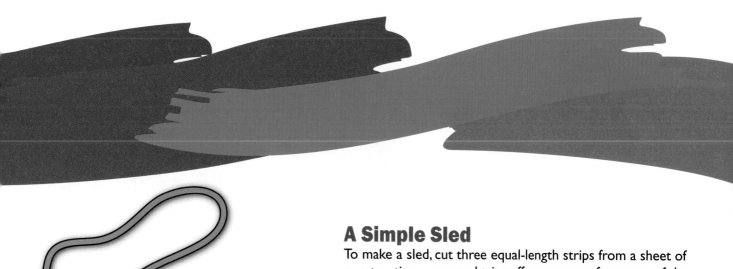

A Simple Sled

To make a sled, cut three equal-length strips from a sheet of construction paper and trim off one corner from two of the strips. Next, cut a 10" x 3" strip from a contrasting sheet of construction paper and personalize it to make a nameplate. Arrange the equal-length strips side by side, leaving a small space between each one as shown. Then glue the nameplate across the top. Finally, add brass fasteners to the nameplate, punch two holes at the top of the sled, and thread yarn through the holes.

Jennifer Mross, Kiel School, Kinnelon, NJ

Snowflake Ornament

This fancy ornament adds beauty to any winter display. Fold three small paper doilies in half and glue all but two halves back to back. Make a loop at one end of a pipe cleaner and slide four beads toward the loop. Place the pipe cleaner in the center of the doilies and then glue the remaining halves together. Slide several more beads on the open end of the pipe cleaner. Then twist that end to secure the beads.

Arts & Crafts

"Un-frog-gettable" Valentine Holder

Students are sure to leap for this cute card collector! Ask your cafeteria director to save some of the large cans for you.

Lynsia Sprouse, Follett Elementary, Follett, TX

Materials for each student:
large, empty coffee can (or a gallon-vegetable or fruit can)
foot and arm templates (patterns on page 18)
3 sheets of green construction paper
strip of green bulletin board paper
construction paper scraps (red, white, pink)
black crayon
scissors
glue

Steps:
1. Wrap the bulletin board paper around the can and glue it in place. Fold any paper taller than the can over the top rim.
2. On green construction paper, trace each foot and arm template twice; then cut out the shapes.
3. To create the legs, fold another sheet of green construction paper in half and cut out a half-heart shape along the open side. Glue one foot on the pointed end of each leg; then glue the legs to the back of the can.
4. Accordion-fold the base of each arm; glue the arms on the front of the can.
5. Cut out and personalize a red paper heart. Glue it on the front of the can.
6. Trim two white circles and draw a black dot on each one to make eyes. Glue each eye onto a slightly larger green circle before gluing both eyes on a large green circle (head). Draw a nose and mouth, then glue the head on the can. Use paper scraps to add other decorations as desired.

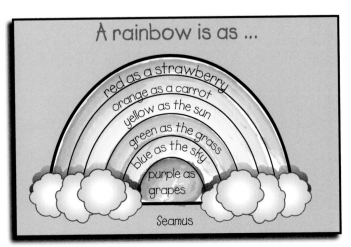

Rainbow Writing

To make this colorful craft, cut out an enlarged copy of the rainbow pattern from page 18. On each arc, use a crayon to write a simile about the corresponding color word to complete the phrase "A rainbow is as…" Then paint over each arc with a watercolor that matches the color word. Next, glue the rainbow to a sheet of light blue construction paper, label it as shown, and add cotton balls or cotton batting to make clouds.

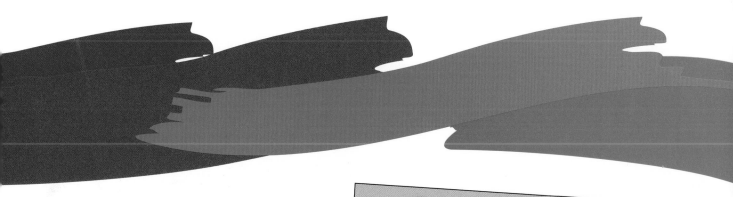

Dandelion Wishes

To inspire your students' creative writing, have them create dandelion cards using the directions below. Then have each student write on her card a brief description of a wish she would make with her flower.

Materials for each student:

2½ yards of white yarn	scissors
6" length of white yarn	glue
4" piece of green pipe cleaner	crayons
half sheet of construction paper	

Steps:

1. To make the flower, loosely wrap the long piece of yarn 20 times around three fingers.
2. Carefully slip the wrapped yarn off your fingers and pinch it in the middle, creating loops on each side.
3. Tie the middle with the short piece of yarn. Trim the excess yarn.
4. Cut each loop in half and shake the yarn.
5. Glue the flower and the pipe cleaner on the construction paper as shown. Use a crayon to draw leaves.

Jane Walsh, Sweetwater Elementary, Lithia Springs, GA

My Wish

I would wish for a brand-new puppy. I would name her Carleigh, and she would be my best friend.

by Jaida

Bunny Basket

Turn a drinking cup into a basket for collecting springtime treats. To begin, a student colors the handle, nose, and ear patterns on a copy of page 19 and then cuts out all the patterns. Next, he glues the eyes and nose on the cup as shown. The child uses a permanent marker to draw a mouth; then he tapes the ears and handle to the inside of the cup. Finally, he glues a cotton ball tail to the back of the cup. If desired, have each student fill his basket with cellophane grass or shredded paper.

Arts & Crafts

Editing Visors

Use these fun visors to encourage students to edit their work before turning it in. Give each student a copy of page 20 and a long pipe cleaner. Have each child personalize his editing visor and cut it out. Instruct him to push a pencil point through the circles on the visor and then gently thread each end of the pipe cleaner through a hole. Next, have the student put on his visor and adjust the fit by sliding the pipe cleaner and bending back the ends to secure it in place. When it is editing time, have each student sport his visor and take on the role of editor.

Jennifer Garvey, The Peck School, Morristown, NJ

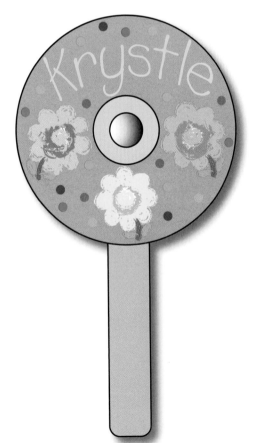

Garden Markers

Mark students' planting areas in your school's flower garden using recycled CDs. Collect a class supply of old CDs and have parents donate self-sticking CD labels. Have each child personalize a label using crayons (the wax repels rain) and place it on the CD. Then help the student hot-glue a craft stick to the back of the CD. Finally, have each student plant his seeds in an assigned area of your school or class garden and label his area with his marker. Come fall, your students will easily identify the flowers that sprouted from the seeds they planted.

Sylvia Yeaton, Cape Cod Hill School, New Sharon, ME

Bookmark Pocket Pattern

Use with “Buggy Bookmarks” on page 7.

Glue.

I made this bookmark especially for you
Because of all the nice things you say and do.

Happy Grandparents Day!

To:

From:

TEC43038

Glue.

I made this bookmark especially for you
Because of all the nice things you say and do.

Happy Grandparents Day!

To:

From:

TEC43038

Fall Is a Colorful Season

List the colors you see on your tree.

Write words that describe the colors.

List things that the colors remind you of.

©The Mailbox® • TEC43039 • Oct./Nov. 2008

Fall Is a Colorful Season

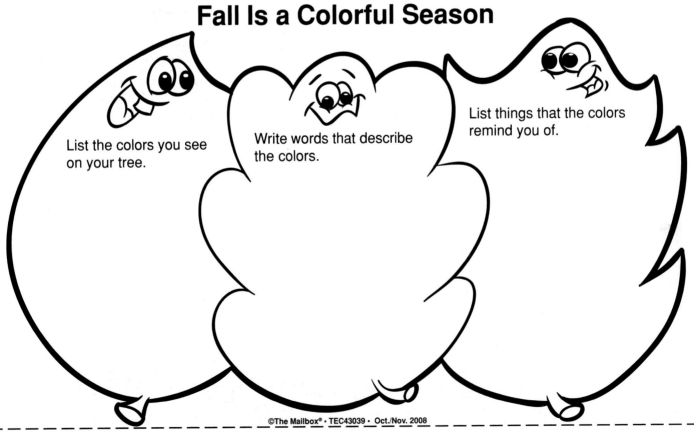

List the colors you see on your tree.

Write words that describe the colors.

List things that the colors remind you of.

©The Mailbox® • TEC43039 • Oct./Nov. 2008

Note to the teacher: Use with "'Puzzle-tively' Pleasing Trees" on page 9.

Save the Dates

PLACE SNOWPAL MAGNET HERE.

TEC43040

Inclement Weather and Emergency School Closing Information

PLACE SNOWPAL MAGNET HERE.

TEC43040

Frog Patterns

Use with "'Un-frog-gettable' Valentine Holder" on page 12.

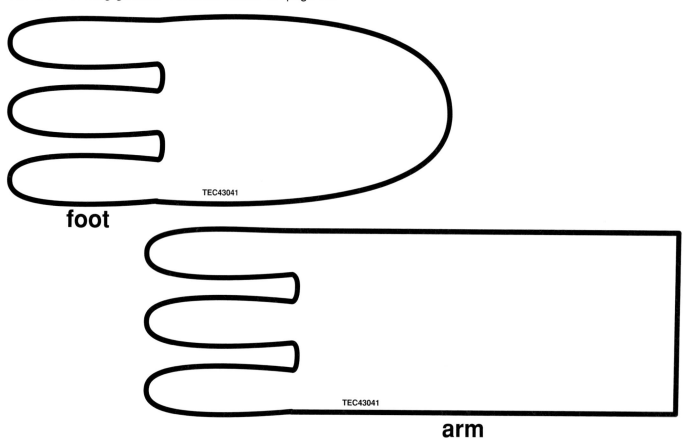

foot

TEC43041

arm

TEC43041

Rainbow Pattern

Use with "Rainbow Writing" on page 12.

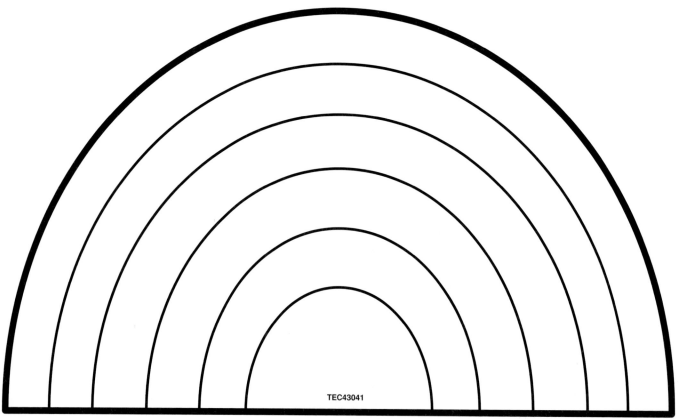

TEC43041

eyes

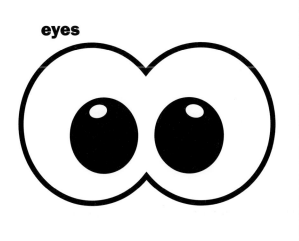

handle

nose

ear

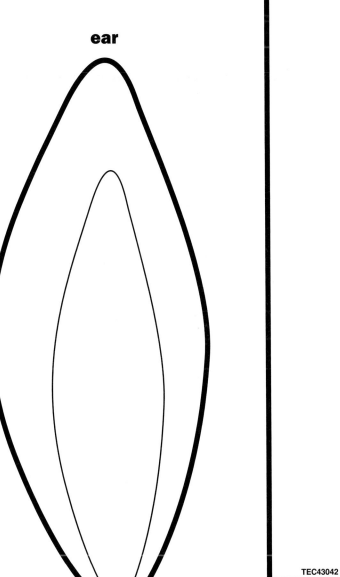

ear

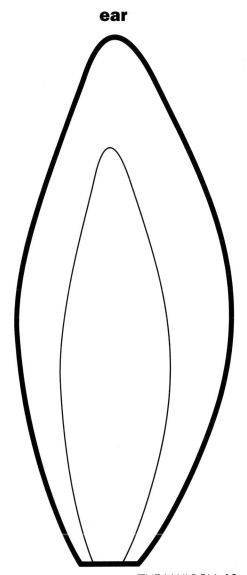

TEC43042

Editing Visor Pattern

Use with "Editing Visors" on page 14.

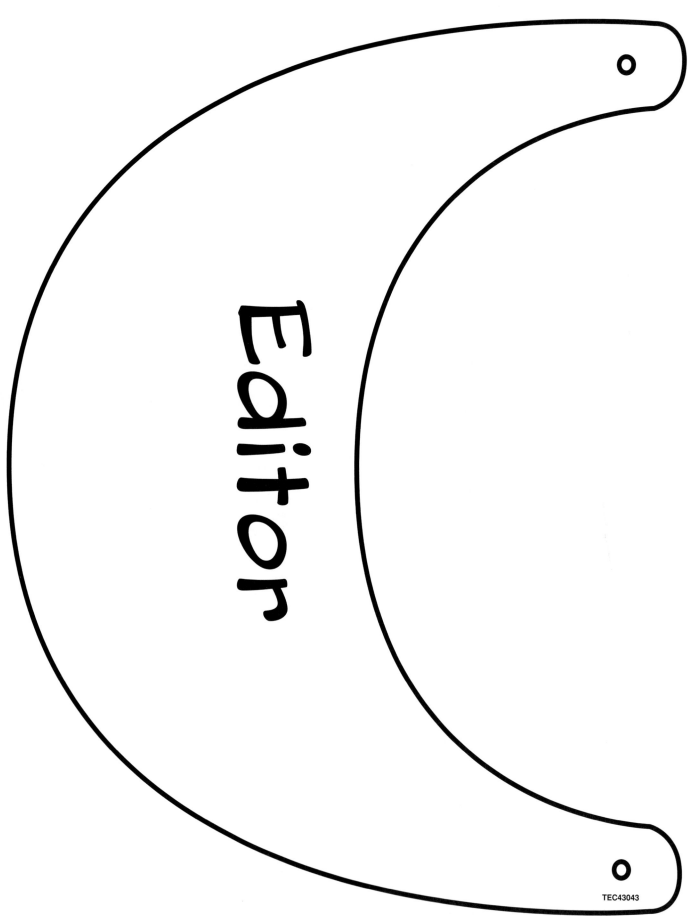

Editor

TEC43043

CELEBRATE THE SEASON!

Celebrate the Season!

Fact

James Madison is known as the father of the Constitution.

Ben Franklin was the oldest man to sign the Constitution.

There were 55 delegates at the Constitutional Convention.

The Constitution was signed on September 17, 1787.

The articles of the Constitution divide the U.S. government into three branches.

The first ten amendments to the Constitution are called the Bill of Rights.

George Washington was the president of the Constitutional Convention.

Opinion

The Constitution is more important today than it was in 1787.

It was not easy to write the Constitution.

George Washington was a good president for the convention.

Ben Franklin was too old to sign the Constitution.

People should be proud of the Constitution.

Contemplating the Constitution
Fact or opinion

A child cuts apart the header cards and sentence strips on his copy of page 33. After he sorts the strips into facts and opinions, he folds a 9" x 12" sheet of construction paper in half vertically to form two sections. He glues one header card at the top of each section and then glues each sentence strip below its matching header card. When the glue is dry, the child rolls his paper from the top and bottom until the rolls meet in the middle. He ties a length of ribbon around his completed project.

Apple-Pickin' Time
Math fact review

For this fresh fall game, tape flash cards on the board. Write a different letter on each of several apple cutouts and then tape each cutout atop one of the flash cards. To play, divide the class into teams and give each team a basket. Call on a team to "pick" an apple by calling out its letter. Lift up the apple to reveal the problem. If the team gives the correct answer, place the apple in the team's basket. If the team gives an incorrect answer, re-cover the flash card. Continue until all the apples have been "picked." The team with the most apples wins.

Kimberly Barnhill, North Highlands Elementary, Shreveport, LA

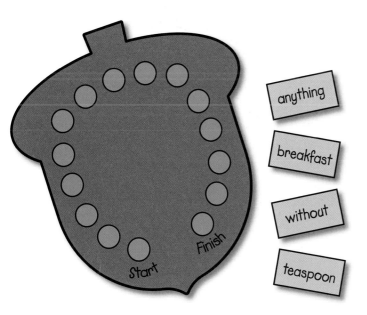

Gathering Acorns
Spelling

In advance, make a gameboard by cutting a large acorn out of poster board. Use adhesive dots to make a simple path around the border of the cutout and then label one dot "Start" and another "Finish" as shown. Program each of a supply of cards with a different spelling word. To play, Player 1 draws a card and reads the word aloud. Player 2 spells the word. Player 1 checks the spelling and, if the word is spelled correctly, Player 2 moves her game marker ahead one space. If the word is spelled incorrectly, Player 2 remains in place. Players continue taking turns until one player reaches the finish space and wins the game.

Debbie Berris, Poinciana Day School, West Palm Beach, FL

Tools for Work
Place value

A child cuts apart the cards on his copy of page 34. He places each crayon below the box that matches the value of its underlined digit. Then he tucks each set of cards into a separate resealable plastic bag.

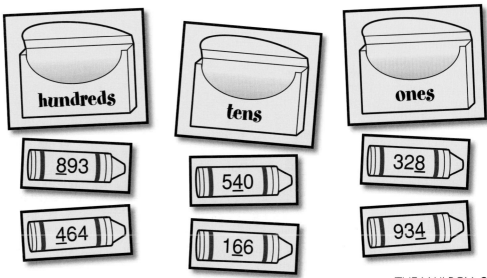

Celebrate the Season!

Vote for me and I will help you.

Vote for My Teacher

My teacher would be a great president. Ms. Cunningham is very fair. She treats everyone the same way. Ms. Cunningham is truthful too. When she says that we will do something, we do it. Ms. Cunningham helps people who need help. She can help you if you forget something important, if you hurt yourself, and especially if you can't do your math. Vote for my teacher for president!

Presidential Qualities

honest	kind
fair	helpful
smart	caring
truthful	

Vote for My Teacher!

Persuasive writing

Start this timely activity with a class discussion of the qualities that make a good president. As students name them, list each quality on the board. Next, encourage each student to imagine that you are running for president. Then direct him to refer to the list as he writes a paragraph titled "Vote for My Teacher." Provide time for each student to illustrate his paragraph and then share his work aloud.

Lisa Cunningham, Joel E. Barber C–5 School, Lebanon, MO

An Eight-Legged Review
Contractions

To make a spider's body, a student traces on construction paper a copy of the pattern from page 35. She cuts out the pattern and labels it with the word *not*. Next, the student folds eight 1" x 8" paper strips in half and unfolds them. She glues four strips (legs) on each side of the spider's body. Then she writes on each leg section closest to the body a word that can be combined with *not* to make a contraction. She writes the corresponding contraction on the outer section of the leg. To complete the spider, the student adds wiggle eyes or other decorations.

based on an idea by Brooke Beverly, Dudley Elementary, Dudley, MA

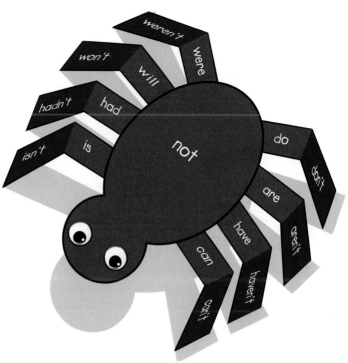

Flavor A:
Caramel

Flavor B:
Cheese

Flavor C:
Butter

Pop! Pop! Popcorn!
Organizing data

Gather samples of three different flavors of popcorn and then guide each child to complete the first step on a copy of page 36. Provide samples of all three flavors to each student; then ask him to decide which flavor he prefers. In turn, read the name of each flavor and have students raise their hands to show their preferences. With students' help, count the raised hands; then guide each student to record the matching number of tally marks on his paper. Finally, have each child use the data to complete the page.

Cali Bendel, Franklin Arts Academy, Mesa, AZ

Jolly Jack-o'-Lanterns
Place value

To make a jack-o'-lantern, a student trims a sheet of orange construction paper into a pumpkin shape. She also cuts a stem from green paper, writes a number on it, and glues the stem on the pumpkin. Next, she traces the patterns from a copy of page 35 to make eyes, a nose, and a mouth. She writes the expanded form of the number on the mouth, cuts out the tracings, and then glues the pieces on her pumpkin. **For an added challenge,** the student cuts a piece of green paper into a long vine shape and writes on it the number in word form. Then she glues the vine to her pumpkin.

Missy Carter, Community R-VI Elementary, Laddonia, MO

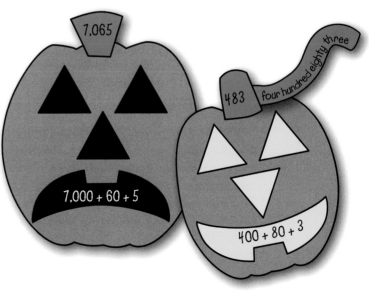

	Penny Pigpen								
1	2	3	4	5	6	7	8	9	10
13	14	15	16	17	18	19			20
24	25	26	27	28	29			30	
34	35	36	37	38	39		40		
44	45	46	47	48	49	50			
54	55	56	57	58	59	60			
	65	66	67	68	69	70			
	75	76	77	78	79	80			
	85	86	87	88	89	90			
	95	96	97	98	99	100			

TEC43040

Pennies for Charity
Counting coins, community service

Share the gift of giving with this class project. In advance, make a class bank by wrapping pink paper around a large container and taping it in place. Color a copy of the pig pattern on page 37, cut it out, and glue it on the container.

To start the project, explain the importance of giving and have the class choose a charity it would like to donate to. Invite students to collect pennies and put them in the bank. At the end of two weeks, divide the class into groups and give each group some pennies and a copy of the recording sheet on page 37. Guide each group to color a square for every penny they have (provide more sheets as needed). Collect the sheets and lead the class in counting by hundreds to find the total number of pennies. Finally, give students coin wrappers and help them wrap the pennies before they donate the money to the charity.

Karen Dufault, Killdeer Public School, Killdeer, ND

Skating Through the Year
Writing, self-evaluation

Invite students to take stock of their academic progress with this reflective activity. Write on the board the questions shown and direct each child to write his answers in complete sentences on a sheet of paper. Next, have each student trim his paper into the shape of an ice-skating pond and glue it onto a sheet of construction paper. Finally, instruct the child to color and cut out a copy of the ice skates from page 38, glue the cutout onto his paper, and title the paper as shown.

Jennifer Mross, Kiel Elementary, Kinnelon, NJ

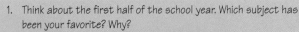

1. Think about the first half of the school year. Which subject has been your favorite? Why?
2. Which subjects do you think are your best? Why?
3. Which subjects do you think need improvement? Why?
4. What is your favorite memory from the first half of the year?
5. Think about the second half of the school year. What are you looking forward to?

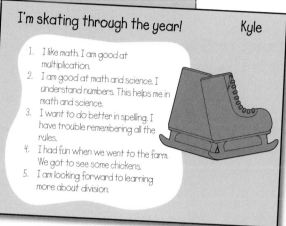

I'm skating through the year!   Kyle

1. I like math. I am good at multiplication.
2. I am good at math and science. I understand numbers. This helps me in math and science.
3. I want to do better in spelling. I have trouble remembering all the rules.
4. I had fun when we went to the farm. We got to see some chickens.
5. I am looking forward to learning more about division.

New Year's Party Pairs

Remember: move across and then up.

(5, 3)

New Year's Party Pairs
Mapping coordinates

To prepare this partner game, copy and cut apart the cards from page 39. Place the cards at a center with a laminated copy of the gameboard from page 40 and two different-colored dry-erase markers. To play the game, Player 1 stacks the cards facedown. She draws a card and marks the matching point with a dot. Player 2 confirms her answer and, if it is correct, Player 1 leaves her dot in place. If the answer is incorrect, Player 1 wipes off her dot. Players continue taking turns until one player marks three dots in a row either vertically, horizontally, or diagonally and wins the round.

Crack Open a Cookie!
Narrative writing

Celebrate Chinese New Year with these story prompts. To prepare, make enough copies of the fortune strips from page 38 so each child has one; then cut out and fold each strip and put them in a bag. Next, have each child draw one strip and use the prompt to write and illustrate a narrative paragraph. Then direct the child to fold a four-inch tan circle in half twice and staple his strip inside it as shown. Finally, have him staple his fortune cookie onto the top corner of his paper and display the projects around the room.

adapted from an idea by Jennifer Mendez, Chapel Trail Elementary
Pembroke Pines, FL

You will win a lot of money.

Michael

My fortune says I will win a lot of money! I am going to buy some new games for my computer. Then I will buy some plane tickets so my family can go to the beach. We will play in the water and build sand castles. I will give some of my money to Bobby. I can't wait to win my money!

Celebrate the Season!

Love to Shop!
Money

A few weeks before Valentine's Day, collect materials to make a class supply of valentine card bags, such as paper lunch bags, heart-shaped stickers, foam hearts, doilies, and glitter pens; then label each set of items with a different price. Display a poster like the one shown, listing the items and their prices. Use a permanent marker to label a resealable plastic bag (wallet) for each child.

Give each child his wallet and tell the class that over the next few weeks each student will earn play money for responsible behaviors. Also explain that they should store their earned money in their wallets to later use to purchase supplies for their valentine card bags. Then, just before Valentine's Day, place the supplies on a table (store). Have each student total his money and refer to the poster to make a list of supplies he wants to purchase. Direct him to calculate the total for his supplies and determine the amount of change he should receive. Have him bring his list and money when he collects his supplies at the store. Then provide time for students to decorate their bags.

Trisha Mohrhusen, Seaford Elementary, Seaford, VA

For Sale

lunch bag = $1.00
(Everyone must purchase a bag.)
stickers = $0.25 each
foam hearts = $0.50 each
doilies = $0.75
glitter pen = $0.75

Madam C. J. Walker was a salesperson and business owner. She sold hair care products. She also trained other women to sell these products. Many people believe that she was the first African American woman to become a millionaire! She left most of her money to charities when she died.

Madam C. J. Walker

1867 – 1919

She was the daughter of former slaves. She lost a lot of her hair in the 1890s. This made her interested in hair care products.

Studying Superstars
Writing, researching

Here's a great way to display research for Black History Month, Presidents' Day, or Women's History Month. After each student gathers information on a chosen individual, he writes on a copy of the star pattern from page 41 a paragraph about the individual's contributions. Next, the child writes the individual's name near the top of a rectangular paper strip. He glues a photo or illustration of the individual beneath the name and then writes below the picture fun facts about the individual. Post each strip under the corresponding star on a board titled "[February or March] Superstars."

Nanci Brochhagen, Willow Road School, Franklin Square, NY

A Lot to List
Poetry

Include a poetry-writing activity on the 100th day of school. Guide the class to name ten things that describe what they love about school. On a sheet of chart paper, make a list poem like the one shown by writing the number 10 in front of each item named. If desired, assign student pairs or small groups one line of the poem to illustrate. Then glue the illustrations around the poem.

Christina Terry, Inman Elementary, Inman, SC

100 Things We Love About School
10 readers' theater plays
10 pizza and chocolate milk lunches
10 freewriting sessions
10 new crayons
10 perfect recess days
10 Magic Tree House books
10 chances to work with a friend
10 cool science investigations
10 guest readers
10 homework-free nights

Golden Opportunity
Fractions of a set

To give your lively leprechauns hands-on practice with fractions, have each student cut apart a copy of the coin patterns on page 42 and place the cutouts in a paper cup. Direct each child to place his hand atop the cup, gently shake it, and then carefully empty the cup on his desktop. Have him write on another sheet of paper the fraction of the coins that landed heads up; then have him write the fraction of the coins that are heads down. Instruct the child to return the coins to the cup and repeat the process four more times. Finally, have the student write at least three sentences about his results.

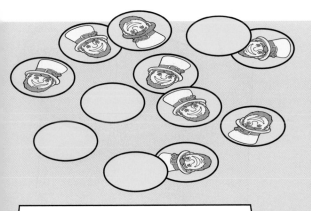

Heads Up $\frac{8}{12}$ Heads Down $\frac{4}{12}$

Goodbye, Winter— Hello, Spring!
Graphs

Use the change of seasons as the topic of a graphing investigation. First, lead students in a discussion of the things they enjoy in winter and spring. With students' help, choose three answers for each season and write them on tally charts as shown. Have students raise their hands to indicate what they will miss most about winter and what they look forward to most in spring; record the results on the tally charts. Next, direct each student to use two copies of the pictograph recording sheet on page 42 to draw graphs that represent each set of data. Finally, instruct each child to write on the back of her papers a sentence about each graph, comparing her personal choices to the results of the whole class.

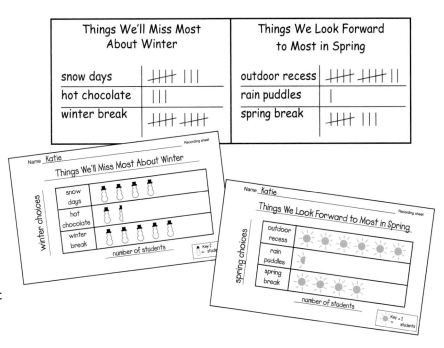

Things We'll Miss Most About Winter	
snow days	‖‖‖ |||
hot chocolate	|||
winter break	‖‖‖ ‖‖‖

Things We Look Forward to Most in Spring	
outdoor recess	‖‖‖ ‖‖‖ ||
rain puddles		
spring break	‖‖‖ |||

Celebrate the Season!

"Eggs-cellent" Attributes
Solid figures

For this project, have each child cut out a copy of the egg and chick patterns on page 43. Next, direct the student to write on the egg two or more sentences that describe a solid figure, followed by the question "What am I?" Instruct the child to write the figure's name on the chick and then color the cutouts. To assemble the egg, have the child fold back the tab on the chick and glue it onto the back of his egg as shown.

adapted from an idea by Sherri McWhorter
Hephzibah Elementary, Hephzibah, GA

I have eight corners.
I have six faces that are each the same size.
What am I?

a cube

light +
+ light

door +
+ door

house +
+ house

A Tisket, a Tasket
Compound words

This easy-to-prepare center helps students form compound words. Cut apart a copy of the egg cards on page 43 and display them at a center, along with three baskets or other containers labeled as shown. A child reads the word on each card and then sorts it into the corresponding basket. After she has sorted the cards, the child writes on a sheet of paper a list of the compound words she made.

Brooke Beverly, Dudley Elementary, Oxford, MA

Bags of Beans
Probability

Celebrate spring with this sweet partner activity. A student cuts apart a copy of the probability cards on page 44, keeps four cards, and gives four to his partner. Next, each student folds a sheet of paper into four equal sections and glues a card onto the bottom of each section. Above each card he draws a bag of jelly beans to match the description on the card. Then the partners share their drawings with each other and explain how each drawing matches its description.

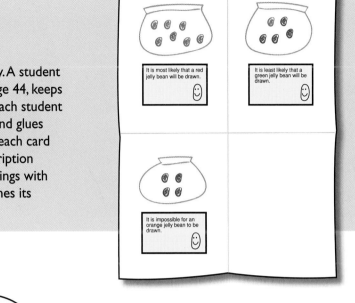

The sad butterfly flew over the pond. He saw the frogs and ducks playing. He wanted to play too, so he stopped. Soon all the friends were playing hide-and-seek. The butterfly was happy.

Janie

Beautiful Butterflies
Narrative writing

To prepare, put small amounts of paint in shallow containers. A child cuts out the butterfly pattern from a copy of page 44 and traces it on white or light-colored construction paper. Then she cuts out the tracing and decorates it by making thumbprints with the paint. She continues painting until she achieves a desired effect. While the paint dries, the child writes a short story on the butterfly pattern. Then she glues the story onto the back of her painting.

Amy Emmons, Enon Elementary, Franklinton, LA

slide   turn   flip   turn   slide

Twisting Tulips
Flips, slides, and turns

This quick idea helps students' geometry skills bloom. To begin, each child makes a simple tulip cutout. He places the cutout on the left end of a sentence strip and traces it. Then he flips, slides, and turns the cutout across the strip, as desired, tracing the cutout each time. He labels each movement along the bottom of the strip and then colors his paper.

Poetry by the Sea
Writing couplets

Have each pair of students cut apart a copy of the cards on page 45. Next, direct the students to choose a card, glue it to their paper, and write a list of words that rhyme with the word on the card. Have the partners refer to the list as they write a couplet using the word. Instruct students to continue with three or more of the remaining cards. To publish their work, have each pair copy its edited couplets on a sheet of paper. Then guide partners to draw seashells and other beachy items for the border. Display their work on a board titled "Poetry by the Sea."

adapted from an idea by Genevieve Petrillo School 10, Belleville, NJ

Summer Schedule
Elapsed time

To begin this camp-themed activity, have each child cut apart a copy of the cards from page 46. Direct her to read each camp activity card and glue the appropriate ending time card on it. **To extend the activity,** have the child order the cards from the beginning of the day to the end, glue the cards to a sheet of paper, and use the ordered cards to write a schedule for the day.

adapted from an idea by Jean Erickson, Milwaukee, WI

Watching Over Words
Reviewing parts of speech

Generate a seasonal word bank with help from your students. To begin, program copies of the pelican pattern from page 45 with different parts of speech. Color and cut out the pelicans and display them in a location easily accessible to students. Next, cut brown construction paper perches and mount one under each pelican. Program a large sun cutout with a summer topic, such as the beach or vacation, and add it to the display. Invite students to write corresponding words on each perch. Then have students refer to the word bank as they write journal entries and complete other assignments.

adapted from an idea by Kathryn Davenport, Partin Elementary, Oviedo, FL

Turn to pages 47–52 for seasonal practice pages.

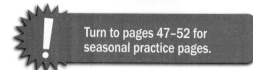

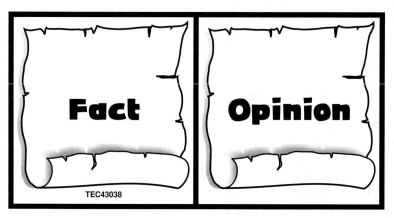

Fact   **Opinion**

TEC43038

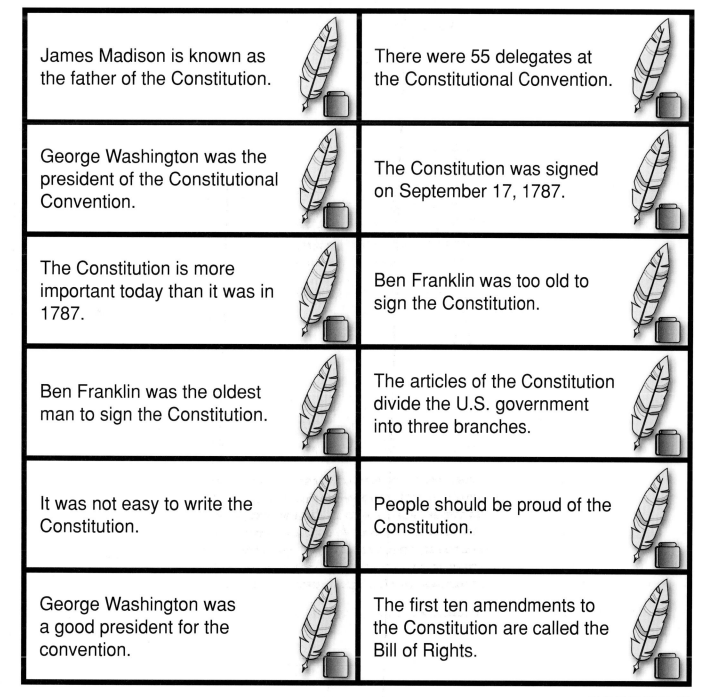

James Madison is known as the father of the Constitution.

There were 55 delegates at the Constitutional Convention.

George Washington was the president of the Constitutional Convention.

The Constitution was signed on September 17, 1787.

The Constitution is more important today than it was in 1787.

Ben Franklin was too old to sign the Constitution.

Ben Franklin was the oldest man to sign the Constitution.

The articles of the Constitution divide the U.S. government into three branches.

It was not easy to write the Constitution.

People should be proud of the Constitution.

George Washington was a good president for the convention.

The first ten amendments to the Constitution are called the Bill of Rights.

Box and Crayon Cards

Use with "Tools for Work" on page 23.

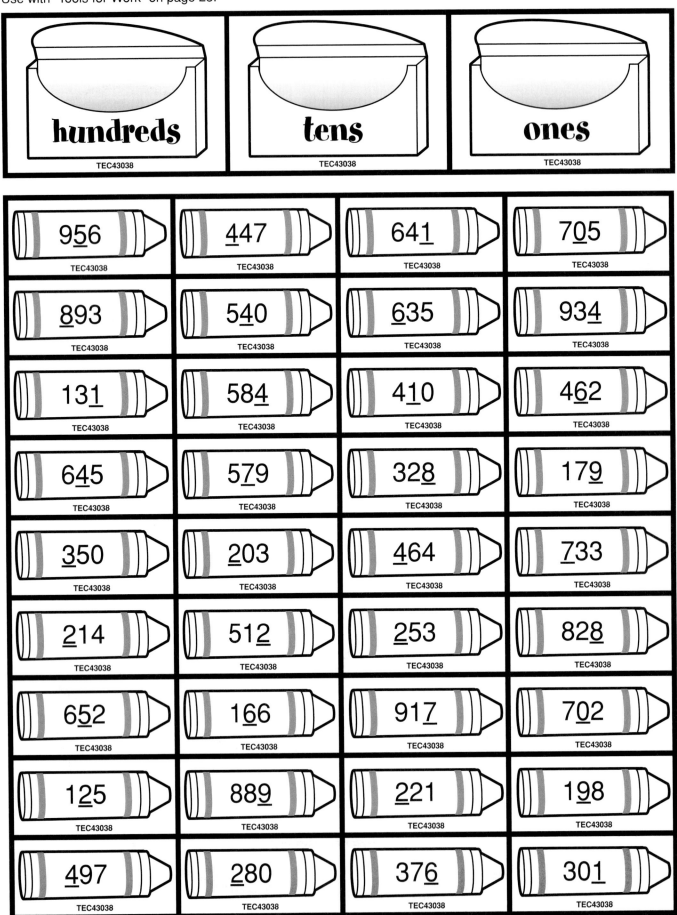

hundreds   TEC43038

tens   TEC43038

ones   TEC43038

9<u>5</u>6	<u>4</u>47	64<u>1</u>	7<u>0</u>5
<u>8</u>93	5<u>4</u>0	<u>6</u>35	93<u>4</u>
131	58<u>4</u>	4<u>1</u>0	4<u>6</u>2
6<u>4</u>5	5<u>7</u>9	32<u>8</u>	17<u>9</u>
<u>3</u>50	<u>2</u>03	<u>4</u>64	<u>7</u>33
<u>2</u>14	51<u>2</u>	<u>2</u>53	82<u>8</u>
6<u>5</u>2	1<u>6</u>6	91<u>7</u>	7<u>0</u>2
1<u>2</u>5	88<u>9</u>	<u>2</u>21	1<u>9</u>8
<u>4</u>97	<u>2</u>80	37<u>6</u>	30<u>1</u>

Spider Body Pattern

Use with "An Eight-Legged Review" on page 25.

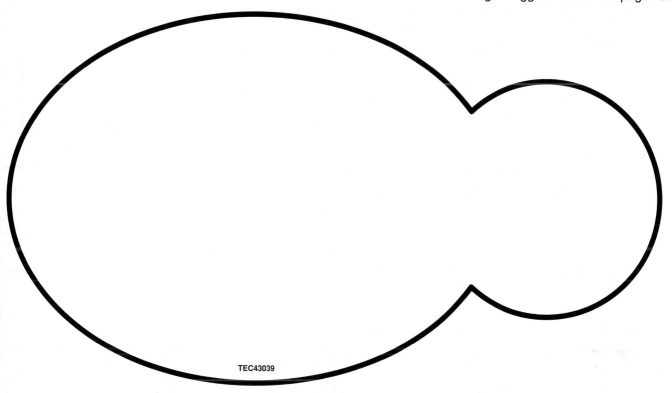

TEC43039

Pumpkin Patterns

Use with "Jolly Jack-o'-Lanterns" on page 25.

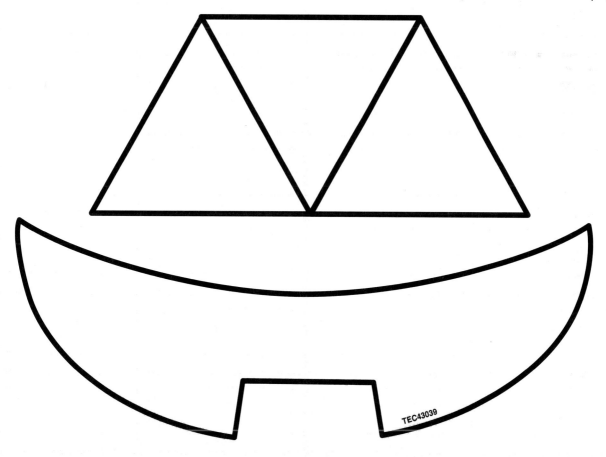

TEC43039

Pop! Pop! Popcorn!

1. Write the names of the popcorn flavors.
   Circle the one you think most people will like.

   Flavor A: _____

   Flavor B: _____

   Flavor C: _____

2. Draw a tally mark for each choice.

Flavor A	
Flavor B	
Flavor C	

3. Complete the bar graph.
   Use the information on the tally chart above to help you.

Our Favorite Popcorn Flavors

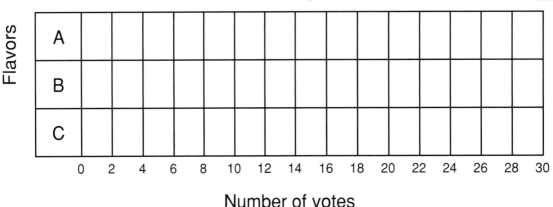

Number of votes

4. Was your prediction correct? _____

   Explain. _____

   _____

   _____

TEC43040

Penny Pigpen

1	2	3	4	5	6	7	8	9	10
11	12	13	14	15	16	17	18	19	20
21	22	23	24	25	26	27	28	29	30
31	32	33	34	35	36	37	38	39	40
41	42	43	44	45	46	47	48	49	50
51	52	53	54	55	56	57	58	59	60
61	62	63	64	65	66	67	68	69	70
71	72	73	74	75	76	77	78	79	80
81	82	83	84	85	86	87	88	89	90
91	92	93	94	95	96	97	98	99	100

TEC43040

Ice Skate Patterns
Use with "Skating Through the Year" on page 27.

TEC43040

Fortune Strips
Use with "Crack Open a Cookie!" on page 27.

You will meet your favorite television star. TEC43040	You will trade places with your teacher for one day. TEC43040
You will travel to another state. TEC43040	You will travel to the moon. TEC43040
You will win a lot of money. TEC43040	You and your family will move to a new town. TEC43040
You will meet a new friend who is very different from you. TEC43040	You will meet a genie who gives you three wishes. TEC43040

Use with "New Year's Party Pairs" on page 27.

(0, 0)	(1, 3)	(3, 0)	(4, 3)
(0, 1)	(1, 4)	(3, 1)	(4, 4)
(0, 2)	(1, 5)	(3, 2)	(4, 5)
(0, 3)	(2, 0)	(3, 3)	(5, 0)
(0, 4)	(2, 1)	(3, 4)	(5, 1)
(0, 5)	(2, 2)	(3, 5)	(5, 2)
(1, 0)	(2, 3)	(4, 0)	(5, 3)
(1, 1)	(2, 4)	(4, 1)	(5, 4)
(1, 2)	(2, 5)	(4, 2)	(5, 5)

TEC43040

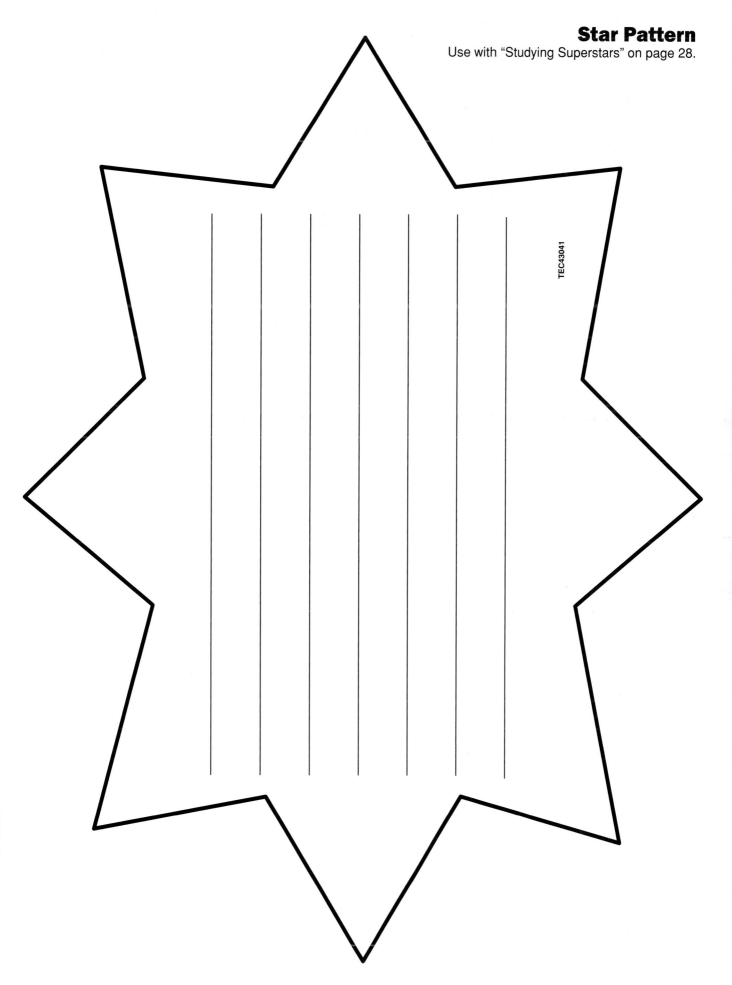

TEC43041

Coin Patterns

Use with "Golden Opportunity" on page 29.

Name _____ Recording sheet

_____

Key
=

Note to the teacher: Use with "Goodbye, Winter—Hello, Spring!" on page 29.

TEC43042

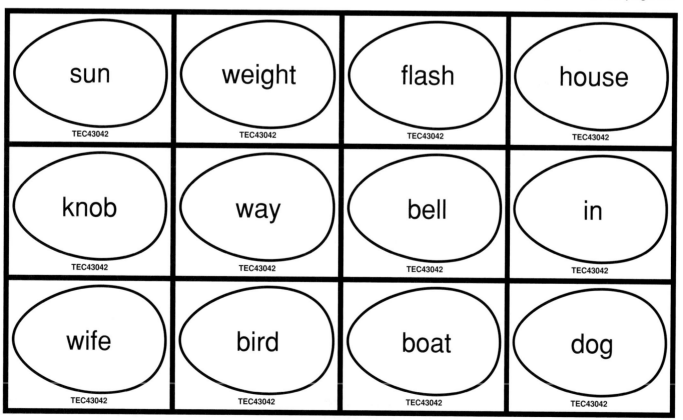

sun	weight	flash	house
TEC43042	TEC43042	TEC43042	TEC43042
knob	way	bell	in
TEC43042	TEC43042	TEC43042	TEC43042
wife	bird	boat	dog
TEC43042	TEC43042	TEC43042	TEC43042

Probability Cards

Use with "Bags of Beans" on page 31.

It is most likely that a red jelly bean will be drawn. TEC43042	It is most likely that a purple jelly bean will be drawn. TEC43042	It is most likely that a yellow jelly bean will be drawn. TEC43042
It is least likely that a yellow jelly bean will be drawn. TEC43042	It is least likely that a green jelly bean will be drawn. TEC43042	It is least likely that a purple jelly bean will be drawn. TEC43042
It is certain that a green jelly bean will be drawn. TEC43042	It is impossible for an orange jelly bean to be drawn. TEC43042	

Butterfly Pattern

Use with "Beautiful Butterflies" on page 31.

TEC43042

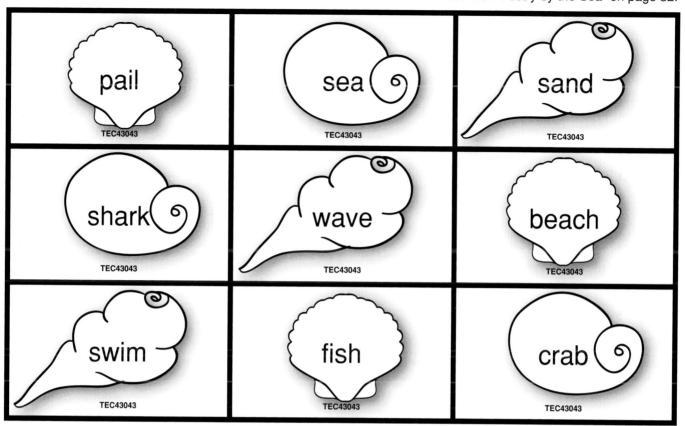

pail — TEC43043

sea — TEC43043

sand — TEC43043

shark — TEC43043

wave — TEC43043

beach — TEC43043

swim — TEC43043

fish — TEC43043

crab — TEC43043

Pelican Pattern

Use with "Watching Over Words" on page 32.

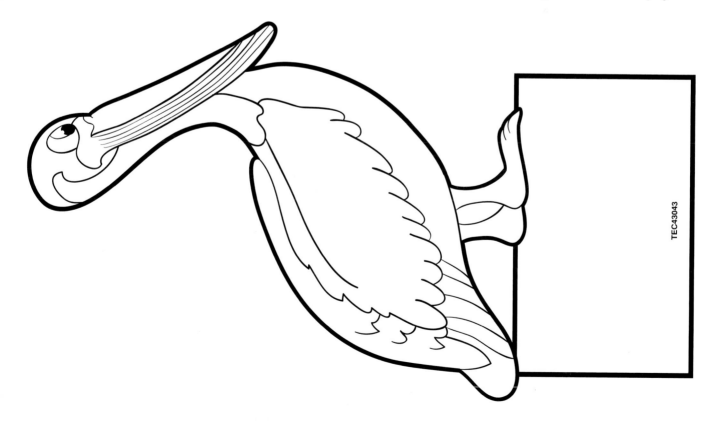

TEC43043

Camp Activity and Ending Time Cards

Use with "Summer Schedule" on page 32.

Camp Cool

D. Snack lasts for 15 minutes.

start time

3:00 PM

end time

TEC43043

Camp Cool

C. Arts and crafts last for 50 minutes.

start time

11:00 AM

end time

TEC43043

Camp Cool

B. Boating safety lasts for 1 hour and 30 minutes.

start time

12:25 PM

end time

TEC43043

Camp Cool

A. Outdoor games last for 1 hour and 15 minutes.

start time

9:45 AM

end time

TEC43043

Camp Cool

H. Free swim lasts for 1 hour and 5 minutes.

start time

1:55 PM

end time

TEC43043

Camp Cool

G. Music lasts for 45 minutes.

start time

9:00 AM

end time

TEC43043

Camp Cool

F. Sing-along lasts for 20 minutes.

start time

3:15 PM

end time

TEC43043

Camp Cool

E. Lunch lasts for 35 minutes.

start time

11:50 AM

end time

TEC43043

11:00 AM
TEC43043

3:00 PM
TEC43043

11:50 AM
TEC43043

9:45 AM
TEC43043

1:55 PM
TEC43043

3:35 PM
TEC43043

3:15 PM
TEC43043

12:25 PM
TEC43043

Fall Funnies

To solve the first riddle, cut off Row 1 below.
Order the numbers. Glue them in order on Pencil 1.
Repeat the steps with each of the rows and pencils.

1. Why do magicians do so well in school?

Pencil 1

2. Where do you go to learn how to make ice cream?

Pencil 2

3. What should you do if you find a gorilla sitting in your desk?

Pencil 3

4. Why did Sammy the snake have to stay after school?

Pencil 4

©The Mailbox® • TEC43038 • Aug./Sept. 2008 • Key p. 309

Row 4	870 bus.	825 Because	846 he	858 the	851 "hissed"
Row 3	678 a	682 different	674 to	636 Move	695 desk!
Row 2	516 You	534 to	531 go	540 school.	535 "sundae"
Row 1	342 trick	311 good	346 questions.	325 at	300 They're

A Pile of Pumpkins

Circle the word that best completes each sentence.
Find each circled word in the puzzle.

1. We (grow, grows) pumpkins on our farm.

2. My Dad (plant, plants) the seeds in the spring.

3. My sister and I (watch, watches) the little plants all summer long.

4. The bees (buzz, buzzes) around the pumpkin blossoms.

5. Soon, the first pumpkin (begin, begins) to grow!

6. The workers (help, helps) my dad pick the pumpkins.

7. I (choose, chooses) one pumpkin and carry it into the house.

8. Mom (cut, cuts) it into pieces and scoops out the seeds.

9. Then she (bake, bakes) a pumpkin pie.

10. My family (love, loves) pumpkin pie!

b	r	l	o	v	e	s	k	b
j	c	a	d	f	t	a	c	e
b	q	z	h	e	l	p	e	g
a	c	h	o	o	s	e	t	i
k	i	g	r	o	w	b	l	n
e	b	a	p	l	a	n	t	s
s	u	o	v	p	t	m	d	u
u	z	e	i	f	c	u	t	s
g	z	y	o	x	h	w	h	n

Planning Ahead

Complete each task.

1. The first day of February is Sunday. There are 28 days in February this year. Number the calendar.

2. Groundhog Day is February 2. Write a *G* in this space.

3. Valentine's Day is February 14. Draw a heart in this space.

4. Presidents' Day is February 16. Write a *P* in this space.

Use the calendar to answer the questions.

5. Greta's class will have a party on the 100th day of school. The party will be four days after Groundhog Day. What day and date will the class have the party?

6. Greta will begin making her valentines one week before Valentine's Day. What is the date that she will start?

7. Greta will be out of school on Presidents' Day. What day of the week will she return to school?

8. On what day of the week will March begin? How do you know?

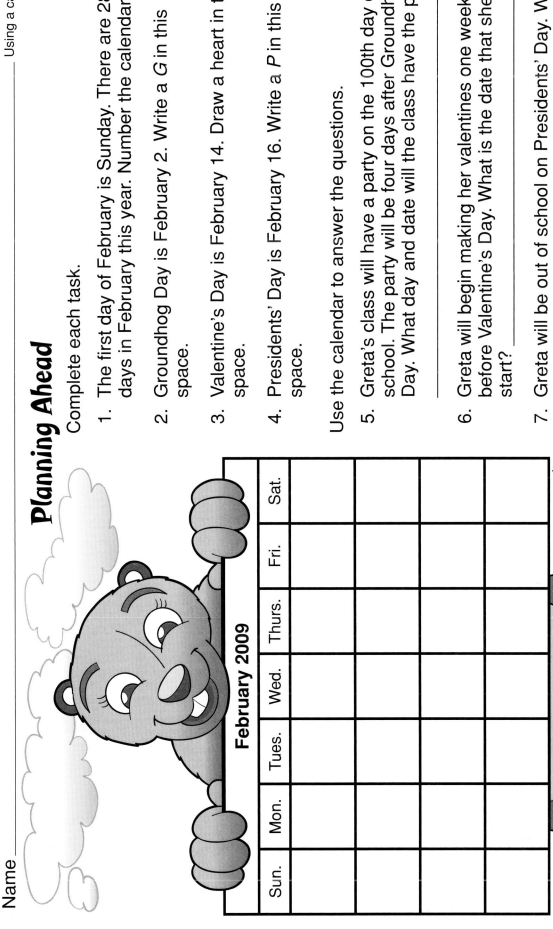

February 2009

Sun.	Mon.	Tues.	Wed.	Thurs.	Fri.	Sat.

Name _____

Windy Hill

Subtract.
Cut apart the squares on the left.
Glue each square over its matching problem on the grid.

25 −19	61 −33	50 −27	74 −48
81 −22	42 −38	34 −16	90 −53
75 −36	23 −18	87 −29	52 −17
60 −27	71 −58	95 −47	84 −15
53 −15	44 −27	70 −24	36 −28

Puzzle pieces: 4, 39, 33, 5, 13, 59, 6, 28, 17, 26, 35, 23, 8, 58, 38, 18, 69, 48, 37, 46

The Frog Hop

Use the contest results to complete the bar graph.

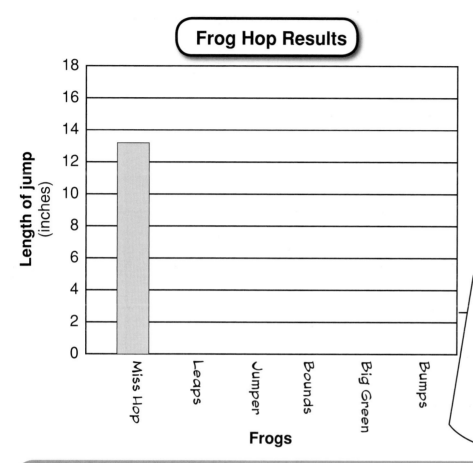

Frog Hop Results

Length of jump (inches)

18
16
14
12
10
8
6
4
2
0

Miss Hop | Leaps | Jumper | Bounds | Big Green | Bumps

Frogs

Contest Results

Miss Hop	= 13 inches
Leaps	= 8 inches
Jumper	= 16 inches
Bounds	= 4 inches
Big Green	= 7 inches
Bumps	= 15 inches

Answer the questions.

1. Which frog won the contest? _____

2. Which frog jumped the shortest distance? _____

3. Which frog jumped farther than Big Green but not as far as Miss Hop?

   _____

4. Which frog jumped farther than Miss Hop but not as far as Jumper?

   _____

5. How much farther did Miss Hop jump than Big Green? _____

6. How many inches did Leaps and Bounds jump in all? _____

7. How many more inches did Bumps jump than Leaps? _____

8. How many inches did Miss Hop and Jumper jump together? _____

Celebrate Earth Day

If the sentence is written correctly, color the box.
If the sentence is not written correctly, color the can.

1. Do you know how Earth Day began. [M] [C]

2. Years ago, people saw that the earth needed help. [W] [T]

3. The ground, the air, and the water were dirty. [R] [O]

4. what would happen if no one started cleaning the earth? [H] [E]

5. People and other living things would get sick. [Y] [D]

6. A holiday named Earth Day was planned. [L] [I]

7. people learned about things that hurt the earth [G] [L]

8. They also learned how to help the earth [N] [E]

9. Some people picked up litter. [Y] [K]

10. Others planted trees and gardens? [P] [A]

11. We should remember to take care of the earth every day. [S] [B]

12. what will you do to help [U] [C]

What is one way you can help the earth?

To find out, write each colored letter from above on its matching numbered line or lines below.

____ ____ ____ ____ ____ ____   ____ ____ ____ ____ ____ ____ ____ !
10   6   2   10   5   11   3   8   1   9   12   7   4

Bonus Box: Look at the sentences above. Choose three that are not written correctly. On the back of this page, write each sentence correctly.

   ©The Mailbox® • TEC43042 • April/May 2009 • Key p. 309

CLASSROOM DISPLAYS

Classroom Displays

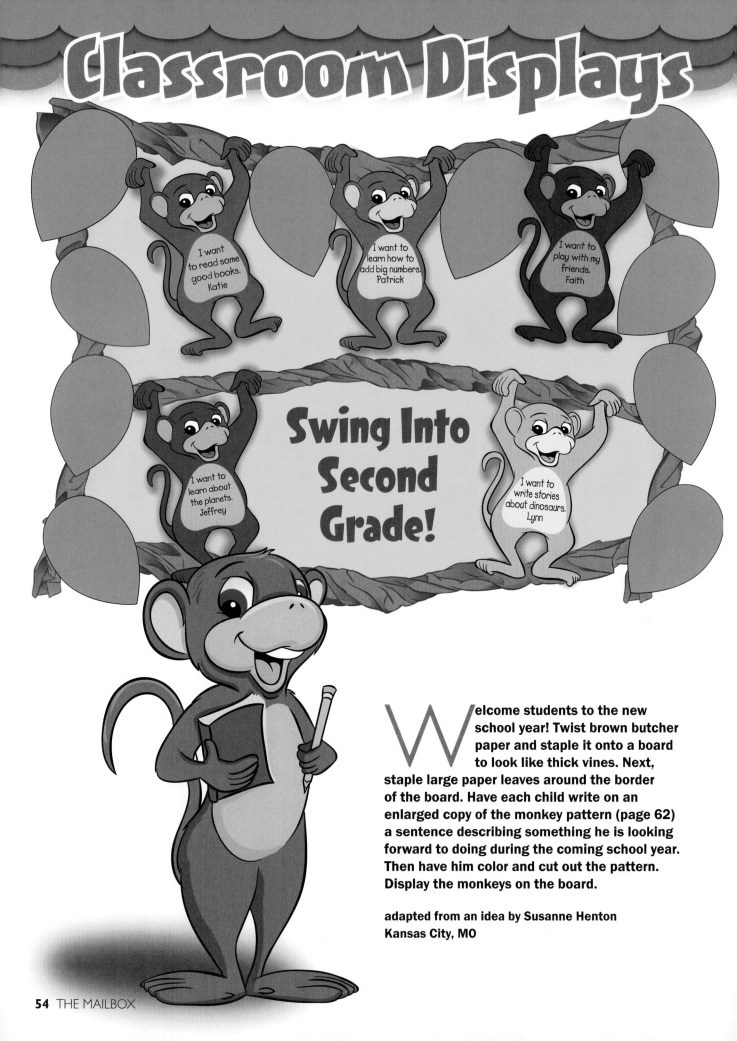

I want to read some good books. Katie

I want to learn how to add big numbers. Patrick

I want to play with my friends. Faith

I want to learn about the planets. Jeffrey

Swing Into Second Grade!

I want to write stories about dinosaurs. Lynn

Welcome students to the new school year! Twist brown butcher paper and staple it onto a board to look like thick vines. Next, staple large paper leaves around the border of the board. Have each child write on an enlarged copy of the monkey pattern (page 62) a sentence describing something he is looking forward to doing during the coming school year. Then have him color and cut out the pattern. Display the monkeys on the board.

adapted from an idea by Susanne Henton
Kansas City, MO

Blasting Off With Great Work

To put the spotlight on students' work, have each child personalize and cut out a copy of the rocket pattern on page 62. Post each rocket above a sheet of construction paper. Then direct each student to choose a sample of his best work and mount it on the paper below his rocket. To complete the display, cut stars from metallic paper and staple them to the board. Throughout the year, invite students to update their samples.

adapted from an idea by Sarah Massey, Blum, TX

This display not only helps students learn their classmates' names, but it's also a great way to learn more about families! First, write each child's name on a paper strip and post it on a display. Next, have each child bring in a family photo. Make a copy of each photo and write the child's name on the back of the copy. Place the copied photos in a resealable plastic bag near the display. A child tacks each photo below the corresponding name. After checking her answers, she removes the photos for the next student.

adapted from an idea by Cortney Ragsdale
Terrace Elementary, Ankeny, IA

Classroom Displays

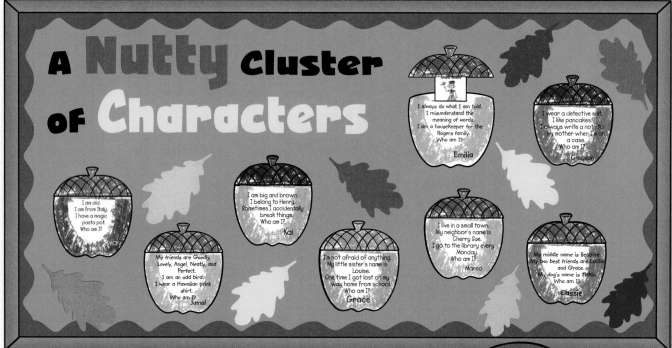

A Nutty Cluster of Characters

I always do what I am told.
I misunderstand the meaning of words.
I am a housekeeper for the Rogers family.
Who am I?

Emilia

I wear a detective suit.
I like pancakes.
I always write a note to my mother when I'm on a case.
Who am I?

Grayson

I am old.
I am from Italy.
I have a magic pasta pot.
Who am I?

I am big and brown.
I belong to Henry.
Sometimes I accidentally break things.
Who am I?

Kai

I live in a small town.
My neighbor's name is Cherry Sue.
I go to the library every Monday.
Who am I?

Marco

My friends are Goodly, Lovely, Angel, Neatly, and Perfect.
I am an odd bird.
I wear a Hawaiian print shirt.
Who am I?

Jamal

I'm not afraid of anything.
My little sister's name is Louise.
One time I got lost on my way home from school.
Who am I?

Grace

My middle name is Beatrice.
My two best friends are Lucille and Grace.
My dog's name is Tickle.
Who am I?

Cassie

Flat Stanley

I was mailed to California in an envelope.
My brother used me as a kite.
I helped catch thieves at a museum.
Who am I?

Jacob

For this amusing riddle display, have each child cut out a copy of the acorn pattern on page 63. Next, direct each student to write on the acorn three sentences that describe an amusing book character followed by the question "Who am I?" Instruct each student to write the character's name on the strip and draw a picture of the character. Then have the child color the rest of the acorn. To assemble the acorn, cut a slit on the acorn's dotted line and then insert the strip. Finally, post each child's acorn on the display.

Cheer for positive group work behavior with this fun display! Make a different-colored copy of a helmet pattern from page 64 for each group. Label each helmet with a different team name, cut out the helmets, and then tack them to the 50-yard line. When a group works well together, move its team helmet ahead to the next 10-yard line. After a team reaches the goalpost, give the team members a small reward and reset the team's helmet to the 50-yard line.

To create this community helper display, each child traces his hand on a piece of paper and cuts out the tracing. He writes the job title of a chosen community helper on the thumb and words or phrases that describe the worker on the remaining fingers. Then the student draws a picture of the worker on the hand's palm and posts it on a board with the title shown.

Katie Leavitt, R. E. Baker Elementary, Bentonville, AR

Classroom Displays

Shining Bright in Second Grade

Showcase students' skills or talents with this illuminating display. Direct each child to fold a piece of construction paper in half, trace on the fold a lightbulb template (pattern on page 65), and cut out the tracing, leaving the fold intact. On the inside of his lightbulb, have each student write a sentence describing something he does well. Then have him color the top of his bulb and glue his photo on the front. Punch a hole at the top of each lightbulb, lace a length of yarn through the holes, and hang the resulting string of lights on the board.

Christina Travers, Little River Elementary, Orlando, FL

Encourage students to think about peaceful solutions for their families, their community, or the world. Have each child stand in front of a sheet of black paper. Use an overhead projector to shine the child's silhouette on the paper; then trace it. Next, direct each child to write on white paper a sentence describing her dream for peace and then trim her paper into a bubble shape. Guide the student to cut out her silhouette and post it under her dream bubble.

Michele Campbell, Fairfield Central Elementary, Fairfield, OH

Use this display to motivate students to share the stories they read. After a child reads a book, he completes a copy of the gingerbread man organizer on page 65. Then he colors the gingerbread man, cuts it out, and attaches it to the board.

Jennifer L. Kohnke, St. Charles, IL

Classroom Displays

On the Writing Process Trail

Prewriting | Rough Draft | Editing | Revising | Publishing

Omar • Bailey • Jada • Landon • Dominic • Madison • Kylie
Cayla • Robert • Carlos • Chloe • Asia
Jose • Ian

This interactive board serves both as a reminder of the steps in the writing process and a visual update on students' progress during a writing project. Label five trail sign cutouts, each with a different step of the writing process, and post them on a board titled as shown. Have each student personalize and cut out a copy of the hiking boot pattern on page 66. Tack each boot under the Prewriting sign. When a student completes a step in the writing process, he moves his boot below the next sign.

Brooke Beverly, Julia Bancroft School, Auburn, MA

To reinforce common and proper nouns, assign half the class to the common nouns category and the other to the proper nouns category. Next, have each student use the pattern from page 67 to make a card similar to the ones shown, writing examples from her assigned category on its front. Then have her write the category name inside the card. Display the cards on a board titled as shown and invite students to use the cards to test their knowledge of common and proper nouns.

Kara Cuomo, F. E. Bellows School, Mamaroneck, NY

Classroom Displays

It's Time For April Showers

May Flowers:
Brought to You by April Showers

Student art transforms into not one but two seasonal displays! Guide each student to blend watercolors of different spring colors on a piece of paper. When the paper is dry, have him use a raindrop template (pattern on page 68) to trace several raindrops and then cut them out. Next, have the child trace an umbrella template (pattern on page 68) on construction paper and cut the tracing out. In April, display the cutouts as a shower of umbrellas and raindrops with the title shown. Then, in May, arrange the raindrops and umbrellas so they resemble flowers and change the title as shown.

Cindy Barber, Fredonia, WI

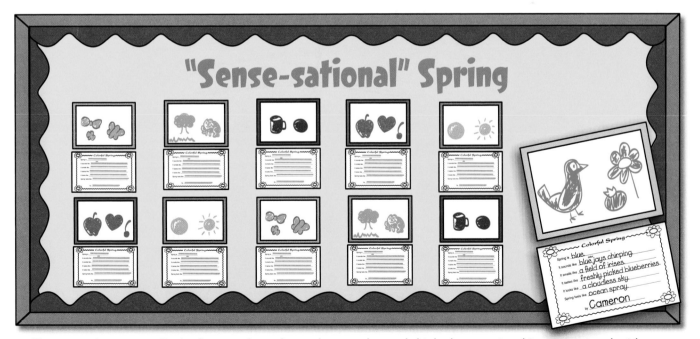

"Sense-sational" Spring

To create this poetry display, have each student select a color and think about spring things associated with it. Next, direct him to complete a copy of the poem outline on page 68. Then have the student use the corresponding colored crayon to draw a picture about his poem and mount the picture on a like-colored piece of construction paper. Finally, display each child's poem with the title shown.

Monkey Pattern

Use with "Swing Into Second Grade!" on page 54.

Rocket Pattern

Use with "Blasting Off With Great Work" on page 55.

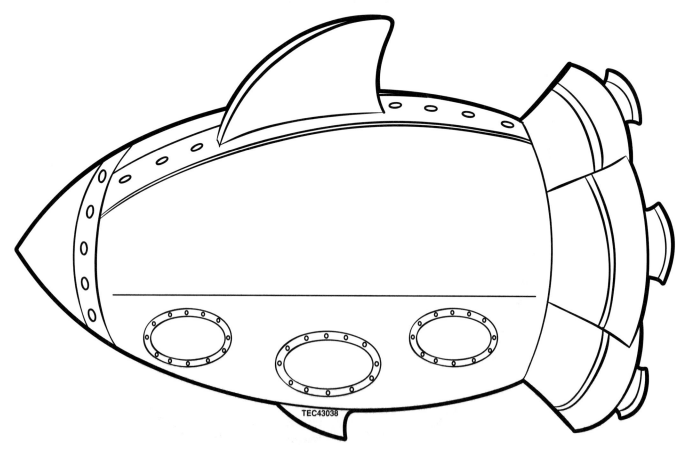

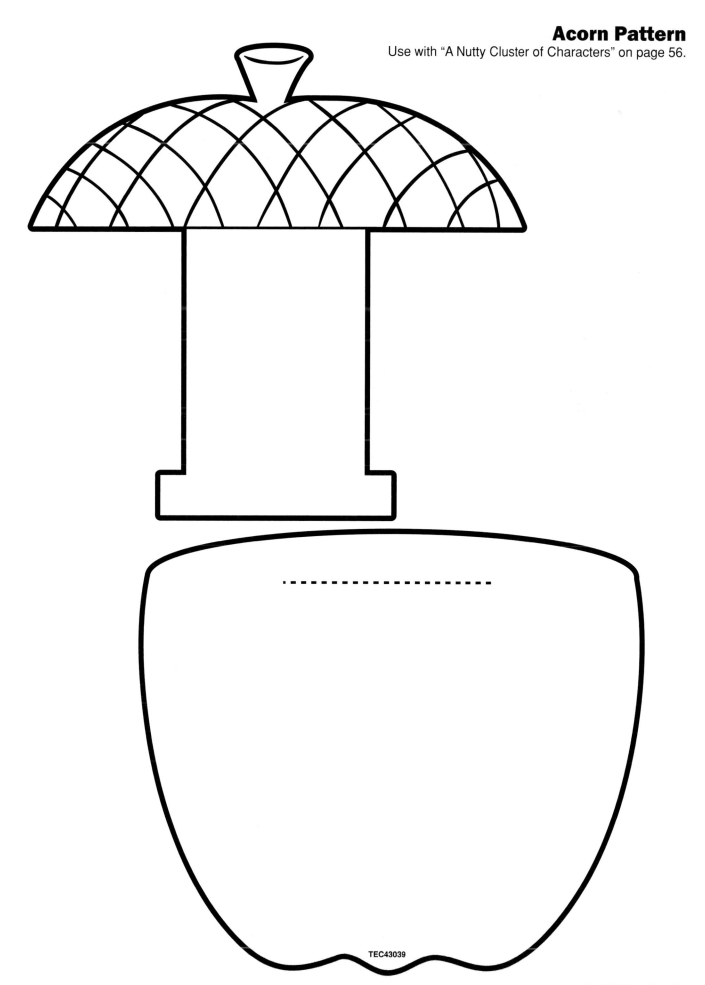

TEC43039

Helmet Patterns

Use with "Be a Team Player" on page 57.

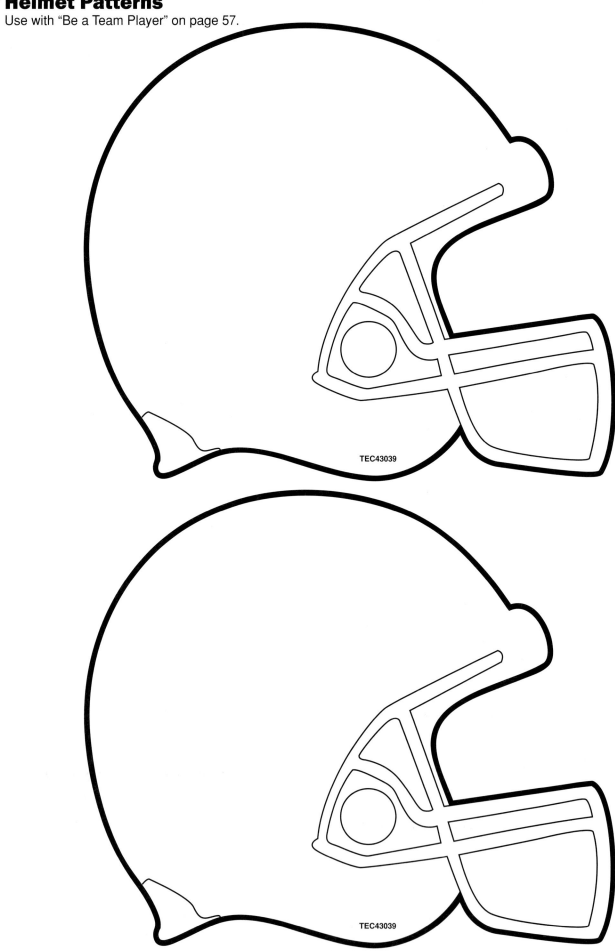

TEC43039

TEC43039

Lightbulb Pattern

Use with "Shining Bright in Second Grade" on page 58.

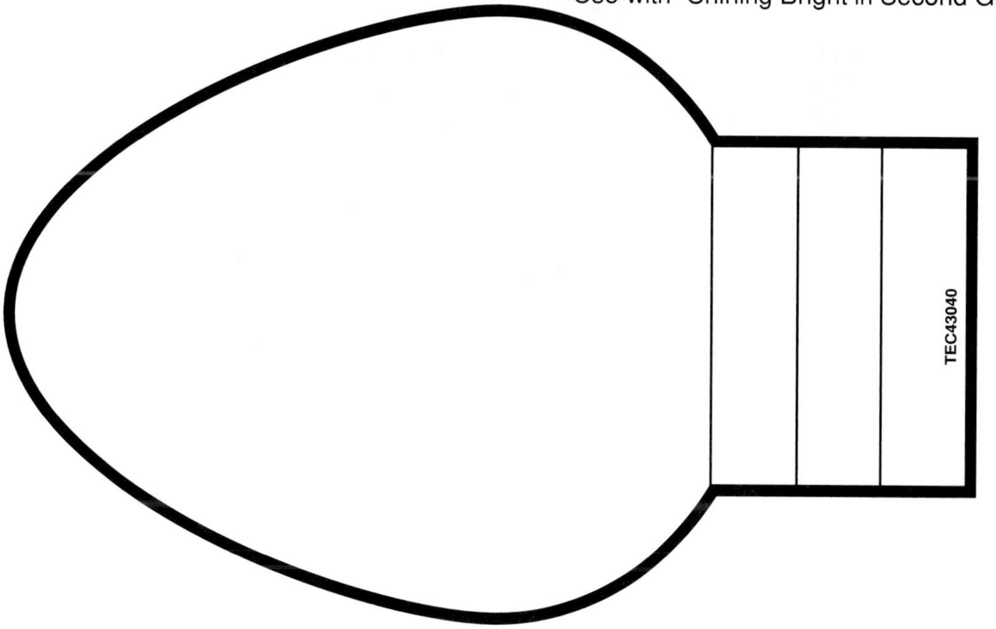

TEC43040

Gingerbread Man Pattern

Use with "Read, Read as Much as You Can!" on page 59.

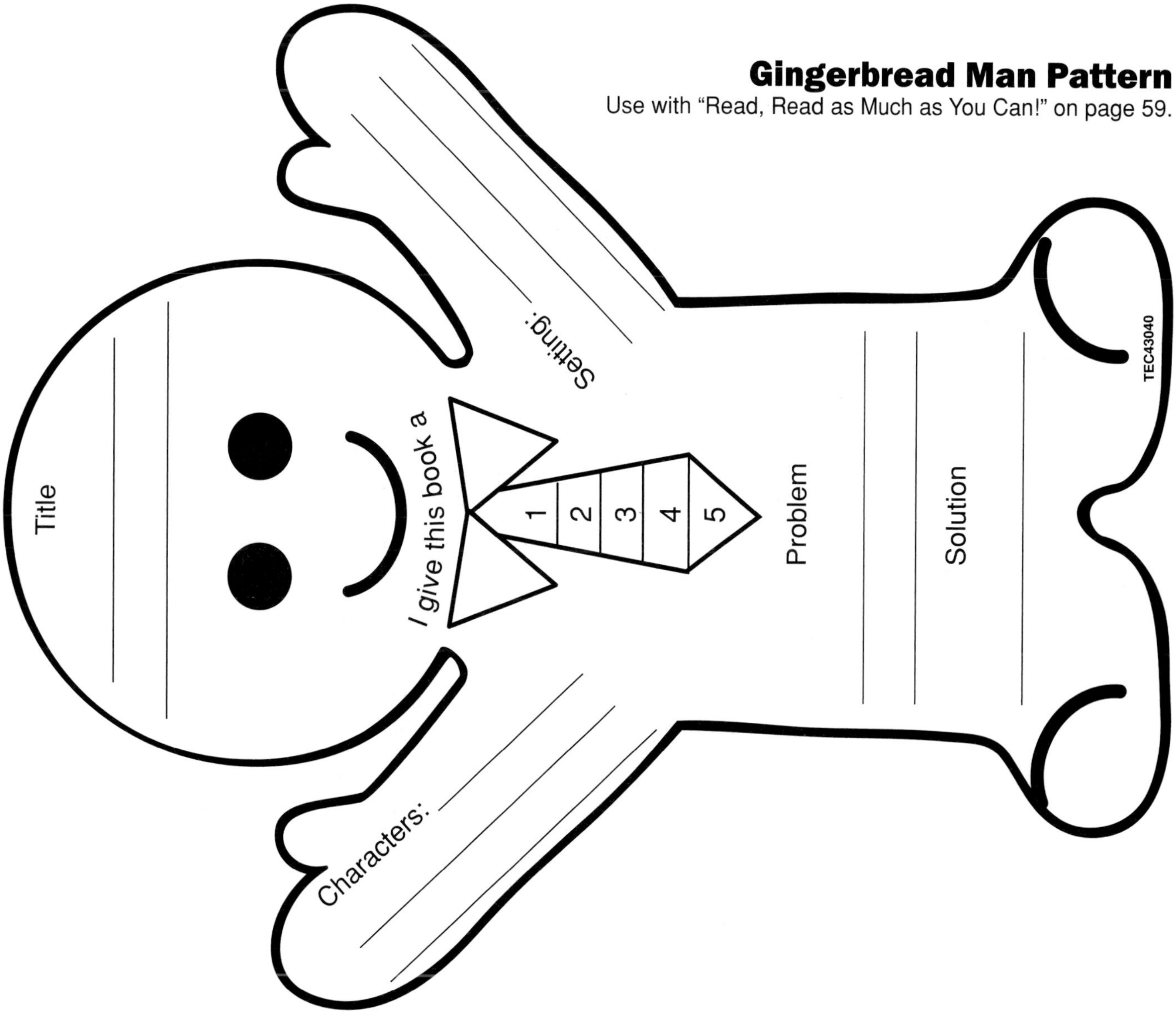

TEC43040

Title

Setting:

I give this book a

1
2
3
4
5

Problem

Solution

Characters:

Hiking Boot Pattern

Use with "On the Writing Process Trail" on page 60.

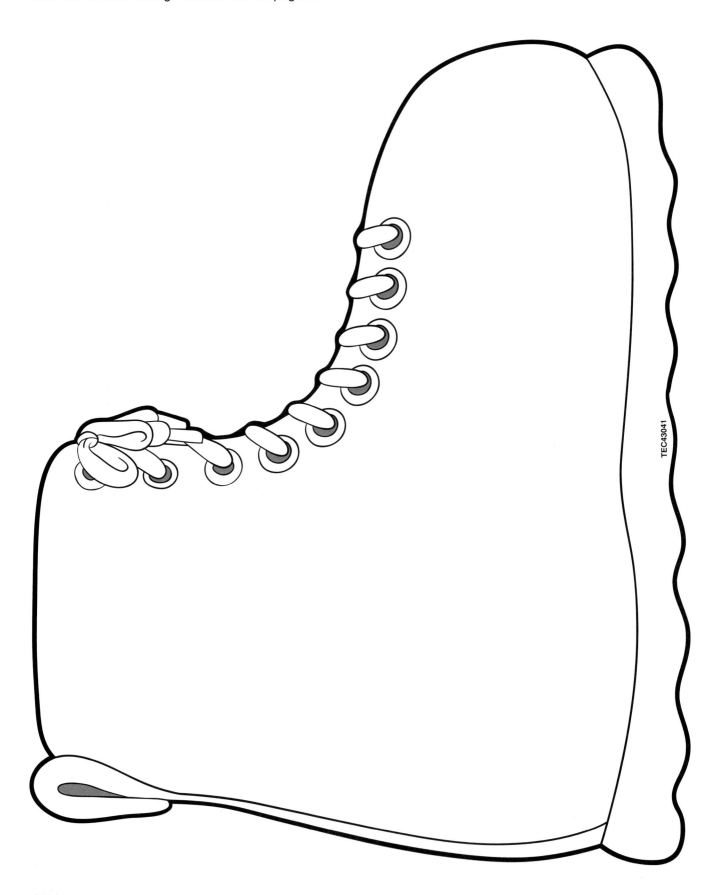

TEC43041

©The Mailbox

Umbrella and Raindrop Patterns

Use with "It's Time for April Showers" and "May Flowers:
Brought to You by April Showers" on page 61.

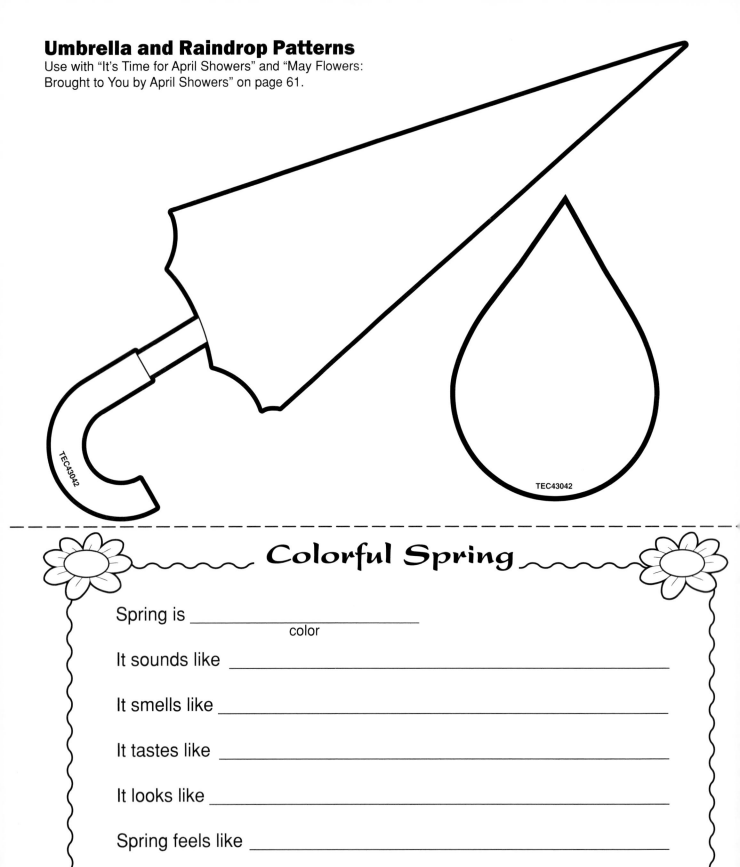

TEC43042

TEC43042

Colorful Spring

Spring is _____
color

It sounds like _____

It smells like _____

It tastes like _____

It looks like _____

Spring feels like _____

by _____

©The Mailbox® • TEC43042 • April/May 2009

Note to the teacher: Use with "'Sense-sational' Spring" on page 61.

Exploring Social Studies

Exploring Social Studies

More Land or More Water?
Geography

This partner activity helps students answer the question, "Is there more land or more water on the earth?" To begin, provide each student pair with an 8½" x 11" copy of a world map and a supply of centimeter cubes in two different colors. Direct each duo to completely cover its map with cubes, using one color for the land areas and the other color for the water. When the map is covered, have the students remove the cubes and sort them by color. Then have them count each set and share their results with the rest of the class.

Lesa Haney, The Colony, TX

Personal Importance
Timeline

Here's an activity that's perfect for the beginning of the school year! Direct each child to fold a 12" x 18" sheet of paper into fourths and then unfold it. Next, have each child select four important events in his life. Instruct him to write on each of four sticky notes sentences about each event. Then have him place the sticky notes in order on his paper. After checking that he's placed them in order, direct the student to add an illustration for each event. Then have him orally share his timeline or post it for others to read. Either way, the timeline will serve as a great getting-to-know-you activity.

Exploring Social Studies

Moving in the Right Direction
Cardinal and intermediate directions

To begin, have each child label a copy of a hundred chart with directional abbreviations as shown. Next, announce a number from 1 to 100 and have each student color the corresponding square on his chart. Then give a direction such as "Go west five spaces" and guide the student to move in that direction on his chart, coloring each space as he goes. After giving several directions, instruct each child to circle the number he stops on; then lead a class discussion about the path taken and the end location.

Karen Potter, Red Oak-Sturgeon Elementary, Alberta, VA

NW					N				NE
1	2	3	4	5	6	7	8	9	10
11	12	13	14	15	16	17	18	19	20
21	22	23	24	25	26	27	28	29	30
31	32	33	34	35	36	37	38	39	40
41	42	43	44	45	46	47	48	49	50
51	52	53	54	55	56	57	58	59	60
61	62	63	64	65	66	67	68	69	70
71	72	73	74	75	76	77	78	79	80
81	82	83	84	85	86	87	88	89	90
91	92	93	94	95	96	97	98	99	100

(W on left, E on right; SW bottom-left, S bottom-center, SE bottom-right)

If you are a rural community, stand up.

If you are a suburban community, clap your hands.

If you are an urban community, snap your fingers.

If your community is just outside a city, pat your back.

If your community can be called a city, stomp your feet.

If your community is outside a suburb and can be called the country, wave your hands.

Meaningful Model
Types of communities

Here's an easy way to get students involved with identifying urban, suburban, and rural communities. First, select a child to sit on a chair in the middle of the room. Tell the child that she represents a city, or an urban community. Next, direct several more students to sit on the floor around the chair. Tell these students that they represent suburban communities. Finally, have the remaining students sit around the students designated as suburban and tell these students that they are rural communities. Then, to reinforce the community characteristics, give directions like the ones shown for students to follow.

Lisa Strieker, St. Paul Elementary, Highland, IL

Exploring Social Studies

A Look Around Town
Goods and services

The end result of this activity is a striking display. In advance, obtain photos of recognizable local businesses. (This is a great task for a parent volunteer!) To start the activity, a student mounts a photo on a piece of paper and writes either "goods" or "services" based on what the business provides. Next, the student draws a picture of himself holding a good from the business or modeling a service. He cuts around his picture and glues it on the photo of the business. Display the projects on a board titled "Goods and Services Around Town."

Jennifer Mross, Kiel Elementary, Kinnelon, NJ

goods

services

Dr. Martin Luther King Jr.

This figure is a man.
He grew up in Georgia.
He was a very good student.
He gave a speech called "I have a dream."
He is honored in January.

The Name of the Game
Historic figures associated with holidays

Students work together to create this class game. First, have each small group choose a different person associated with a holiday and write the person's name on an index card. Next, direct the group to write a general clue to describe the person, three more-specific clues about the person, and then a final clue that tells when the figure is honored. After all the groups have finished, direct a representative from each group to read the group's clues aloud while students in the other groups try to name the figure. When a student correctly identifies the figure, points are awarded to his group based on the number of clues read before he determined the answer. For example, if a figure is correctly named after the first clue, the group gets five points; if all the clues must be read to determine the answer, the group receives only one point.

Jean Erickson, Grace Christian Academy, West Allis, WI

Exploring Social Studies

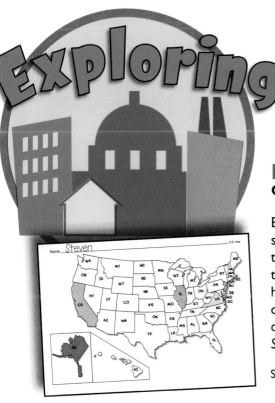

Booking Through the USA
Geography

Expose students to each state's location. After reading a story or a social studies lesson that mentions a U.S. state, have each child locate the state on a copy of page 76. Select a child to indicate the state's location on an overhead copy or an enlarged version of the map; then have him color it in. Direct students to use the same color to shade the state on their own maps. Repeat the activity each time a reading includes a different state until all states are identified. If needed, read *The Scrambled States of America* by Laurie Keller to complete the map.

Susan Marsh, White Township Consolidated, Belvidere, NJ

Sweet Tooth Island
Landforms, bodies of water, map skills

Here's a hands-on activity students will want to sink their teeth into! Gather edible materials to represent landforms and bodies of water, such as large cookies (islands), chocolate icing (soil), chocolate kisses (mountains), chocolate chips (hills), miniature candy bars (plateaus), green coconut (plains), and blue icing (water features). Display a key that explains what each material represents and have each student refer to it as she constructs an island that uses at least three of the materials. When her island is complete, have her place it on a sheet of blue construction paper or a blue napkin. Then direct her to create a map that details the island's features. If desired, take a photo of each island before inviting students to have a taste.

Malinda Pryor, Pine Ridge Elementary, Ellerslie, GA

Looking Back
Community in the past

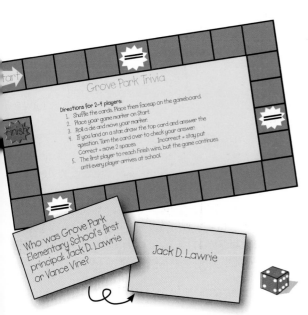

To help students learn more about their school community, have them make a game! First, direct small groups of students to use references—such as information in the media center, facts from the district Web site, and conversations with community citizens—to obtain facts about the history of your school. Have students use the facts to write game questions on index cards, including each question's answer on the back of the card. Also guide students to draw a gameboard and write the game's directions on a 11" x 18" sheet of paper. Store the game cards with the corresponding gameboard and encourage students to play during free time.

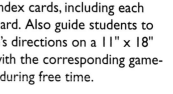

Rebecca Graves, Grove Park Elementary, Burlington, NC

Exploring Social Studies

Ups and Downs of Invention
Effects of technology

In advance, write an example of a type of technology on a sentence strip and tape it to the board. Also cut two arrows from 12" x 18" paper and tape the arrows behind the sentence strip as shown. Next, direct small groups of students to discuss ways the particular technology has helped people and communities (ups) as well as how it has hurt them (downs). After the discussions, record students' ideas on the corresponding arrow. Repeat the activity at another time with a different technology example.

Ups
- People can work from home, so there is less air pollution from cars.
- People can send emails to keep in touch.
- People can play games for fun.
- Students learn new things for school.

Internet

Downs
- People might not talk face-to-face.
- Not everyone has it, so some people might feel left out.

Three Government Branches
(sung to the tune of "Three Blind Mice")

Three branches,
Three branches:
Here's how they work,
Here's how they work!

The legislative branch
Makes all the laws.
The judicial branch
Makes sure they're obeyed.
The executive branch
Carries them out.
Three branches!

Branching Out
Government

Introduce this song to your students to help them identify the three branches of government.

adapted from an idea by Andrea Crawford, Montvale Elementary, Montvale, VA

History in a Box
Changes in a community, timeline

To help students explore the history of your community, assign each small group one period from your community's past. Then provide access to research materials and guide the group to research that period. Next, have the group create a diorama to show what it learned. Lead the groups in chronological order to present their work and then staple the dioramas together to form a sequenced, three-dimensional display of your community's history.

Carol Buning, Northern Michigan Christian School, McBain, MI

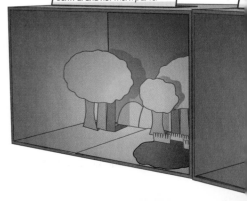

1840: Missaukee County was first surveyed

Forests were found all over the county. There were swamplands in the southern and eastern parts. There were hills in the central and northern parts.

Exploring Social Studies

Class Collection
Time and change

Assign student pairs to gather digital photos or newspaper clippings that reflect favorite foods, clothing trends, games, technology, and important news events from the school year. Have the students attach a sticky label to the back of each item, explaining what it is and why it's important. Store the resulting artifacts in a large mailing envelope and label it with the school year and your school's name and location. Place the envelope in a specially marked container or file. Repeat the activity each year, sharing previous collections with students and leading them in a discussion of time and change.

Barack Obama was elected president. He is our country's first African American president.

Do you first travel north, south, east, or west on your way home?

Do you pass any landmarks, such as parks or recreation areas, on your way?

Tell a friend how to get from school to your house. Use directional words.

Use your map to tell a classmate how you would travel from home to school.

Weekday Trip
Map skills

Take advantage of computer technology to practice a variety of map and geography skills. Under your supervision, guide students to a mapping Web site. Direct each child to enter the school address as the starting address and then his own address as the destination. Have the student print the resulting directions and map. Then have him use the map to respond to questions and tasks like the ones shown.

Laura Turner, Cashell Donahoe Elementary, Sandston, VA

Seeds of Knowledge
State community

To begin, explain to students that each state has symbols that represent and have meaning to the state. Introduce some of your state's symbols and share your state's flower. Next, have each student complete a copy of the seed packet on page 77 with information about your state and a picture of the state flower. Guide each student to cut out the pattern, fold on the thin lines, and glue it together. If desired, provide each child with a small number of seeds to place inside the packet.

Linda Masternak Justice, Kansas City, MO

Missouri
state

White Hawthorn Blossom
flower

USA Seed Company

State _____ Missouri
Capital city _____ Jefferson City
State symbols

bird = bluebird

fish = channel catfish

insect = honeybee

Name _____ Terrance

Go to pages 78-82 for social studies practice pages.

Name _____

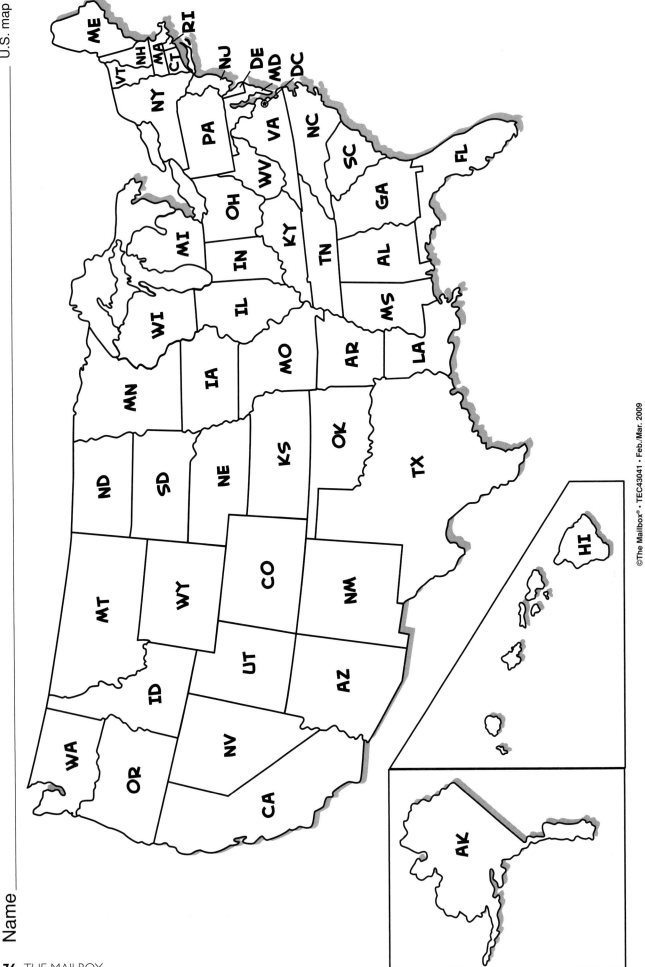

©The Mailbox® • TEC43041 • Feb./Mar. 2009

Note to the teacher: Use with "Booking Through the USA" on page 73.

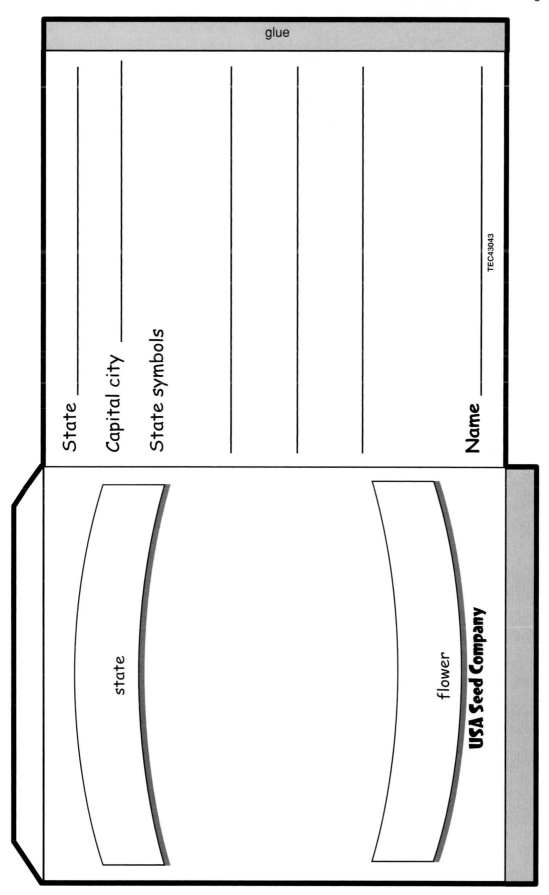

glue

State _____

Capital city _____

State symbols _____

_____

_____

_____

Name _____

TEC43043

state

flower

USA Seed Company

A Place for the President

Read each sentence below.

If the sentence tells about the president's job duties, write the matching number on a window on the left side of the White House.

If the sentence tells another fact about the president, write the matching number on a window on the right side of the White House.

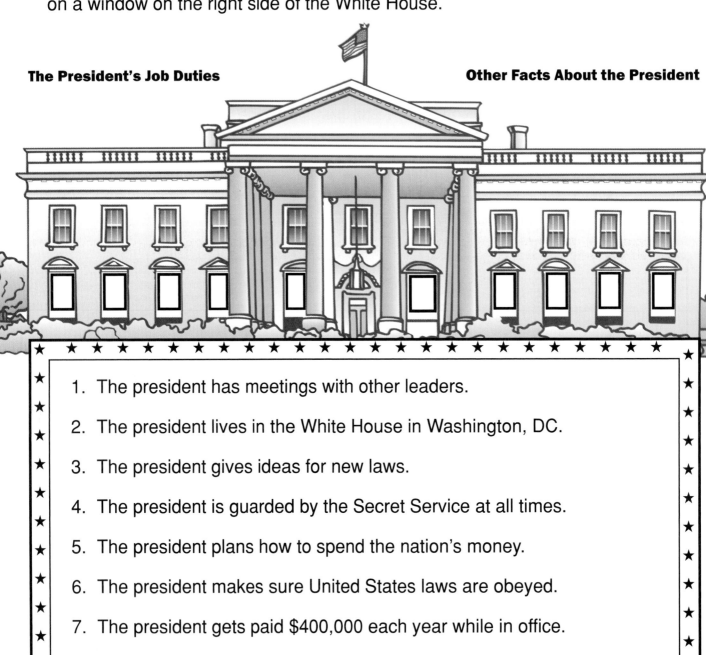

The President's Job Duties

Other Facts About the President

1. The president has meetings with other leaders.

2. The president lives in the White House in Washington, DC.

3. The president gives ideas for new laws.

4. The president is guarded by the Secret Service at all times.

5. The president plans how to spend the nation's money.

6. The president makes sure United States laws are obeyed.

7. The president gets paid $400,000 each year while in office.

8. The president is the commander in chief of the armed forces.

9. The president has a getaway retreat called Camp David.

10. The president travels to faraway places on a jet called Air Force One.

©The Mailbox® • TEC43039 • Oct./Nov. 2008 • Key p. 309

Shopping Around

Write the word for each definition.
Use the word bank.

1. when something is wanted by many, but there is only a small supply

2. things that people make or grow and then sell

3. things a person must have to survive

4. things a person would like to have but does not need

5. things used to make goods or to provide services

6. money made from selling goods or services

7. a job done for another person

8. someone who makes goods or provides services

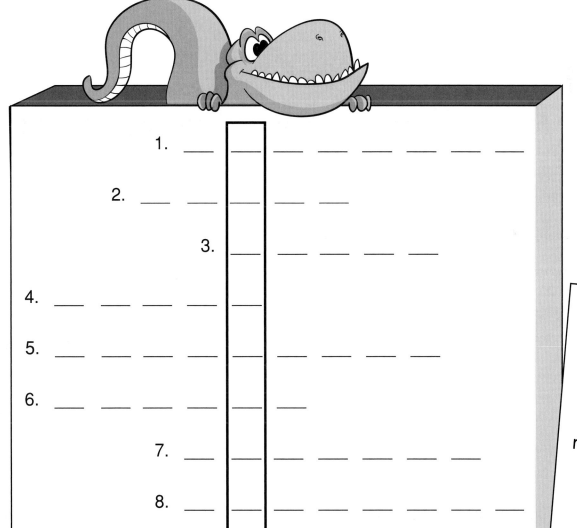

1. _ _ _ _ _ _ _ _ _

2. _ _ _ _ _

3. _ _ _ _ _

4. _ _ _ _

5. _ _ _ _ _

6. _ _ _ _ _

7. _ _ _ _ _ _ _

8. _ _ _ _ _ _ _

Word Bank
goods
income
needs
producer
resources
scarcity
service
wants

What do you call a buyer of goods or services?
To find out, write the letters from the bold box, in order, on the lines below.

_ _ _ _ _ _ _ _

A Day for Dolls

Families in Japan celebrate with dolls each year on March 3.

Hina-Matsuri is the name of a holiday in Japan. It is also known as Doll Festival or Girls' Festival. Hina-Matsuri is held on the third day of the third month each year. On this day, families pray for their daughters to be healthy and happy. They set up dolls in their houses. These dolls wear costumes. Each family's dolls are placed on steps that are covered with red felt. Often there are five or seven steps. The top step is saved for two very special dolls. They are the emperor and empress dolls. They are placed there to look like they are sitting on a throne. Some families set up only these two dolls on this day. No matter how they set up the dolls, the families place food in front of the dolls. They hope this will bring good luck to their daughters. Then the dolls are put away until the next year.

Write a question about the passage using each question starter.
Answer each question.

1. Who _____?
   _____

2. What _____?
   _____

3. When _____?
   _____

4. Where _____?
   _____

5. Why _____?
   _____

Name _____

How Movies Began

The first motion picture, or movie, was shown over 100 years ago.

Answer the questions.
Use the timeline.

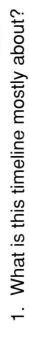

1877–1888
Photos were taken of a horse as it ran. The photos were the first to show an object in motion.

1893
Thomas Edison showed his kinetoscope. It was a machine that played a movie for just one person at a time. The person looked through a small hole in a cabinet to see the movie. There was no sound.

1895
A movie screening for a large group of people was held in Paris, France. A projection machine was used.

1905
People saw movies in small theaters called nickelodeons. It cost just a nickel to see the movie!

1928
Steamboat Willie was made by Walt Disney. It was a cartoon movie with sound.

1929
Many movies had sound.

1. What is this timeline mostly about?

_____

2. How many people could watch a movie on a kinetoscope?

_____

3. What was used to show a movie to a large group in 1895?

_____

4. When did people start seeing movies at nickelodeons?

_____

5. What happened in 1928?

_____

6. What is the first year shown on the timeline?

_____

What is the last year shown?

_____

©The Mailbox® • TEC43042 • April/May 2009 • Key p. 310

From Cow to Consumer

About 900 million gallons of ice cream are made in the USA each year.

Ice cream is made from milk products, sugar, and flavorings. Milk comes from cows. But how does the milk become ice cream and make it to your house? Read on to find out!

Cows are milked at a farm. Products from the milk, like cream, are sent by truck to a factory.

At the factory, machines mix and stir the milk products with other ingredients. This helps make the ice cream safe to eat. The ice cream mixture is cooled. Flavorings are added. Then the ice cream is frozen. The ice cream is put in cartons, and the cartons are put in a hardening room. This makes the ice cream frozen solid. The cartons are checked to be sure they are just right for selling. The cartons are grouped in sets. They are sent to stores.

When the ice cream cartons arrive at the store, the ice cream is placed in freezers. The consumer selects his favorite flavor, pays for it, and goes home to eat it!

Complete the chart. Use the passage.

At the Farm

1. Cows are milked at a farm.

2. _____

At the Factory

1. Machines mix the ingredients.

2. Flavorings are added.

3. _____

4. _____

5. The cartons are checked and shipped to stores.

At the Store

1. _____

2. The consumer pays for the ice cream.

LEARNING CENTERS

Way to Go!
Cougar Football
World Champs

D. one hundred thirty-seven

Christopher

A. 45

B. 98

C. 150

D. 137

A Winning Combination

Help students become champions at reading and writing numbers! Copy the strip on page 96 onto tagboard and cut it out. Next, copy and color the center mat from page 97. Then laminate the strip and mat. Cut slits on the mat where indicated and use a permanent marker to program each line of the strip with a number word. Thread the strip through the slits and place it at a center with a supply of paper. A child pulls the strip to reveal each number word and writes the corresponding number on his paper. To change the number words, simply use hair spray or nail polish remover to wipe away the programming before writing new words.

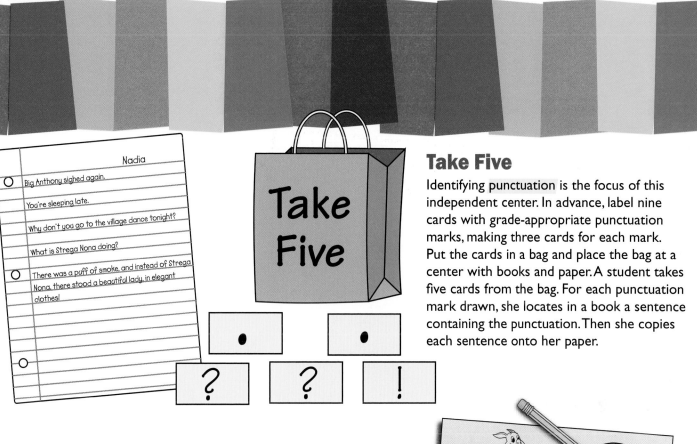

Take Five

Identifying punctuation is the focus of this independent center. In advance, label nine cards with grade-appropriate punctuation marks, making three cards for each mark. Put the cards in a bag and place the bag at a center with books and paper. A student takes five cards from the bag. For each punctuation mark drawn, she locates in a book a sentence containing the punctuation. Then she copies each sentence onto her paper.

Handwritten paper:

> Nadia
>
> Big Anthony sighed again.
>
> You're sleeping late.
>
> Why don't you go to the village dance tonight?
>
> What is Strega Nona doing?
>
> There was a puff of smoke, and instead of Strega Nona, there stood a beautiful lady, in elegant clothes!

Punctuation cards: . . ? ? !

Getting There

This partner game leads students to a better understanding of even and odd numbers. Place at a center student copies of page 98, crayons, and a paper clip. To play, each partner chooses a path to follow and writes in each space of his path a different even or odd number. Player 1 uses the paper clip and a pencil to spin the spinner. He reads the resulting term aloud and then colors a corresponding space on his trail. If no numbers match the term spun, he loses a turn. Player 2 takes a turn in a similar manner, and play alternates until one player has colored all the spaces on his trail.

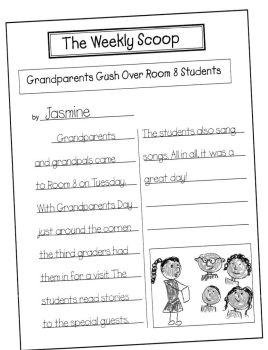

The Weekly Scoop

Grandparents Gush Over Room 8 Students

by Jasmine

Grandparents and grandpals came to Room 8 on Tuesday. With Grandparents Day just around the corner, the third graders had them in for a visit. The students read stories to the special guests. The students also sang songs. All in all, it was a great day!

What's Happening?

Here's a ready-to-go activity that gives students something to write about! Place at a center student copies of the newspaper page on page 99, a class or school calendar of events, and crayons. A child titles her newspaper page and then uses the calendar to select a topic for an expository article about a recent class activity or a fictional article based on an upcoming event. After she's finished writing her article, she draws a picture related to her text.

Kelli Higgins, P. L. Bolin Elementary, East Peoria, IL

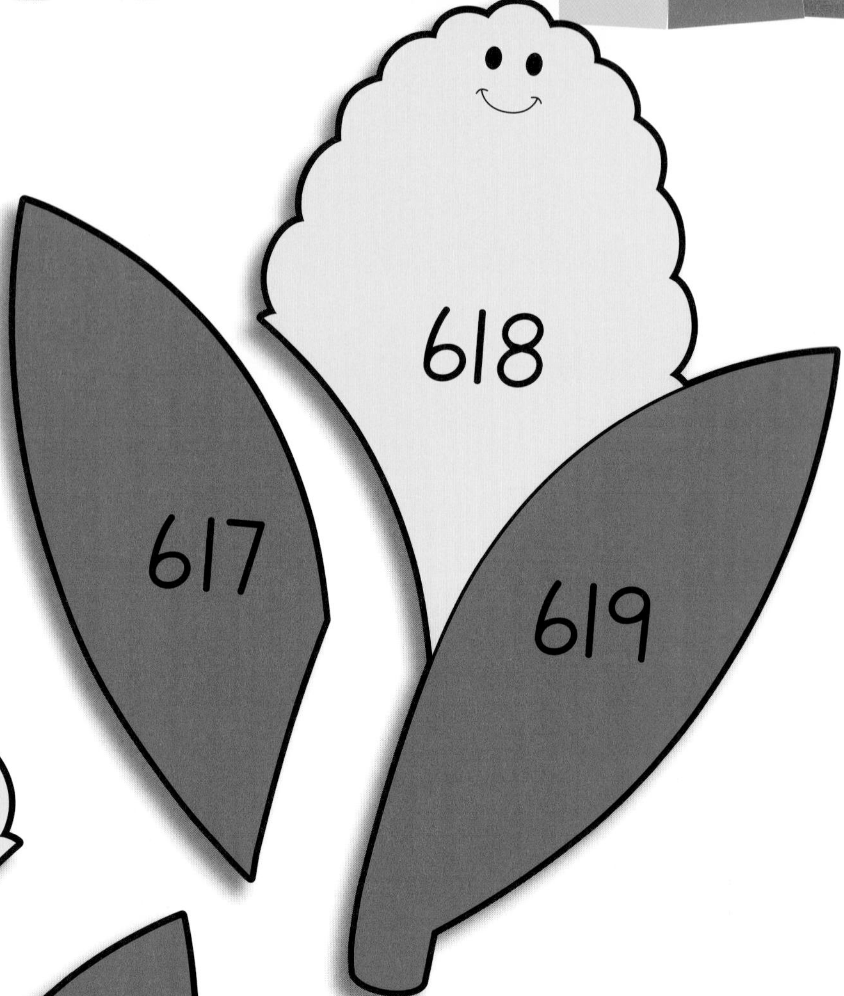

Learning Centers

618

617

619

83

84

82

"A-maize-ing" Arrangement

Give students a taste of ordering numbers! In advance, make several copies of the corncob and husk pattern from page 100. Program each set with three consecutive numbers, with the middle number on the corncob; then color and cut out the corn apart from the husks. If desired, make the center self-checking by putting a like-colored dot on the back of each piece in a set. A child chooses a husk set and locates the corncob that has the missing number. He places the corncob between the husks. When all matches have been made, he turns over each set to check his work. To vary the activity, cut out one husk, leaving the cob and other husk as one piece. The child matches the number that comes before or after the pair.

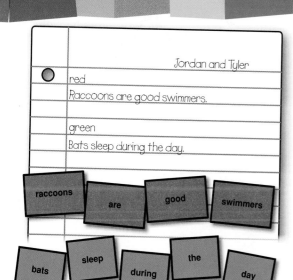

Getting the Facts Straight

Students work together to order words in sentences. To prepare, copy page 101, color each row of cards a different color, and cut apart the cards. Place each colored set in a separate plastic bag. A student pair chooses a bag and writes the color of the cards on a sheet of paper. The twosome orders the cards so the words make a complete sentence. Then one student writes the resulting sentence on the paper, adding capital letters and punctuation marks as needed. After returning the cards to the bag, the students choose another bag and repeat the process. Partners take turns writing the sentences until all sentences have been completed. **For an added challenge,** encourage students to test each set to see if the cards can be arranged to form a question.

Results Will Vary

Reinforce computation skills with this easy-to-prepare activity. Program two sets of cards: one set with the numbers 1–5 and the other set with numbers that are answers to grade-appropriate addition, subtraction, multiplication, or division problems. Put each set in a separate resealable bag and label the bags as shown. A child chooses a card from each bag. He uses the card drawn from the "Problems" bag to determine the number of problems he must write that result in the answer found on the other card. After he records his answers, he returns the cards to the bags; then he selects a new pair.

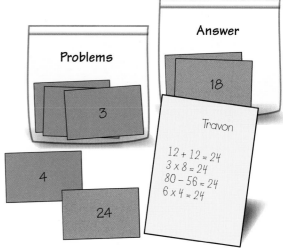

Easy as Pie!

This hands-on center helps students identify correct plural endings. Label one paper plate "s" and another plate with "es." Then divide two more plates into equal sections. Label each section of a divided plate with words to which an s is added to show the plural form; label each section of the final plate with words to which an es is added. Cut apart the sections from the divided plates and place the cutouts in a bag. A student takes each cutout from the bag and places it on the corresponding plate. When she's placed each cutout, she writes each word with its plural ending on a sheet of paper.

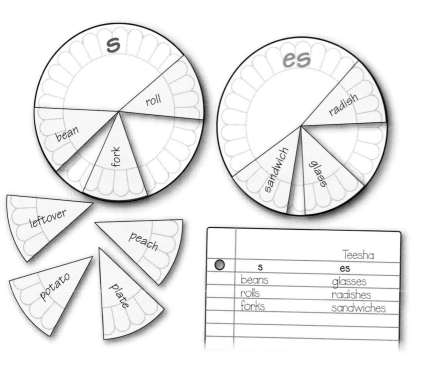

Learning Centers

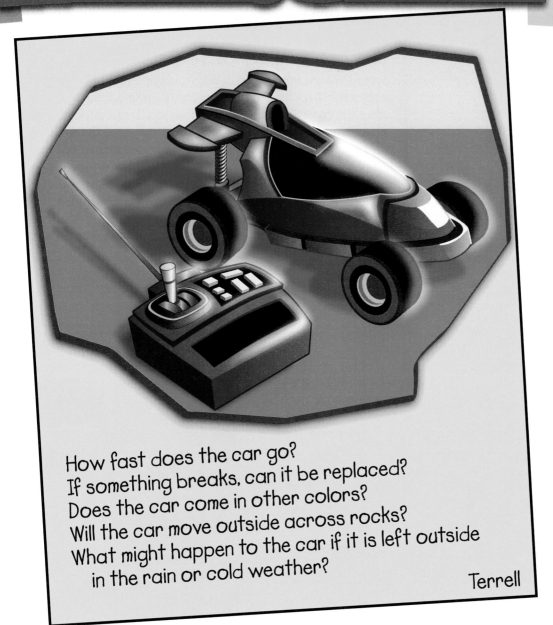

How fast does the car go?
If something breaks, can it be replaced?
Does the car come in other colors?
Will the car move outside across rocks?
What might happen to the car if it is left outside
   in the rain or cold weather?

Terrell

Products to Ponder

To provide practice generating questions, set out a supply of sales circulars. A student selects an interesting product from a circular, cuts it out, and glues it to the top of a sheet of paper. Then the child writes five questions he could ask the manufacturer about the product.

Leslie Grohmann, St. John's Catholic School, Red Bud, IL

Directory Assistance

Students identify two-digit addition problems that require regrouping when they work on this independent activity. Place at a center a local phone book and a supply of paper. A student chooses a business from the phone book; then she writes its name and phone number across the top of her paper. She uses the digits in the phone number to make a list of two-digit numbers. Then she chooses two numbers to add together and writes the problem on her paper. The student solves the problem and, if it requires regrouping, circles it. She continues in this manner until she has solved at least five problems that require regrouping.

adapted from an idea by Jenice Pearson, Coalfield Elementary, Coalfield, TN

Geographically Speaking

This activity provides practice with capitalizing the names of geographic places. Cut apart the cards from a copy of page 102 and store them in a resealable plastic bag. A child numbers his paper from 1 to 10; then he chooses a card from the bag. He identifies the landform or body of water and makes up a proper name for it. The student writes the name on his paper next to the corresponding number, making sure he uses the correct capitalization. Then he continues with each remaining card.

Jean Erickson, Grace Christian Academy, West Allis, WI

What's It All About?

Identifying the main idea of short paragraphs is the focus of this self-checking center. To prepare, cut apart the cards from a copy of page 103. Write on the back of each card the letter that corresponds to the paragraph's main idea; then place the cards at a center. A child selects a card and reads the paragraph. She chooses the paragraph's main idea and then turns the card over to check her answer. If her response was incorrect, she rereads the passage before selecting another card.

Elaine Sanchez, Spring Place Elementary, Chatsworth, GA

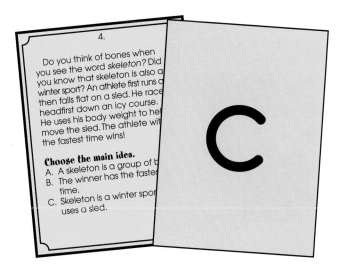

4.

Do you think of bones when you see the word *skeleton*? Did you know that skeleton is also a winter sport? An athlete first runs then falls flat on a sled. He race headfirst down an icy course. He uses his body weight to he move the sled. The athlete wit the fastest time wins!

Choose the main idea.
A. A skeleton is a group of b
B. The winner has the faste time.
C. Skeleton is a winter spor uses a sled.

C

Learning Centers

Stacked Up

Reinforce rounding three-digit numbers to the nearest ten with this center. Copy the center mat from page 105 and color it. Then cut apart a copy of the cards on page 106 and put them in a resealable plastic bag. Set out the bag, the center mat, and a class supply of copies of the recording sheet on page 104. A student reads each card, locates the number on the mat that would be rounded to the number on the card, and places the card on the mat. After he's placed all the cards, he copies the number from each card onto the corresponding section of his recording sheet.

Stacked Up

Round each number to the nearest ten.
Place the matching card on the box.

906	163		739	591
274	359		847	165
586	618		584	902
844	597		611	429
			352	275

Name Christian   Recording sheet

Stacked Up

Write the number shown on each card in its matching section.

910	160		740	590
270	360		850	170
590	620		580	900
840	600		610	430
730	420		350	280

Get Rolling

Help students identify the sounds of -ed. Place at a center a copy of the code and word list on page 106, a die, and a supply of paper. A child divides a sheet of paper into three columns and labels each column as shown. Next, the student rolls a die and looks at the code. Then she writes a word from the list in the matching column. If she has written all the words that match her roll, she rolls again. She continues until she writes at least ten words in all.

adapted from an idea by Jennifer Cripe
James Bilbray Elementary, Las Vegas, NV

/d/	/id/	/t/
rolled	sorted	napped
learned	waited	tripped
slammed	lifted	helped
stirred	ended	parked
giggled	handed	walked

Code
roll 1 or 2 = /d/
roll 3 or 4 = /id/
roll 5 or 6 = /t/

ended
giggled
handed
helped
learned
lifted
napped
parked
rolled
slammed
sorted
stirred
tripped
waited
walked

Classroom Experts

Give students practice with writing directions as they show off all they know about daily classroom tasks. Program the two blank cards from a copy of page 104 with any tasks unique to your classroom; then cut all eight cards apart. Place the cards at a center with a supply of 9" x 12" paper and markers. A child chooses a card and writes each step of the task in pencil on a sheet of paper. He proofreads his work, making changes or corrections as needed. Then he uses markers to trace his writing.

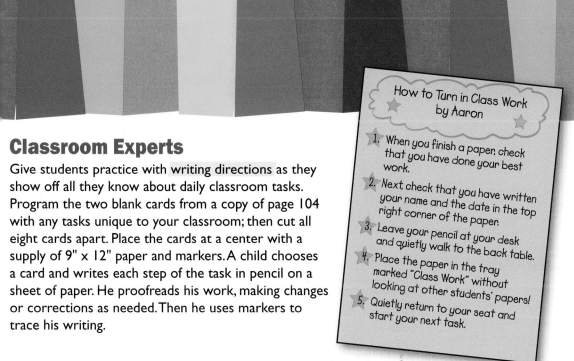

How to Turn in Class Work
by Aaron

1. When you finish a paper, check that you have done your best work.
2. Next, check that you have written your name and the date in the top right corner of the paper.
3. Leave your pencil at your desk and quietly walk to the back table.
4. Place the paper in the tray marked "Class Work" without looking at other students' papers!
5. Quietly return to your seat and start your next task.

A. Seth has three homework sheets. He has a spelling sheet, a math sheet, and a science sheet. How many different ways can he order his homework sheets?

Show each combination.

Spelling   Math   Science

Puzzling Permutations

To challenge students' problem-solving skills, copy the permutation and key cards on page 107 and cut them apart; then laminate the five blank cards at the bottom of the page and cut them out. Place the cards, a dry-erase marker, and a supply of paper at a center. A student reads card A and uses the marker to write each person or object in the problem on a separate blank card. She manipulates the programmed cards to make all possible combinations, writes each combination on her paper, and answers the question. Then the child wipes each programmed card clean before solving the next problem. When she finishes, she uses the key to check her work.

Silent Dialogue

This quiet partner activity provides plenty of fun practice with quotation marks. A student writes a brief statement or question in the form of a direct quotation as shown. He passes the paper to his partner, who reads the sentence and writes a reply in the same format. Students continue as time allows. As a quiet alternative, have students type their sentences on a computer instead.

Rebecca Graves, Grove Park Elementary, Burlington, NC

"I'm so sleepy today," said Colby.

Josh replied, "Me too."

Colby said, "I had a basketball game last night."

"I was up all night doing make-up work from when I was absent," said Josh.

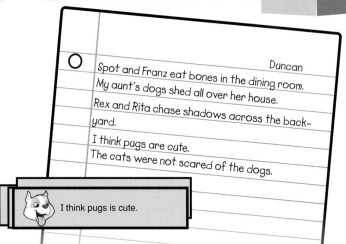

Categories for Canines

This center provides practice with plural subjects and predicates. First, color and cut apart the mat and sentence cards on page 108; then place them at a center. A student reads each sentence and determines if the subject and verb agree. If they do, he places the card on the dog. If they do not agree, he places the card on the doghouse. After he has sorted all the cards, he turns them over to check his work. Then he writes each incorrect sentence, altering the predicate to make the sentence correct.

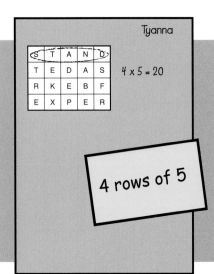

Cutting Columns and Rows

Reuse word searches to make arrays. Label each of a supply of index cards with a different direction to make an array. Place the cards and word searches at a center stocked with paper, scissors, and glue. A child selects a card and cuts a matching array from a word search. She glues the cutout to her paper and writes the corresponding multiplication fact. The student then selects a different card and repeats the steps.

Larry Landscaper

Dig into perimeter and area with this easy-to-prepare center. Cut apart the notepad pages from a copy of page 109 and staple them in order. (To make the notepad more realistic, bind the pages with a plastic binding comb instead.) A child reviews the landscaper's notes and then, on a sheet of paper, solves each project.

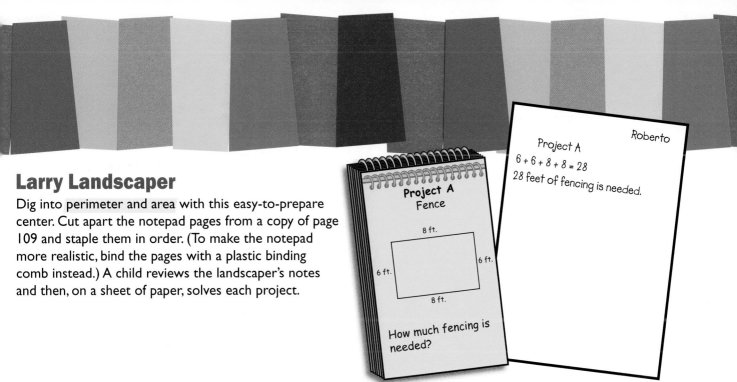

Roberto

Project A
6 + 6 + 8 + 8 = 28
28 feet of fencing is needed.

Project A
Fence

8 ft.

6 ft.   6 ft.

8 ft.

How much fencing is needed?

Get Cracking!

To help students decode multiple-meaning words, cut out the decoder strip and code cards from a copy of page 110. Fold the strip to make a tent and stack the cards facedown. A child draws the top card, refers to the decoder to match each symbol with its letter, and writes each letter on his paper to decode the word. Then he writes the word in two different sentences before drawing another card. Need to extend the activity for an early finisher? Direct the child to generate a list of other multiple-meaning words and write the code for each.

Julie Hamilton, The da Vinci Academy, Colorado Springs, CO and Molly Lynch, Arundel School San Carlos, CA

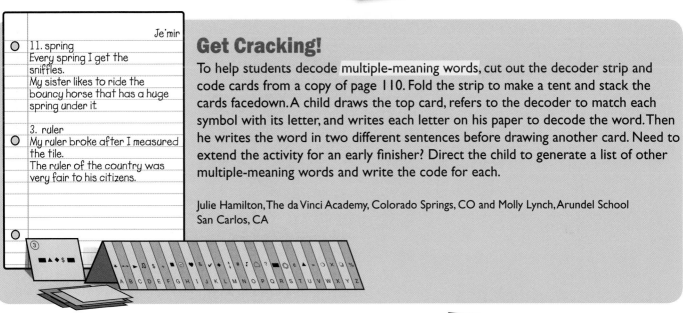

Je'mir

11. spring
Every spring I get the sniffles.
My sister likes to ride the bouncy horse that has a huge spring under it.

3. ruler
My ruler broke after I measured the tile.
The ruler of the country was very fair to his citizens.

Going Places

This partner activity guides students toward a better understanding of coordinate maps and helps improve their listening skills. Place two copies of the coordinate map from page 111 at a center with a supply of index cards. Each student refers to a map as she writes at least four directions, each from one coordinate location to another. Next, one student reads her directions aloud as her partner uses his finger to follow them on his map. Then students switch roles.

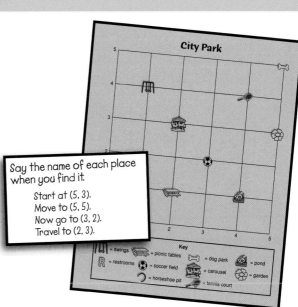

City Park

Say the name of each place when you find it.
Start at (5, 3).
Move to (5, 5).
Now go to (3, 2).
Travel to (2, 3).

Key
= swings   = picnic tables   = dog park   = pond
R = restrooms   = soccer field   = carousel   = garden
= horseshoe pit   = tennis court

Learning Centers

Referenced Rewrite

Students use a thesaurus to generate synonyms with this easy-to-set-up activity. Simply place at a center a thesaurus, classroom books, and a supply of paper. A child locates an interesting sentence in one of the books. He writes the book title and author on his paper and copies the sentence. Next, the student uses the thesaurus to find synonyms for two or more words from the sentence. He rewrites the sentence using the synonyms. Then the child chooses another sentence and repeats the steps.

Jen Goldman, Cheltenham, PA

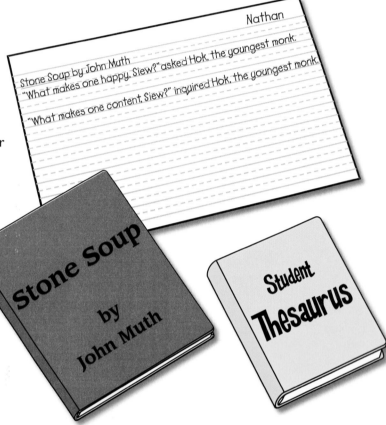

Nathan

Stone Soup by John Muth
"What makes one happy, Siew?" asked Hok, the youngest monk.

"What makes one content, Siew?" inquired Hok, the youngest monk.

Who Rules?

This partner center has students measuring with inches. To prepare, cut apart a copy of the cards on page 112. Place the cards in a bag; then put the bag at a center with two rulers and a supply of paper. To start the activity, each student draws a dot anywhere on his paper. Player 1 takes a card from the bag, uses her ruler to draw a corresponding line segment from her initial dot, and labels the line segment with its measurement. She returns the card to the bag and then Player 2 takes a turn in the same manner. Students alternate play, each time drawing a new line segment from the end of the previous one without going off the page or crossing another line. The first player who cannot draw a line segment loses the round, and play starts again on new sheets of paper.

Ann Fisher, Toledo, OH

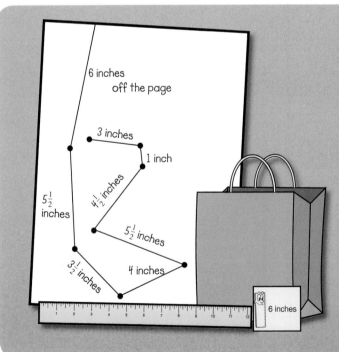

Lucky Draw

Here's a fun activity for three to five students that provides alphabetizing practice. Place at a center a supply of previously studied word cards, such as sight words, vocabulary words, or spelling words. One student in the group stacks the cards facedown. Then each child takes a card and turns it faceup. The students work together to arrange the words in alphabetical order. The child whose card comes first in alphabetical order takes all the cards from that round. Students start a new round and continue until all cards are played. The child with the most cards wins.

Marcia Wuest, Port Byron, IL

gas | matter | solid

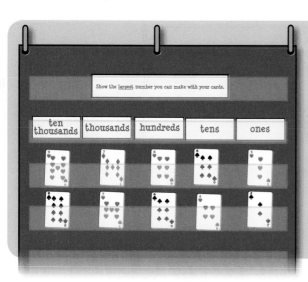

Show the *largest* number you can make with your cards.

| ten thousands | thousands | hundreds | tens | ones |

In Their Place

To review place value skills, cut apart a copy of the cards on page 113 and place one direction card in the top row of a pocket chart. Next, put the place value cards that match your grade-level curriculum in the second row. Remove the face and ten cards from a deck of cards and place the remaining cards near the pocket chart. A student draws one card for each place value position and builds a number to match the direction. He continues until he makes a number on each row. Then the student copies each number on a sheet of paper.

Rebecca Loduca, St. Procopius School, Chicago, IL

Figurative Language Sort

Build knowledge of similes and metaphors with this sorting activity. Copy and cut apart the cards on page 114 and place them in a resealable bag. A child sorts the cards into two stacks, one for similes and one for metaphors. After all the cards are sorted, she checks her work by arranging the cards from each stack to make a picture. If she does not make a heart picture with the simile cards and a star picture with the metaphor cards, she rereads the cards and resorts them.

adapted from an idea by Jennifer Cripe
James Bilbray Elementary, Las Vegas, NV

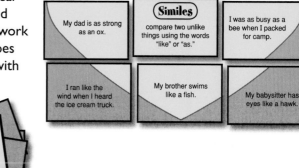

Her smile was as bright as the sun. | My baby sister is as cute as a button. | Aunt Tia looked as pretty as a picture.

My dad is as strong as an ox. | **Similes** compare two unlike things using the words "like" or "as." | I was as busy as a bee when I packed for camp.

I ran like the wind when I heard the ice cream truck. | My brother swims like a fish. | My babysitter has eyes like a hawk.

Metaphors compare two unlike things so that one thing becomes the other. TEC43843

Center Strip

Use with "A Winning Combination" on page 84.

A.

B.

C.

D.

E.

F.

G.

H.

I.

J.

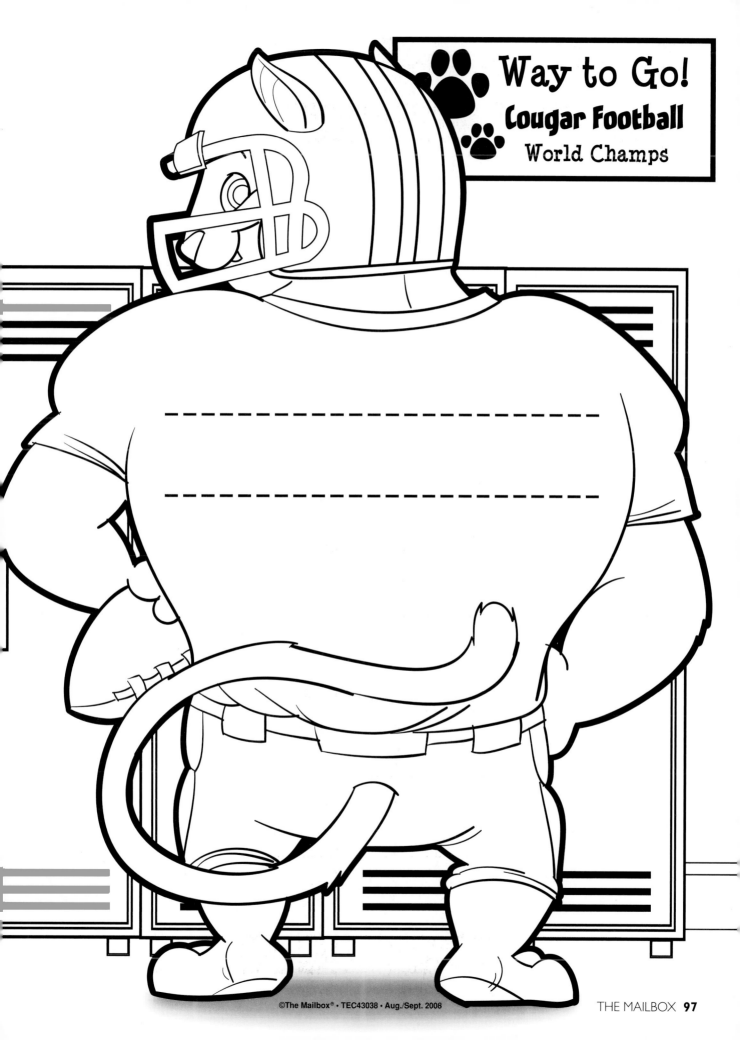

Way to Go!
Cougar Football
World Champs

Player 1

Player 2

odd • even

Even numbers have **0, 2, 4, 6,** or **8** in the ones place.

Odd numbers have **1, 3, 5, 7,** or **9** in the ones place.

©The Mailbox® • TEC43038 • Aug./Sept. 2008

Note to the teacher: Use with "Getting There" on page 85.

by _____

Note to the teacher: Use with "What's Happening?" on page 85.

THE MAILBOX **99**

Corncob and Husk Pattern

Use with "'A-maize-ing' Arrangement" on page 86.

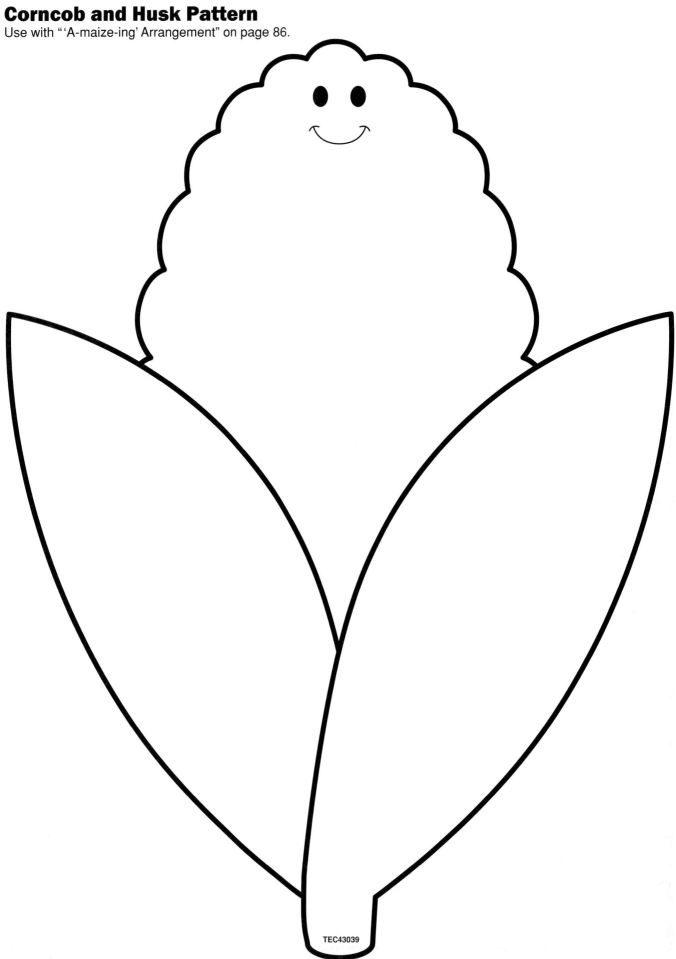

TEC43039

raccoons	are	good	swimmers
crows	are	smart	birds

most	spiders	eat	insects

bats	sleep	during	the	day
squirrels	build	nests	in	trees

owls	hunt	for	food	at	night
cats	use	their	whiskers	to	touch
wild	turkeys	can	run	and	fly

Geography Cards

Use with "Geographically Speaking" on page 89.

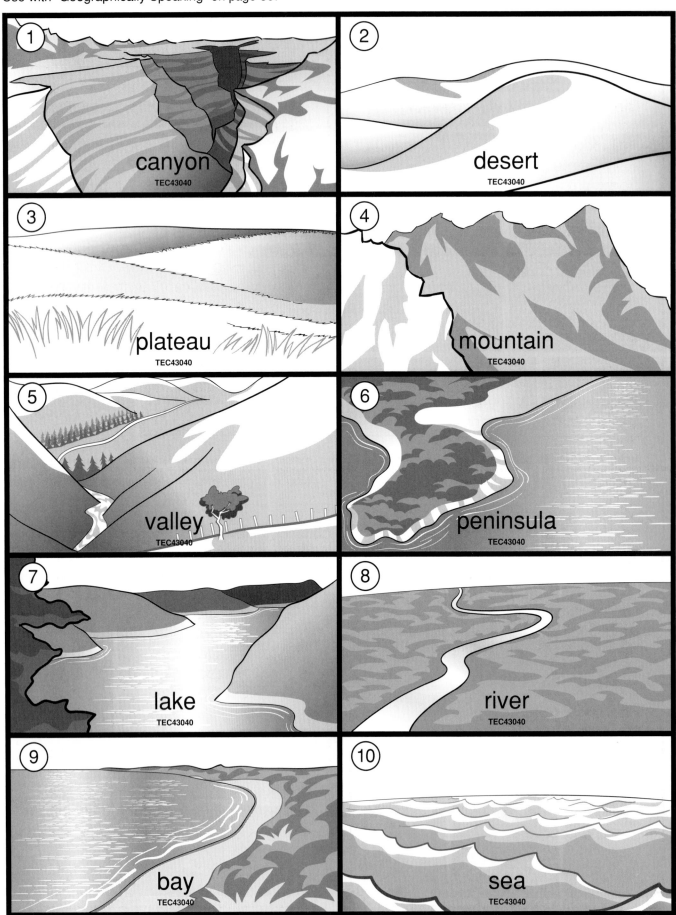

1. canyon
TEC43040

2. desert
TEC43040

3. plateau
TEC43040

4. mountain
TEC43040

5. valley
TEC43040

6. peninsula
TEC43040

7. lake
TEC43040

8. river
TEC43040

9. bay
TEC43040

10. sea
TEC43040

1.

Do you play video games? Did you know that over 50 years ago a scientist named William Higinbotham invented what some say was the first video game? The game was called *Tennis for Two.* Players bounced an electronic ball back and forth over a net. This game couldn't be played at home, though. It could only be played at the lab where it was made.

Choose the main idea.
A. The game was made in a lab.
B. William Higinbotham invented what some say was the first video game, called *Tennis for Two.*
C. *Tennis for Two* was made over 50 years ago.

2.

Each year, gray whales migrate. This means they make a long trip to another place. The whales spend their summers in the seas near Alaska and Russia. Then they move south. Where do they go? They travel as far south as Mexico! Gray whales move close to the shore as they migrate. People who live along or visit the Pacific coast like to watch them.

Choose the main idea.
A. Gray whales go to Mexico.
B. Gray whales migrate from northern seas to the waters by Mexico.
C. Whale watching is fun.

3.

Snowshoes are a kind of footwear for walking over snow. They are about two feet long and about one foot wide. Their size helps spread a person's weight over a large space. This keeps the person from sinking in the snow.

Choose the main idea.
A. Snowshoes help people walk on snow without sinking.
B. Snowshoes are long and wide.
C. Snowshoes are worn in the snow.

4.

Do you think of bones when you see the word *skeleton?* Did you know that skeleton is also a winter sport? An athlete first runs and then falls flat on a sled. He races headfirst down an icy course. He uses his body weight to help move the sled. The athlete with the fastest time wins!

Choose the main idea.
A. A skeleton is a group of bones.
B. The winner has the fastest time.
C. Skeleton is a winter sport that uses a sled.

Classroom Task Cards

Use with "Classroom Experts" on page 91.

○	How to Get Settled in the Morning TEC43041	○	How to Turn in Homework TEC43041
○	How to Turn in Class Work TEC43041	○	How to Line Up to Leave the Room TEC43041
○	How to Share an Answer With the Class TEC43041	○	How to Get Ready to Go Home TEC43041
○	TEC43041	○	TEC43041

Name _____ Recording sheet

Stacked Up

Write the number shown on each card in its matching section.

Stacked Up

Round each number to the nearest ten.
Place the card on the matching box.

591	739
THE MAILBOX	THE MAILBOX
165	847
THE MAILBOX	THE MAILBOX
902	584
THE MAILBOX	THE MAILBOX
429	611
THE MAILBOX	THE MAILBOX
275	352
THE MAILBOX	THE MAILBOX

163	906
THE MAILBOX	THE MAILBOX
359	274
THE MAILBOX	THE MAILBOX
618	586
THE MAILBOX	THE MAILBOX
597	844
THE MAILBOX	THE MAILBOX
424	733
THE MAILBOX	THE MAILBOX

©The Mailbox® • TEC43041 • Feb./Mar. 2009

Number Cards

Use with "Stacked Up" on page 90.

160 TEC43041	170 TEC43041	270 TEC43041	280 TEC43041
350 TEC43041	360 TEC43041	420 TEC43041	430 TEC43041
580 TEC43041	590 TEC43041	590 TEC43041	600 TEC43041
610 TEC43041	620 TEC43041	730 TEC43041	740 TEC43041
840 TEC43041	850 TEC43041	900 TEC43041	910 TEC43041

Code and Word List

Use with "Get Rolling" on page 90.

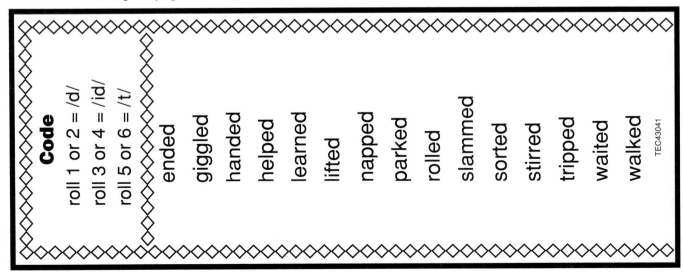

Code
roll 1 or 2 = /d/
roll 3 or 4 = /id/
roll 5 or 6 = /t/

ended
giggled
handed
helped
learned
lifted
napped
parked
rolled
slammed
sorted
stirred
tripped
waited
walked

TEC43041

A. Seth has three homework sheets. He has a spelling sheet, a math sheet, and a science sheet. How many different ways can he order his homework sheets?

Show each combination.

B. Luke is ready to eat lunch. He has a sandwich, a pear, and a carrot. How many different ways can he order what he eats?

Show each combination.

C. Grace has three heart stickers. She has a pink heart sticker, a red heart sticker, and a purple heart sticker. How many different ways can she order her stickers?

Show each combination.

D. Quinn is getting ready for school. She can wear a green shirt, a yellow shirt, or a pink shirt. She can also wear black pants or blue pants. How many different outfits can she make with these clothes?

Show each combination.

Answer Key

A. Six combinations
spelling, math, science
spelling, science, math
math, spelling, science
math, science, spelling
science, math, spelling
science, spelling, math

B. Six combinations
sandwich, pear, carrot
sandwich, carrot, pear
pear, sandwich, carrot
pear, carrot, sandwich
carrot, pear, sandwich
carrot, sandwich, pear

C. Six combinations
pink heart, red heart, purple heart
pink heart, purple heart, red heart
red heart, pink heart, purple heart
red heart, purple heart, pink heart
purple heart, pink heart, red heart
purple heart, red heart, pink heart

D. Six combinations
green shirt, black pants
green shirt, blue pants
yellow shirt, black pants
yellow shirt, blue pants
pink shirt, black pants
pink shirt, blue pants

Center Mat and Cards

Use with "Categories for Canines" on page 92.

Spot and Franz eats bones in the dining room.	Did you hear the hounds howl at the fire trucks?
My aunt's dogs sheds all over her house.	I think pugs is cute.
The bulldogs were watching the cats play.	Ted's puppies lick their paws after eating.
Rex and Rita chases shadows across the backyard.	The cats was not scared of the dogs.
Leah's dogs bark whenever I come to visit.	Linus, Lucy, and Patty were sleeping on the couch.

Project B
Fence

4 ft.
4 ft.
7 ft.

How much fencing is needed?

Project A
Fence

6 ft.
8 ft.
8 ft.
6 ft.

How much fencing is needed?

Fence Projects

Find the distance around the yard.

perimeter = l + l + w + w

Sod Projects

Find out how much grass is needed to cover the yard.

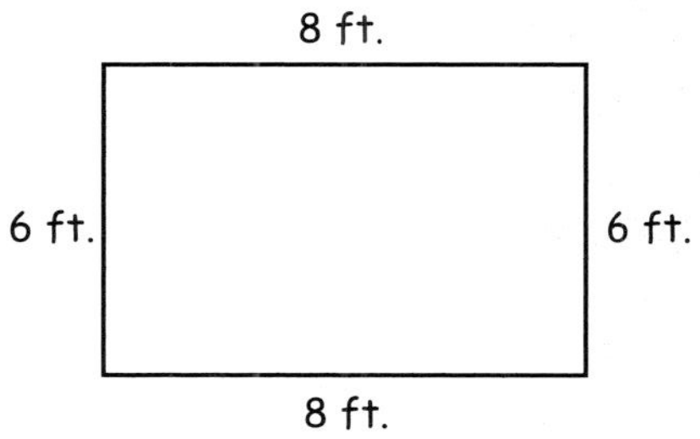

area = l × w

Notes

Larry Landscaper   TEC43042

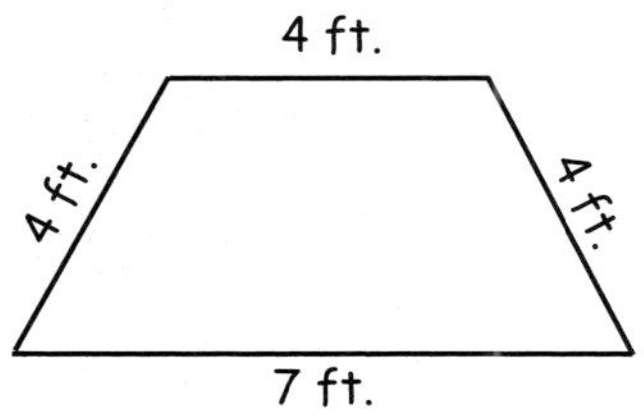

Project F
Sod

12 ft.
5 ft.

How much sod is needed?

Project E
Fence

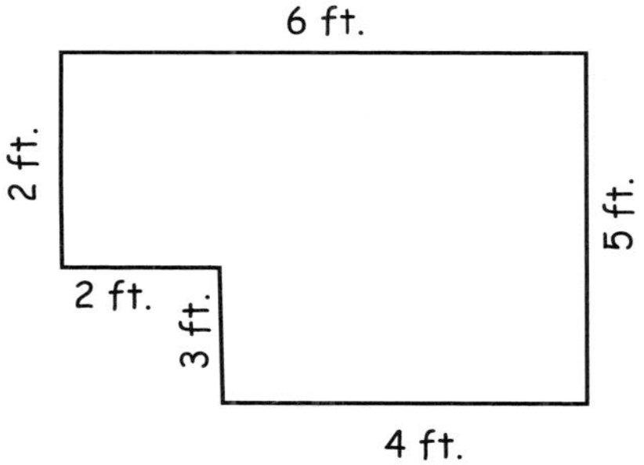

5 ft.
6 ft.
2 ft.
3 ft.
2 ft.
4 ft.

How much fencing is needed?

Project D
Sod

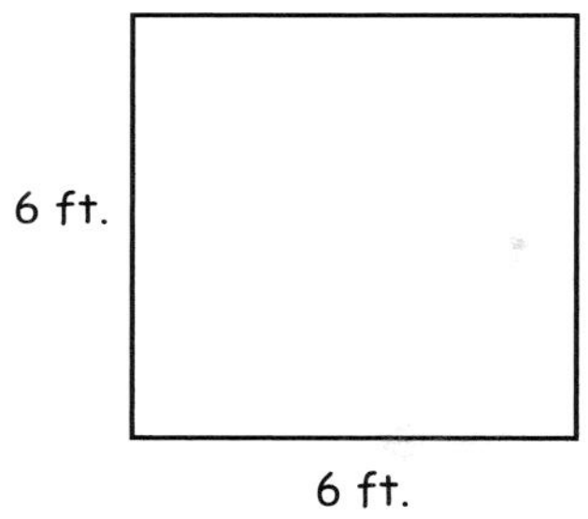

6 ft.
6 ft.

How much sod is needed?

Project C
Sod

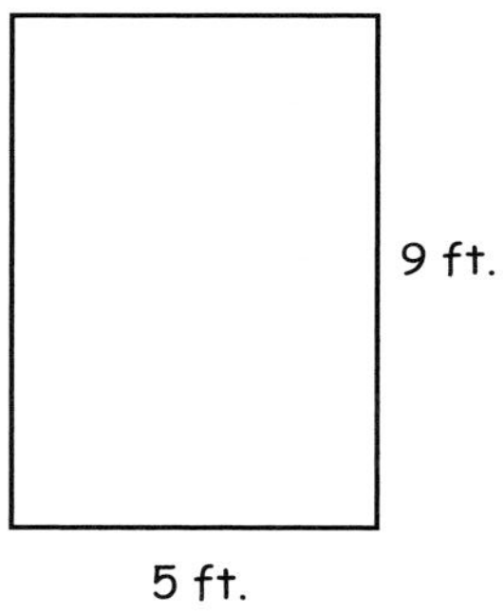

9 ft.
5 ft.

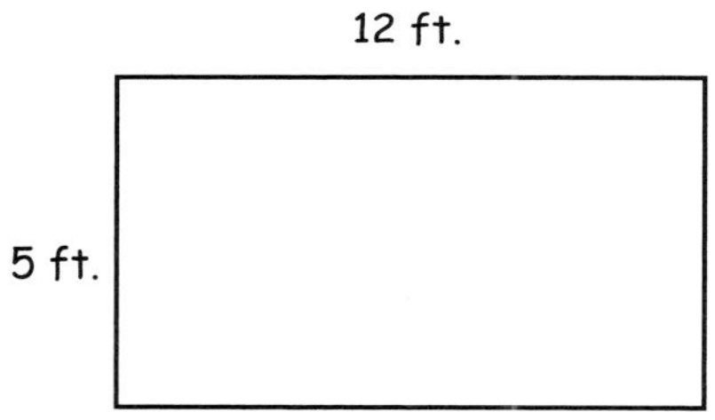

How much sod is needed?

Decoder Strip and Code Cards

Use with "Get Cracking!" on page 93.

Symbol	Letter
%	z
❑	y
✕	x
◯	w
=	v
◀	u
¢	t
☼	s
▮	r
؟	q
◁	p
♪	o
#	n
↔	m
◆	l
♪	k
&	j
❤	i
☺	h
■	g
+	f
$	e
♫	d
▲	c
↕	b
★	a

1 ☼ # ★ ⌂

2 ↔ ▲ ■

3 ■ ▲ ◆ $ ■

4 ⌂ ◆ ★ #

5 ¢ ❤ $

6 + ♪ ♪ ¢

7 ☼ ¢ ★ ↕ ⌂

8 ☼ ❤ ■ #

9 ¢ ■ ❤ ⌂

10 ↔ ❤ ◆ ◆

11 ☼ ⌂ ■ ❤ # ■

12 ◯ ★ = $

13 ■ ♪ ▶ ✔

14 ☼ ★ + $

City Park

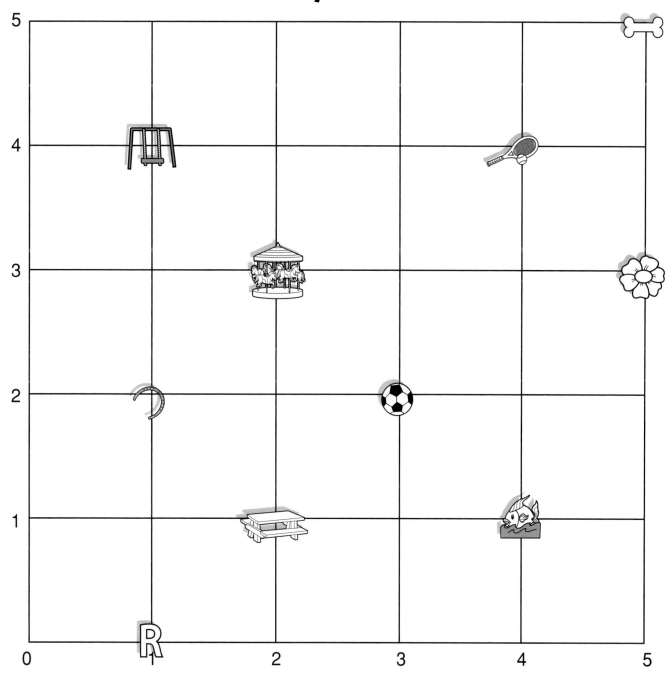

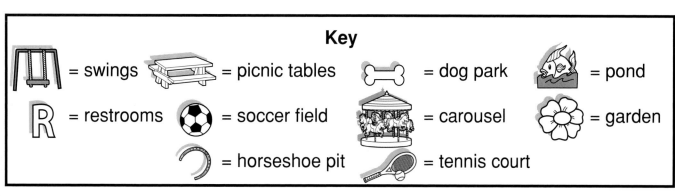

Key

swings = swings   = picnic tables   = dog park   = pond

R = restrooms   = soccer field   = carousel   = garden

= horseshoe pit   = tennis court

Measurement Cards

Use with "Who Rules?" on page 94.

$\frac{1}{2}$ inch TEC43043	$\frac{1}{2}$ inch TEC43043	1 inch TEC43043	1 inch TEC43043
$1\frac{1}{2}$ inches TEC43043	$1\frac{1}{2}$ inches TEC43043	2 inches TEC43043	2 inches TEC43043
$2\frac{1}{2}$ inches TEC43043	$2\frac{1}{2}$ inches TEC43043	3 inches TEC43043	3 inches TEC43043
$3\frac{1}{2}$ inches TEC43043	$3\frac{1}{2}$ inches TEC43043	4 inches TEC43043	4 inches TEC43043
$4\frac{1}{2}$ inches TEC43043	$4\frac{1}{2}$ inches TEC43043	5 inches TEC43043	5 inches TEC43043
$5\frac{1}{2}$ inches TEC43043	$5\frac{1}{2}$ inches TEC43043	6 inches TEC43043	6 inches TEC43043

Use with "In Their Place" on page 95.

Show the largest number you can make with your cards.

TEC43043

Show the smallest number you can make with your cards.

TEC43043

ones

TEC43043

tens

TEC43043

hundreds

TEC43043

thousands

TEC43043

ten thousands

TEC43043

Simile and Metaphor Cards

Use with "Figurative Language Sort" on page 95.

Her smile was as bright as the sun.

TEC43043

My baby sister is as cute as a button.

TEC43043

Aunt Tia looked as pretty as a picture.

TEC43043

My dad is as strong as an ox.

TEC43043

Similes

compare two unlike things using the words "like" or "as."

TEC43043

I was as busy as a bee when I packed for camp.

TEC43043

I ran like the wind when I heard the ice cream truck.

TEC43043

My brother swims like a fish.

TEC43043

My babysitter has eyes like a hawk.

TEC43043

My friend Cara is a songbird.

TEC43043

The scouts slept under a blanket of stars.

TEC43043

The room was an icebox.

TEC43043

Today was a dream.

TEC43043

Metaphors

compare two unlike things so that one thing becomes the other.

TEC43043

His dad is a brain.

TEC43043

My hair is a rat's nest in the morning.

TEC43043

Homework is a breeze.

TEC43043

Her room was a pigsty until she cleaned it.

TEC43043

MANAGEMENT TIPS
& TIMESAVERS

Management Tips & Timesavers

What's for Lunch?

Here's a clever way to keep track of student lunch counts. Staple a tablecloth onto a bulletin board, but leave the bottom edge loose. Write each lunch choice on a paper plate and tack the plates to the board. If desired, mount napkins and plastic utensils next to the plates to create place settings. Next, write each student's name on a clothespin and clip the clothespins along the bottom of the tablecloth. When each student arrives, have him remove his clothespin from the tablecloth and clip it to the plate of his lunch choice.

Amanda Madden, Brushy Creek Elementary
Taylors, SC

A Pocketful of Supplies

Keep extra student supplies accessible and organized with this easy-to-use storage idea. Hang a shoe organizer on a classroom door and label one pocket for each student. During the first week of school, have each student place any extra pencils, markers, scissors, or glue sticks inside the pocket labeled with her name. When a child needs a specific supply, she retrieves it from her pocket.

Andrea Leverton, Alpac Elementary, Pacific, WA

Dial-a-Helper

Classroom job assignments are simple to maintain with this spinning display. First, cut a class supply of yellow paper strips (rays) and label each one with a different student's name or number. Next, tape the rays around the edge of a large tagboard circle to form a sun. Then trim a smaller yellow circle for the sun's center and label it with job titles. Tape a small triangle behind each job title as shown. Finally, place the center circle on top of the large circle and insert a brass fastener. Once a week, turn the dial to assign jobs to a new group of students.

Elizabeth Morgan, Polk County Christian School, Bolivar, MO

Convenient Calling Cards

This organizational tip keeps student contact information at your fingertips. For each student, prepare an index card with his personal contact information, and place the cards in an accordion-style coupon organizer. Anytime you need to make a phone call to a parent, just grab your organizer and head to the phone.

Kristy Dennison, Warsaw Elementary, Warsaw, NC

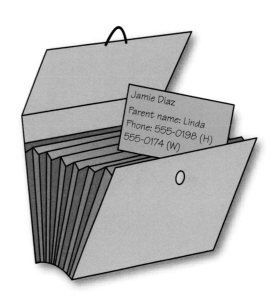

Nice Dice

Encourage students to practice good manners with this daily routine. Label each side of a cube with a different polite phrase, as shown. Each morning, select a student to roll the cube to determine the phrase of the day. Acknowledge students with a high five or another form of recognition as they use the phrase appropriately throughout the day.

Madeline M. Spurck, Neil Armstrong School, Richton Park, IL

Management Tips & Timesavers

Blizzard of Good Behavior

Here's a creative way to reinforce positive behavior and decorate the classroom at the same time. Throughout the day, reward students who are on task with white paper squares. During a break, have each child fold and cut his paper to make a snowflake. Hang the snowflakes around the classroom, and in no time students will see a blizzard of good behavior.

Marcia Horvat, Westvale Public School, Waterloo, Ontario, Canada

Need a Hand?

Students ask for help without raising a hand using this simple idea. Have each child trace her hand on red and green construction paper. Guide her to cut out the hands, glue them back to back, and punch a hole as shown. Lead each student to thread a length of yarn through the hole, tie a knot, and tape the yarn's end to her desktop. At the beginning of seatwork time, have each student put her hand cutout green-side up on her desk. If she needs assistance, have her turn the hand over to the red side.

Natalie Lamb, Battlefield Primary, Fort Oglethorpe, GA

Constant Praise

Here's a great way to bolster students' self-esteem. Make a chart like the one shown. Throughout the month, send home a note, make a phone call home, or give each student a certificate of achievement. Each time a child is recognized for his efforts or good behavior, record it on the chart. Check the chart often to guarantee that each child has received at least one form of praise.

Kim Pohlman, Fort Recovery School, Fort Recovery, OH

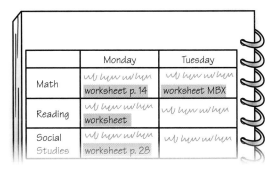

student name	phone call		note home		certificate	
	date	reason	date	reason	date	reason
1. Malcolm						
2. Carly						
3. Anwar						

Positive Communication Record — October 2008

Kiyoko
- ☑ Sorting Sounds
- ☑ Flipping for Numbers
- ☑ Board Work for Two
- ☐ Problem-Solving Center
- ☐ Computer

In Plain View

Control the flow of paper traffic during center time with this organizational tip. For each student, insert a list of the week's center activities inside a clear vinyl folder. Direct each student to check off each activity on her list as she completes it and then put her finished work inside the folder. When it's time to check the student's center work, everything will be in one place.

Brooke Beverly, Dudley Elementary, Dudley, MA

Helpful Highlights

Here's a great way to keep an at-a-glance inventory of reproducibles! While writing a lesson plan, highlight the assignments that will require copies of worksheets. Planning ahead just got a little easier.

Heather Shaffer, Leeton R-X Elementary, Leeton, MO

	Monday	Tuesday
Math	worksheet p. 14	worksheet MBX
Reading	worksheet	
Social Studies	worksheet p. 28	

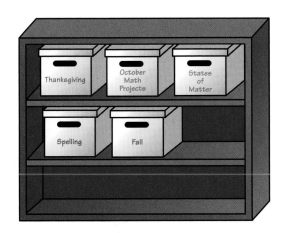

Storage Solutions

Organize seasonal and thematic items in cardboard storage boxes instead of a traditional filing cabinet. Label the outside of each box according to subject, season, or theme. Fill resealable plastic bags with books, manipulatives, and worksheets; then place the items inside the box. Store the boxes in an accessible place.

Madeline M. Spurck, Neil A. Armstrong Elementary, Richton Park, IL

Management Tips & Timesavers

Gold Rush

Here's a golden way to maintain a positive classroom environment. In advance, spray a supply of small stones (nuggets) with gold paint and allow them to dry. Store the nuggets in a resealable plastic container near your desk and place an empty bucket in an accessible area. At the beginning of each week, set a goal for the number of nuggets the class should earn. Each time the class demonstrates a positive behavior, add a gold nugget to the bucket. At the end of the week, select a student to count the nuggets. Reward students with a small treat or special activity if the goal is reached.

Ann Fisher, Toledo, OH

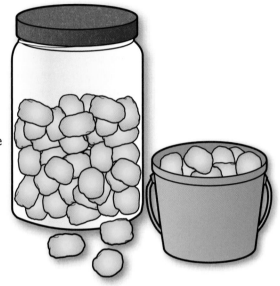

YES WATER NO TOILET

The Sound of Silence

Use hand signals to avoid interruptions during lessons and tests. Model for students a few simple signs, such as TOILET to represent "bathroom" and WATER to symbolize "getting a drink." Also show signs for "yes" and "no." If a student needs to use the bathroom or get a drink, she raises her hand and signs the word rather than speaking. Then the student waits for a YES or NO sign from you.

Anne Kimmey, Crystal Lakes Elementary, Boynton Beach, FL

Lucky Stars

Reinforce responsible behavior with this luck-of-the-draw reward system. Write five different incentives on star cutouts and glue each star on a paper bag. Display the opened bags on a shelf or bulletin board. Throughout the week, give students tickets as rewards for completing homework, following the rules, or other responsible acts. Have each student write his name on the back of the ticket and place it in one of the bags. At the end of the week, select one ticket from each bag and award each corresponding prize. Before emptying the bags for the next week, review the tickets in each bag to assess individual student behavior.

Tara Piccione, Winslow Elementary, Vineland, NJ

Table for Two

Designate spaces for two centers with this practical tip. Label each side of a metal bookend with the name of a different center. Place the bookend in the middle of a large table and put the necessary materials for each center on the corresponding side.

Meredith Black, Augusta Christian School, Augusta, GA

Give Two Cents

Here's a valuable idea to develop listening and speaking skills during small-group instruction. Give each student two pennies. When a student wants to share an idea, direct him to give up a penny before he speaks. After a student uses both pennies, remind him to listen politely to the other students. At the end of the session, give each student who has a penny remaining an opportunity to share his thoughts.

Beth Sine, Dr. Brown Elementary, Waldorf, MD

Got Milk Caps?

Here's a great way to assign student partners. Label a class supply of plastic milk caps with synonyms or antonyms. Before starting a partner activity, distribute the caps and have students quietly find the student with the matching cap.

Nancy Lewis, Our Lady Help of Christians, Abington, PA

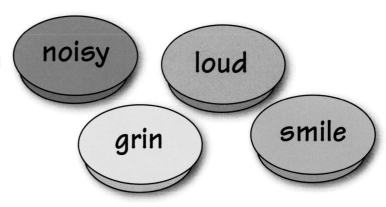

Mystery Walker

There's no secret to maintaining proper hallway behavior with this fun tip. Write each student's name on a craft stick and place the sticks in a container near the door. Also hang a laminated sheet of poster board on the door. Before leaving the room, remove one stick without revealing the mystery walker's name. After returning to the room, name the mystery walker only if he behaved properly. (If he did not behave properly, return the stick to the container.) Direct the student to use a dry-erase marker to sign his name on the poster. Encourage the class to list on the paper as many names as possible during the week. On Friday, count the number of signatures and wipe the poster clean.

Gretchen Vogelei, Martell Elementary, Troy, MI

Management Tips & Timesavers

Clean Desk Fairy

Encourage students to keep their desks neat and orderly with this sweet reward. Before students enter the building in the morning, randomly check desks for organization. On each deserving desk, leave a small treat and a copy of the reward ticket on page 124. After a few days, students will catch the hint to keep their desks tidy and work to earn the fairy's reward at the next inspection.

Susan Jay, Edison Elementary, Hammond, IN

YOU PASSED THE INSPECTION!
The Clean Desk Fairy was impressed with your desk today. Here is a treat to reward you in a sweet way!

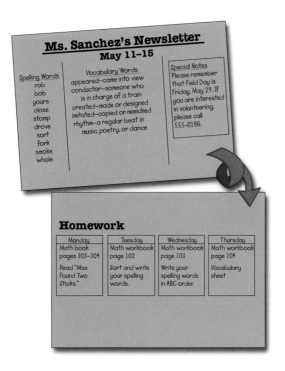

Homework and Happenings

Communicate with parents the week's important information using only one sheet of paper. Simply print your students' weekly homework assignments on the back of your classroom newsletter. Parents will appreciate the single handout and remain informed.

Elaine Sanchez, Spring Place Elementary, Chatsworth, GA

"Egg-ceptional" Behavior

Promote positive behavior by using this incentive basket. Program slips of paper with rewards such as homework passes, free-time choices, or classroom privileges. Insert each slip inside a plastic egg and place the eggs in a basket. When you see excellent behavior, reward the student by having him choose an egg from the basket to reveal his prize.

Patty Frano, Crawford Central School District, Meadville, PA

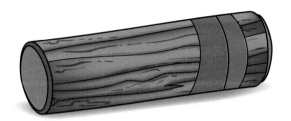

Can You Hear It?

Here's an easy way to signal students to reduce the noise level! Show students a rain stick and explain that whenever you turn it over, you should hear only the sound of rain. Keep your rain stick in an accessible location and enjoy it when your students lower their voices to hear the patter of raindrops.

Janet Godfrey, Golbow Elementary, Katy, TX

Water Fountain Tip

Use skip-counting to monitor your class's water fountain time. To ensure equal drinking time, instruct students to skip-count by a certain number for each person at the fountain, such as "Start at zero and count by twos until you get to eight." Periodically change increments ("Count by fives…") or starting points ("Start at eight and count by fours to…") to provide practice with multiple numbers. This tip allows plenty of time for students to get water and keeps the line moving!

Sarah Burris, Summerwood Elementary, Houston, TX

Expert Tickets

Motivate students to do their best by awarding them inexpensive tickets bought at a discount store. Explain to students that they can earn tickets by showing that they are experts at being responsible. When a student answers a tough question or stays on task, give him an expert ticket. Have the student write his name on the ticket and put it in a basket. Once a week, select five students to receive a small reward, such as a toy from the treasure box or a homework pass; then remove the remaining names. These tickets will keep students working week after week for the honor of being named experts!

Helene Rish, Longwood Elementary, Longwood, FL

Ready Resources

Have your references handy when a parent asks you to recommend an online resource for extra practice. Organize a rotating file according to subject and place it near your computer. Whenever you encounter and test a new student-friendly website, add its address to the file.

Jean Hiller, Canton Charter Academy, Canton, MI

Reward Tickets
Use with "Clean Desk Fairy" on page 122.

YOU PASSED THE INSPECTION!
The Clean Desk Fairy was impressed with your desk today. Here is a treat to reward you in a sweet way!

TEC43042

YOU PASSED THE INSPECTION!
The Clean Desk Fairy was impressed with your desk today. Here is a treat to reward you in a sweet way!

TEC43042

YOU PASSED THE INSPECTION!
The Clean Desk Fairy was impressed with your desk today. Here is a treat to reward you in a sweet way!

TEC43042

YOU PASSED THE INSPECTION!
The Clean Desk Fairy was impressed with your desk today. Here is a treat to reward you in a sweet way!

TEC43042

YOU PASSED THE INSPECTION!
The Clean Desk Fairy was impressed with your desk today. Here is a treat to reward you in a sweet way!

TEC43042

YOU PASSED THE INSPECTION!
The Clean Desk Fairy was impressed with your desk today. Here is a treat to reward you in a sweet way!

TEC43042

YOU PASSED THE INSPECTION!
The Clean Desk Fairy was impressed with your desk today. Here is a treat to reward you in a sweet way!

TEC43042

YOU PASSED THE INSPECTION!
The Clean Desk Fairy was impressed with your desk today. Here is a treat to reward you in a sweet way!

TEC43042

YOU PASSED THE INSPECTION!
The Clean Desk Fairy was impressed with your desk today. Here is a treat to reward you in a sweet way!

TEC43042

YOU PASSED THE INSPECTION!
The Clean Desk Fairy was impressed with your desk today. Here is a treat to reward you in a sweet way!

TEC43042

Math Mailbag

Math Mailbag

Seeing Double
Lines of symmetry

A student positions a sheet of paper horizontally and folds it two times as shown. He starts at the fold and draws half of a body with an arm extending out to the paper's edge as shown. He cuts through the four layers of paper as he trims around the drawing, keeping the fold intact. Then he unfolds his cutout and decorates it to look like identical twins. To make the background, the student folds another sheet of paper in half, unfolds it, and glues the paper cutouts to it. Then he draws a background that is symmetrical on both sides.

adapted from an idea by Kelly Goodwin, Washington Elementary
Mattoon, IL

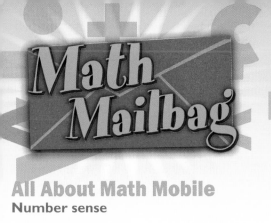

Math Mailbag

All About Math Mobile
Number sense

In advance, prepare templates in the following shapes: a circle, square, rectangle, and triangle. To make a mobile, a student traces each template on three sheets of construction paper, cuts out the shapes, and folds them in half. He unfolds the shapes and then draws a self-portrait on one side of each circle. Then, on the remaining shapes, he writes numbers that tell something about him, such as his birthday, age, favorite number, and height. To assemble the mobile, the student glues together two circle halves, lays a length of yarn down the center as shown and then glues the third circle in place. He repeats the process along the same length of yarn for each of the remaining shapes. Then the student ties loops in the yarn at the top and bottom of his mobile.

adapted from an idea by Natalie Marie Fisher, Sylvania, Ohio

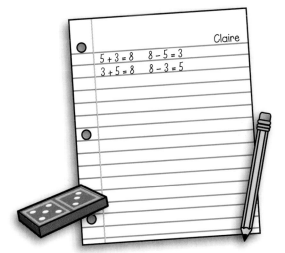

Musical Math Facts
Fact families

Get the whole class moving as students identify and write related addition and subtraction facts. Have each student refer to a domino to write on her paper addition and subtraction facts that correspond with her domino's dots. Next, direct each student to keep the domino at her desk and stand with her paper. Instruct her to wait for the music to begin and then walk around the room until the music stops. Have the student sit at the closest desk and write the fact family for the domino. When she finishes writing, guide her to stand and wait to play another round.

adapted from an idea by Krista Hatten, Forks Elementary, Easton, PA

That Makes "Cents"
Counting coins

Help students successfully identify coin values with this simple strategy. Model for students how to label each type of silver coin with lines as shown, explaining that each line has a value of five. Next, provide each student with a set of coins and a sheet of paper. Have her arrange on her paper the silver coins, from the greatest value to the least, and place any pennies at the end of the line. Guide her to draw the correct number of lines above each silver coin. Then lead the student to skip-count each line by fives until she comes to the pennies. The student stops counting by fives and counts the pennies by ones.

Linda Morel, Amite Elementary, Amite, LA

≡≡ ≡ | | |
50¢   25¢   10¢   5¢   1¢

Math Mailbag

Caleb

This hexagon was made with many different shapes.
two hexagons
four trapezoids
eight rhombuses
14 triangles

Kaleidoscope Fun
Combining geometric shapes to make other shapes

In advance, place in separate resealable bags each set of pattern blocks listed. Direct a student to select a bag; then have the student cut out a copy of the hexagon pattern from page 141. Guide the student to use all the pattern blocks to cover the hexagon cutout. Instruct him to carefully slide the design off the hexagon when he finishes. Have the student trace each block of his design on the hexagon pattern, color each tracing to match the block, and then write a brief description of his design on an index card.

Sets of Pattern Blocks
- three hexagons, six trapezoids, six triangles, six rhombuses
- three rhombuses, three hexagons, six trapezoids, 12 triangles
- three hexagons, six rhombuses, eight trapezoids
- six trapezoids, nine rhombuses, 18 triangles
- six triangles, six rhombuses, six hexagons
- two hexagons, four trapezoids, eight rhombuses, 14 triangles

Math Mailbag

Today's Lineup
Odd and even numbers

Divide the class into two groups, designating students in one group "odd" and the other group "even." When it's time for students to line up, call out a random number. Have each student use a copy of the chant on page 141 to silently determine if the number is odd or even. Direct students from the appropriate group to line up first. Then have the remaining students get in line behind the first group. What a great way to review numbers and practice listening skills!

Paula Panarese, Twin Pines Elementary, Brentwood, NY

Odds and Evens

I'll stand up, push in my chair, and walk to the line
Since an **odd** number ends with **1, 3, 5, 7,** or **9.**

It's time for me to get in a line that is straight
Since an **even** number ends with **0, 2, 4, 6,** or **8.**

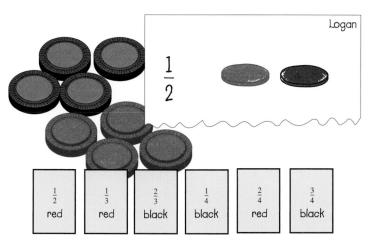

Logan

$\frac{1}{2}$

$\frac{1}{2}$ red	$\frac{1}{3}$ red	$\frac{2}{3}$ black	$\frac{1}{4}$ black	$\frac{2}{4}$ red	$\frac{3}{4}$ black

Check Your Checkers
Fractional parts of a group

In advance, program six index cards with the fractions shown. Also put four red and four black checkers in a resealable plastic bag. To begin, a child reads the fraction on an index card. He makes a model of the fraction with checkers, traces the model on his paper, and colors the fractional parts. Then the student places the index card to the side, selects a new card, and repeats the process until he models the fractions on all the cards.

Jenice Pearson, Oak Ridge, TN

Got Your Number
Reading numbers and number words

To begin this partner game, have students cut apart a copy of the cards and gameboards from page 142, and then stack the cards facedown. To begin, Player 1 turns a card over, looks at the number, and checks his gameboard for the matching number word. If he finds a match, the student places the card on the matching square. If he does not find a match, the student returns the card to the bottom of the stack and his turn ends. Play continues until one player's gameboard is filled. If time allows, students switch gameboards and play again.

adapted from an idea by Anna Hicks, W. R. Odell Elementary, Concord, NC

Player 1

| sixteen | nineteen | twenty- | twenty- | thirty- | forty |

47

Player 2

twelve	fifteen	twenty	twenty-six	thirty-one	forty-three	forty-nine	eighty-two
fifty-four	58	sixty-five	sixty-seven	seventy	seventy-two	eighty	

Math Mailbag

Team 1

Expanded Form	Standard Form
2,000 + 100 + 20	2,120
1,000 + 200 + 10	1,210
300 + 20	320

Bowling for Numbers
Writing numbers in expanded and standard forms

In advance, label ten empty water bottles (pins) with the following base ten values: "1,000" (three pins), "100" (three pins), and "10" (four pins). To play, divide the class into two teams and select a child from one team to roll a ball toward the pins. Have a student from the opposing team record on the board the value of each pin knocked down, showing the value in both expanded and standard forms. After each student takes a turn, lead the class in computing the final score for both teams. To make the game more authentic, label a set of plastic bowling pins (available at discount stores) instead.

Maria Holloway, Reese Road Elementary, Columbus, GA

Pattern Play
Number sequence

This one-on-one activity helps students review skip-counting and number patterns. Cut out a copy of the cards on page 143 and place each set in a plastic bag. Have a student arrange the cards from one set in numerical order. Then direct the student to turn away while you remove a few cards from the series. Refocus the child on the cards and have him identify the missing numbers. As an alternative, use the review as a partner activity.

Mary Davis, Keokuk Christian Academy, Keokuk, IA

What's in a Year?
Calendar

Reinforce problem-solving skills with this partner activity. Give each pair of students a calendar and a copy of a recording sheet from page 144. Guide each duo to complete the questions with information from the calendar. Then have the students exchange papers and calendars with another set of partners. The students read the questions and use the calendar to answer them on the lines provided.

Jean Erickson, Grace Christian Academy, West Allis, WI

Walk the Line
Area and perimeter

Use the classic game of musical chairs to introduce the concept of perimeter and area. Place two rows of three chairs back-to-back and put a rectangular border of tape around the group of chairs. Have six students stand on the border and face the same direction; then start the music. Guide students to walk on the tape and softly repeat the word *perimeter* until the music stops. Then direct each student to sit on a chair and say, "Area." Provide time for each student to have a turn.

Karen Slattery, Marie of the Incarnation School, Bradford, Ontario, Canada

Math Mailbag

A Recipe for Numbers
Writing a two-digit number

Help students discover different ways to show a number using tens and ones. Provide each student with a copy of the recipe card pattern on page 145 and direct her to write a two-digit number at the top of her card. Next, have the student write the value of her number in tens and ones; then have her show it equal to a number sentence. Direct the child to continue writing different increments of tens and ones that equal the original number and include the corresponding number sentences. Have each student cut out her card and display it on a board titled "Cooking Up Numbers."

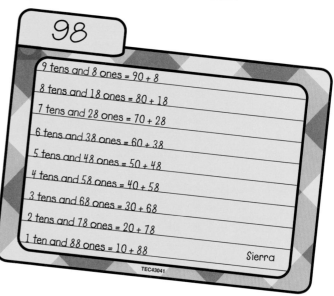

98

9 tens and 8 ones = 90 + 8
8 tens and 18 ones = 80 + 18
7 tens and 28 ones = 70 + 28
6 tens and 38 ones = 60 + 38
5 tens and 48 ones = 50 + 48
4 tens and 58 ones = 40 + 58
3 tens and 68 ones = 30 + 68
2 tens and 78 ones = 20 + 78
1 ten and 88 ones = 10 + 88

Sierra

TEC43041

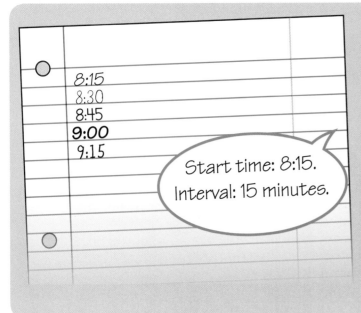

8:15
8:30
8:45
9:00
9:15

Start time: 8:15.
Interval: 15 minutes.

Time Flies
Elapsed time

Have groups of four or five students sit in small circles; designate a recorder for each group. Announce a start time and direct the recorder to write that time at the top of a sheet of paper. Then announce an interval of time, such as 15 minutes. On your signal, the recorder adds the interval time to the start time, writes down the new time, and passes the paper to the next student. Each child takes a turn recording the next time in the interval. When each group finishes, check the answers together and then repeat with a new time and interval. **As an added challenge**, announce an ending time and an interval; then direct the students to find the times that come before the ending time.

Laura Wagner, Menachem Hebrew Academy, Austin, TX

Keys to Multiplying
Multiplication facts

Motivate students to memorize the multiplication tables. Direct each student to color and personalize the car and key patterns on a copy of page 146 and then cut out the patterns. Display the cars on a board titled "On the Road to Mastering Multiplication" by stapling around the bottom perimeter of each car to form a pocket. After a student masters a set of multiplication facts, have her place in her car the key corresponding to the multiplication set she learned. After a student has earned all ten keys, allow her to use a calculator to check her multiplication seatwork at specified times.

Ashley Powell, Mansfield Christian School, Mansfield, OH

Name That Change
Counting coins up to a dollar

In advance, label each of a class supply of envelopes with a different letter and fill them with different amounts of plastic coins totaling up to a dollar each. Keep a list of the envelopes' coin totals as a reference. To begin the activity, have each student count the coins in an envelope and write the total on a piece of paper. Call out one of the coin totals from the list and direct the student with the matching amount to stand up. Have him name the coins in his envelope and count the coins out loud. Continue until each student has had a turn. Repeat the activity at other times to familiarize students with different coin combinations.

Terry Healy, Marlatt Elementary, Manhattan, KS

Computation Challenge
Addition and subtraction

To prepare this teacher-versus-students game, divide the board into six or eight sections and number each section. Select a student to stand at each section; assign one problem to the students in the the odd-numbered sections and a different problem to the students in the even-numbered sections. Direct each child to write his assigned problem on the board, solve it, and return to his seat. When all the students are seated, check each answer and give the students' team one point for each correct response. If all the odd-numbered answers or all the even-numbered answers are correct, the students' team gets a bonus point. If any answer is incorrect, give yourself a point. Record the score on the board with tally marks and then play another round.

1	2	3	4	5	6
37 + 48	73 − 56	37 + 48	73 − 56	37 + 48	73 − 56

Paula Panarese, Twin Pines Elementary, Brentwood, NY

Xs and Os
Division

For this partner game, draw on the board a tic-tac-toe grid with nine dividends. Direct one player in each student pair to copy the grid onto a sheet of paper. To begin, Player 1 chooses a dividend and recites a related division fact. Player 2 uses a calculator to check the answer. If Player 1 is correct, he marks the space with an X and Player 2 takes a turn. If Player 1 is incorrect, his turn ends. The duo continues playing, with Player 2 marking his correct answers with an O, until one player connects three spaces in a line. If all the spaces are marked without a player making a line, the player with the most total marks wins.

adapted from an idea by Kelly Allabach, Kratzer Elementary, Allentown, PA

36	15	21
54	81	72
12	27	40

Part of a Whole
Identifying and ordering fractions

To prepare, program for each small group a set of index cards with common denominator fractions from 0 to 1. Also write 0 and 1 on separate index cards and tape the cards a short distance apart on the floor. Distribute a set of fraction cards to a group of students. Direct the students to hold the cards with the fractions facing out and work together to form a line between the 0 and 1 that shows the fractions in sequential order. Once the line is formed, have the remaining students check the order and make any necessary corrections. Then collect the cards and distribute a new set of fractions among another group of students.

$\frac{0}{5}$	$\frac{1}{5}$	$\frac{2}{5}$	$\frac{3}{5}$	$\frac{4}{5}$	$\frac{5}{5}$

0   1

Math Prompts

Program a copy of the recording sheet on page 145 with one of the prompts below. Then make a class supply of the sheet and direct each student to complete it.

- A plane leaves from New York City at 2:15. If it takes 90 minutes to get to Richmond, what time will the plane arrive?

- Aidan has 21 marbles. Nathan has 38 marbles. About how many more marbles does Nathan have than Aidan? Estimate.

- If you have two white T-shirts and four blue T-shirts, what fraction of the shirts are white?

- Colton has 21 trading cards. He wants to put the cards into groups of 3. How many groups can he make?

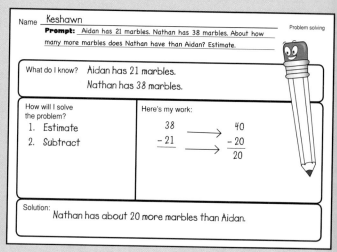

Name __Keshawn__

Prompt: Aidan has 21 marbles. Nathan has 38 marbles. About how many more marbles does Nathan have than Aidan? Estimate.

Problem solving

What do I know? Aidan has 21 marbles.
Nathan has 38 marbles.

How will I solve the problem?
1. Estimate
2. Subtract

Here's my work:

$$38 \longrightarrow 40$$
$$-21 \longrightarrow -20$$
$$ 20$$

Solution: Nathan has about 20 more marbles than Aidan.

Two Parts of a Word
Fractional parts

Give each student a copy of page 147 and direct him to write eight different words with varying numbers of letters in the first column. Have the child count the total number of letters in the first word and write that number (denominator) in the second column. Then have him individually count the consonants and vowels (numerators) and record each number in its appropriate column. Next, guide the child to write a fraction for each part of the word. Remind the student to check that the sum of the numerators equals the denominator. Finally, have him complete the rest of the chart.

Name _Kyle_

Fractions
Fractional parts of a whole

Whole Words

Word	Number of Letters	Consonants	Vowels	What fractional part of the word is consonants?	What fractional part of the word is vowels?
1. flower	6	4	2	$\frac{4}{6}$	$\frac{2}{6}$
2. ladybug	7	5	2	$\frac{5}{7}$	$\frac{2}{7}$
3. April	5	3	2	$\frac{3}{5}$	$\frac{2}{5}$
4. fractions	9	6	3	$\frac{6}{9}$	$\frac{3}{9}$
5.					
6.					
7.					
8.					

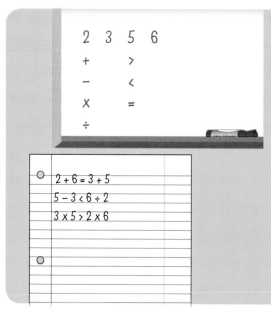

Fill in the Blanks
Equalities and inequalities

Write on the board four numbers along with the operation and comparison symbols shown. Guide each student to use the numbers and operation symbols to write three pairs of equal or unequal equations. Then direct her to write the corresponding comparison symbol for each pair. Select students to write their equations on the board without the comparison symbols. Have each child call upon another student to solve her equations.

Jean Erickson
Milwaukee, WI

Math Mailbag

Hands in Motion
Slides, flips, and turns

Assign each student one of the following terms: *slide, flip,* or *turn*. Next, have the child trace his hand twice on a sheet of paper, cut out the tracings, and color an identical pattern on each cutout. Guide the child to glue the cutouts on a large sheet of paper to demonstrate his assigned transformation and label the paper with the corresponding term. Post the papers on a bulletin board titled "Slides, Flips, and Turns."

Betsy Liebmann, Gotham Avenue School, Elmont, NY

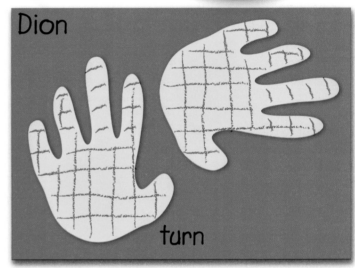

Dion

turn

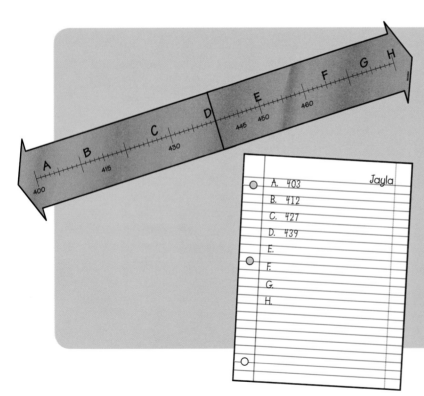

A. 403
B. 412
C. 427
D. 439
E.
F.
G.
H.

Jayla

400 A B 415 C 430 D 445 E 450 F 460 G H

Mystery Numbers
Number sense

In advance, cut apart a copy of the number line pattern on page 148, glue the ends together, and laminate it. Use a permanent marker to label the lines with letters and grade-appropriate numbers as shown. Place the number line at a center with a supply of paper. A student copies the number line's letters on a sheet of paper. Then she writes the missing number that corresponds with each letter.

TIP

When you're ready to provide practice with another set of numbers, use rubbing alcohol or nail polish remover to wipe the strip clean.

Decimal Derby
Decimals and fractions

Help students understand that the words used to name fractions are the same words used to name decimals. Give each twosome a copy of the gameboard on page 149, a copy of the game cards and answer key on page 150, and an envelope. Have the duo cut apart the cards and then follow the directions on the gameboard. When the game ends, direct each pair to put the game cards and answer key in the envelope. To extend the activity at another time, have a student read each card, write on a sheet of paper the matching fractions and decimals, and check his work with the key.

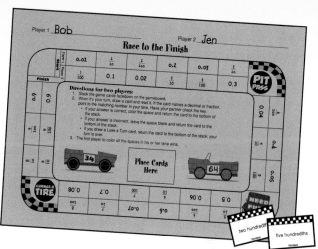

Yummy Yards
Length

Give each student a Fruit by the Foot snack. Direct him to measure with a ruler one foot of the snack and to tear off that length of snack, leaving the paper lining. Invite the child to eat or set aside the first foot of the snack and then repeat the measuring process two more times. After the third foot of snack is measured and removed, guide each student to move around the room with his paper lining and find an object with a height or width equal to the paper lining's length. Make a chart to share students' discoveries.

Karen Britton, Calvary Christian School, Fruitport, MI

How Big Is a Yard?	
Width	Height
desk window	chair bookshelf

Cubes in a Tube
Patterns

Use Unifix cubes and a cardboard tube to reinforce predicting patterns. Connect ten cubes to make a pattern rod. Slide the rod through a tube so half the pattern is shown and the other half is hidden by the tube. Direct each student to write on a sheet of paper the pattern shown and then record his prediction of the next cube's color. Slowly slide the rod to reveal the next cube and direct each student to confirm or adjust his prediction. Continue in the same manner, revealing one cube at a time until all the cubes in the pattern are shown; then provide time for students to share their predictions and conclusions. As time allows, repeat the activity using a different set of cubes.

Pattern shown:
green, blue, yellow, green, blue

Prediction:
yellow

Two of a Kind
Associative property of addition

To prepare for this partner activity, program six paper strips with three addends each. Next, cut a pipe cleaner into four pieces and bend the pieces to look like parentheses. Place the strips, parentheses, and a supply of paper at a center. Each student selects a strip and two parentheses. He places the parentheses around two of the addends, copies the problem on a sheet of paper, and writes the sum. The student exchanges strips with his partner. Each child moves the grouping of the parentheses, copies the new problem, and writes the sum. The children compare their sums and then repeat the activity with two different strips.

Jenice Pearson, Oak Ridge, TN

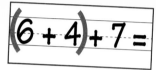

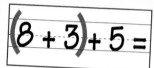

Cooper

$8 + (3 + 5) = 16$
$(6 + 4) + 7 = 17$

Emmanuel

$6 + (4 + 7) = 17$
$(8 + 3) + 5 = 16$

Marcelina

Hidden Solutions
Computation practice

Here's a fun and easy way for students to check answers to daily review problems. In advance, write on each of five sticky notes a different computation problem with its answer, and post the notes around the room. Give each student a copy of the same five problems to solve. When a student is ready to check her work, have her walk around the room to find the matching problem and its answer.

Jennifer Nelson, McDonough, GA

Math Prompts

- Draw a Venn diagram on a sheet of paper. Label the left side 293 and the right side 392. Compare the two numbers. What do the numbers have in common? What makes them different?

- It takes 35 minutes to bake a cake, 45 minutes for the cake to cool, and 20 minutes to frost the cake. If the cake is put in the oven at 2:30, when will it be ready to eat?

- Draw 24 jelly beans. Divide the jelly beans into eight equal groups. Color $\frac{1}{8}$ of the jelly beans yellow, $\frac{1}{8}$ of the jelly beans orange, $\frac{2}{8}$ of the jelly beans red, and $\frac{4}{8}$ of the jelly beans green.

- Draw a picture of an object in the classroom that looks like each of the following shapes: square, circle, triangle, rectangle, cube, sphere, rectangular prism, and cylinder. Label each object with its shape name.

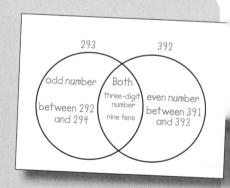

Count On It
Input/output tables

Draw on the board an input/output table without numbers. Give each student a set of counters and a small container; then write a number in the first input section of the table. Direct each student to put the same number of counters in his container. Next, name a rule, such as "add two." Guide each child to put two more counters in his container and then recount them. Write the output number on the table and continue the activity until the table is complete. Then have each child empty his container and repeat the activity using a different input number. **To extend the activity,** program a number in every space and have each student use his manipulatives to determine the rule.

Suzann Falgione, Warrenwood Elementary, Fayetteville, NC

| Input | 5 | 6 | 7 | 8 |
| Output | 7 | 8 | 9 | |

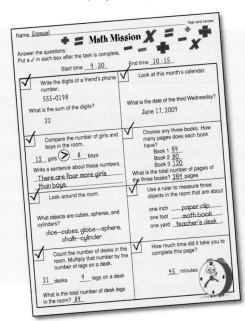

Find It!
Year-end review

Here's an intriguing way to review math skills at the end of the school year. Have each student complete the tasks on a copy of page 151. Encourage him to use classroom items to help him complete the tasks and remind the student to record his start and end times where indicated.

adapted from an idea by J. J. Markle
Rolling Acres Elementary, Littlestown, PA

Pour More
Capacity

To prepare for this demonstration, gather several clear containers of different sizes (ranging from cups to gallons) and shapes. Also give each student a copy of the recording sheet from the bottom of page 152. Select two containers and lead students to predict which container holds more liquid. Use a measuring cup to pour water into each container as students count the number of cups poured. When each container is full, have students record their conclusions. Repeat the process several more times with different pairs of containers. Vary the activity to predict which container will hold less or which containers hold equal amounts. **As an added challenge,** have students arrange the containers from least to greatest volume.

Laura Wagner, Menachem Hebrew Academy, Austin, TX

Summer Destinations
Graphs

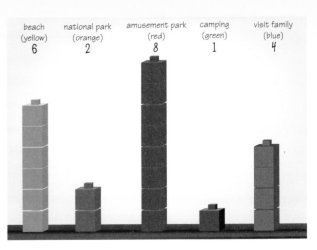

beach (yellow)	national park (orange)	amusement park (red)	camping (green)	visit family (blue)
6	2	8	1	4

To begin, write on the board a color code for five summer vacation destinations. Also place around the room a class supply of Unifix cubes for each color in the code. On your signal, direct each child to choose a cube that matches his preferred vacation destination and then to stand with other students who have the same color cubes. After the five groups have formed, have the students in each group count and connect their cubes. Direct each group to place its connected cubes on the board's ledge under the corresponding vacation destination and write the number of cubes on the board. Then have each student make a bar graph that represents the data shown.

Julie Hamilton, The da Vinci Academy, Colorado Springs, CO

Series of Numbers
Range

Cut out an enlarged copy of the Mini and Max cards on page 152 and tape the cards to the board, leaving a large space between them. Place similar objects in a clear jar and have each student write on a sticky note his estimate for the number of objects in the jar. Guide each child to place his sticky note between Mini and Max, moving other notes as needed to order the estimates from the minimum to maximum. When all the notes are placed in the correct order, select a student to calculate the range.

Stephanie Wanek, Bentwood Elementary, Overland Park, KS

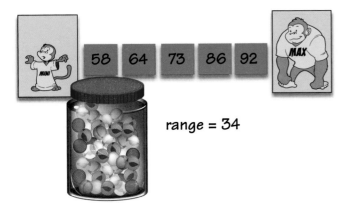

range = 34

Math Prompts

- Think about summer events that are *certain, likely, unlikely,* and *impossible.* Give an example of each, such as "It is likely that the weather will be hot."

- Ben has 10 cups and 7 pints of milk. Two cups equal one pint and two pints equal one quart. How many quarts of milk does Ben have?

- Make an input/output table. Label the input numbers "3," "6," "9," and "12." Label the first two output numbers "6" and "12." Finish the table and write the rule.

- Jenna collects 32 seashells. She has 4 jars. Jenna wants to put the same number of seashells in each jar. How many seashells should she put in each jar so all the seashells are used?

- Matt spent $2.50 on a soft drink and $2.75 on popcorn. He has $4.75 left. How much money did Matt bring to the snack shop?

Turn to pages 153–158 for math practice pages.

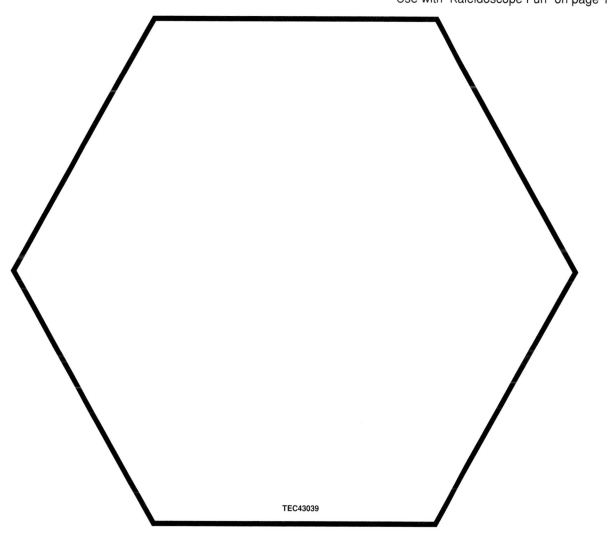

TEC43039

0 1 2 3 4 5 6 7 8 9 0 1 2 3 4 5 6 7 8 9 0 1 2 3 4 5 6 7 8 9 0 1 2 3

Odds and Evens

I'll stand up, push in my chair, and walk to the line
Since an **odd** number ends with **1, 3, 5, 7,** or **9.**

It's time for me to get in a line that is straight
Since an **even** number ends with **0, 2, 4, 6,** or **8.**

TEC43039

Note to the teacher: Use with "Today's Lineup" on page 129.

THE MAILBOX 141

Game Cards and Gameboards

Use with "Got Your Number" on page 129.

Player 1

sixteen	nineteen	twenty-five	twenty-eight	thirty-four	forty	forty-seven
fifty-two	fifty-six	sixty-one	sixty-six	seventy-three	seventy-nine	eighty-two

©The Mailbox® • TEC43039 • Oct./Nov. 2008

Player 2

twelve	fifteen	twenty	twenty-six	thirty-one	forty-three	forty-nine
fifty-four	fifty-eight	sixty-five	sixty-seven	seventy	seventy-two	eighty

©The Mailbox® • TEC43039 • Oct./Nov. 2008

12	15	16	19	20	25	26
TEC43039	TEC43039	TEC43039	TEC43039	TEC43039	TEC43039	TEC43039
28	31	34	40	43	47	49
TEC43039	TEC43039	TEC43039	TEC43039	TEC43039	TEC43039	TEC43039
52	54	56	58	61	65	66
TEC43039	TEC43039	TEC43039	TEC43039	TEC43039	TEC43039	TEC43039
67	70	72	73	79	80	82
TEC43039	TEC43039	TEC43039	TEC43039	TEC43039	TEC43039	TEC43039

2 TEC43040	22 TEC43040	3 TEC43040	33 TEC43040	5 TEC43040	55 TEC43040
4 TEC43040	24 TEC43040	6 TEC43040	36 TEC43040	10 TEC43040	60 TEC43040
6 TEC43040	26 TEC43040	9 TEC43040	39 TEC43040	15 TEC43040	65 TEC43040
8 TEC43040	28 TEC43040	12 TEC43040	42 TEC43040	20 TEC43040	70 TEC43040
10 TEC43040	30 TEC43040	15 TEC43040	45 TEC43040	25 TEC43040	75 TEC43040
12 TEC43040	32 TEC43040	18 TEC43040	48 TEC43040	30 TEC43040	80 TEC43040
14 TEC43040	34 TEC43040	21 TEC43040	51 TEC43040	35 TEC43040	85 TEC43040
16 TEC43040	36 TEC43040	24 TEC43040	54 TEC43040	40 TEC43040	90 TEC43040
18 TEC43040	38 TEC43040	27 TEC43040	57 TEC43040	45 TEC43040	95 TEC43040
20 TEC43040	40 TEC43040	30 TEC43040	60 TEC43040	50 TEC43040	100 TEC43040

Calendar Search

NOVEMBER 23

NOVEMBER 22

1. On what day is the _____ of _____?
   date   month

   _____

2. How many days are in _____? _____
                          month

3. On what day does _____ begin? _____
                      month

   On what day does _____ end? _____
                      same month

4. How many holidays are in _____? _____ Name them.
                             month

   _____

5. Does _____ have more _____ or
          month   day of the week

   _____? _____
   different day of the week

6. In which month is _____? _____
                      holiday

©The Mailbox® • TEC43040 • Dec./Jan. 2008–9

Calendar Search

Names _____ Calendar

NOVEMBER 23

NOVEMBER 22

1. On what day is the _____ of _____?
   date   month

   _____

2. How many days are in _____? _____
                          month

3. On what day does _____ begin? _____
                      month

   On what day does _____ end? _____
                      same month

4. How many holidays are in _____? _____ Name them.
                             month

   _____

5. Does _____ have more _____ or
          month   day of the week

   _____? _____
   different day of the week

6. In which month is _____? _____
                      holiday

©The Mailbox® • TEC43040 • Dec./Jan. 2008–9

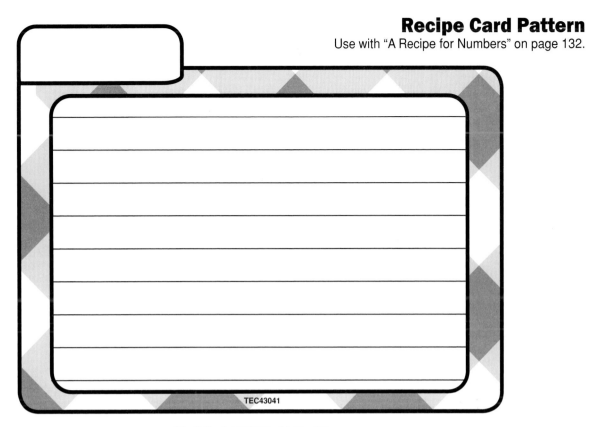

TEC43041

©The Mailbox® • TEC43041 • Feb./Mar. 2009

Name _____ Problem solving

Prompt: _____

_____

What do I know?

How will I solve the problem?	Here's my work:

Solution:

Note to the teacher: Use with "Math Prompts" on page 134.

Key and Car Patterns

Use with "Keys to Multiplying" on page 133.

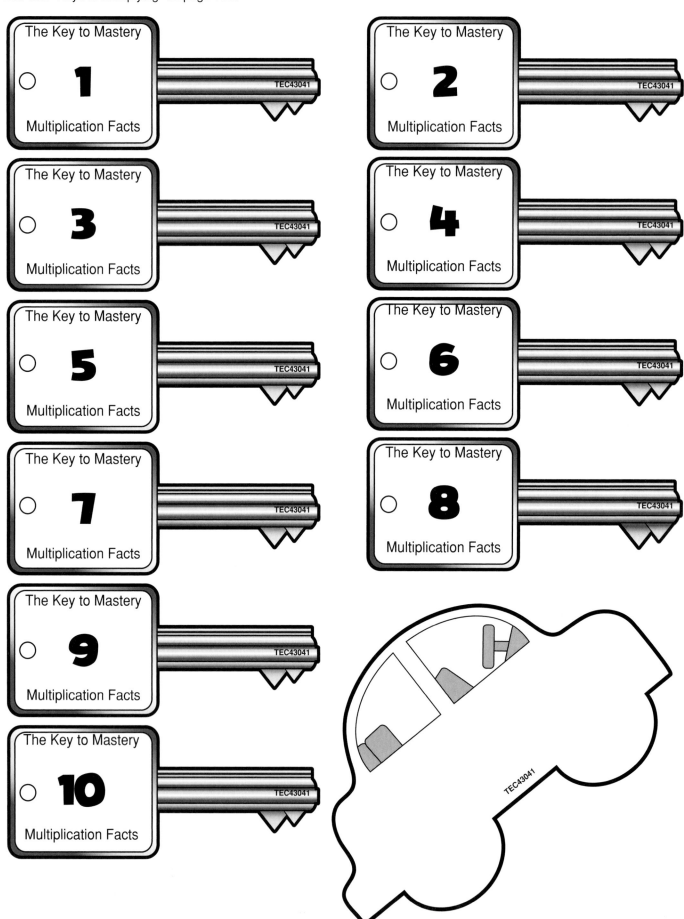

The Key to Mastery

1

Multiplication Facts

TEC43041

The Key to Mastery

2

Multiplication Facts

TEC43041

The Key to Mastery

3

Multiplication Facts

TEC43041

The Key to Mastery

4

Multiplication Facts

TEC43041

The Key to Mastery

5

Multiplication Facts

TEC43041

The Key to Mastery

6

Multiplication Facts

TEC43041

The Key to Mastery

7

Multiplication Facts

TEC43041

The Key to Mastery

8

Multiplication Facts

TEC43041

The Key to Mastery

9

Multiplication Facts

TEC43041

The Key to Mastery

10

Multiplication Facts

TEC43041

TEC43041

Fractions
Fractional parts of a whole

Whole Words

Word	Number of Letters	Consonants	Vowels	What fractional part of the word is consonants?	What fractional part of the word is vowels?
1.					
2.					
3.					
4.					
5.					
6.					
7.					
8.					

©The Mailbox® • TEC43042 • April/May 2009

Note to the teacher: Use with "Two Parts of a Word" on page 135.

Number Line Pattern
Use with "Mystery Numbers" on page 136.

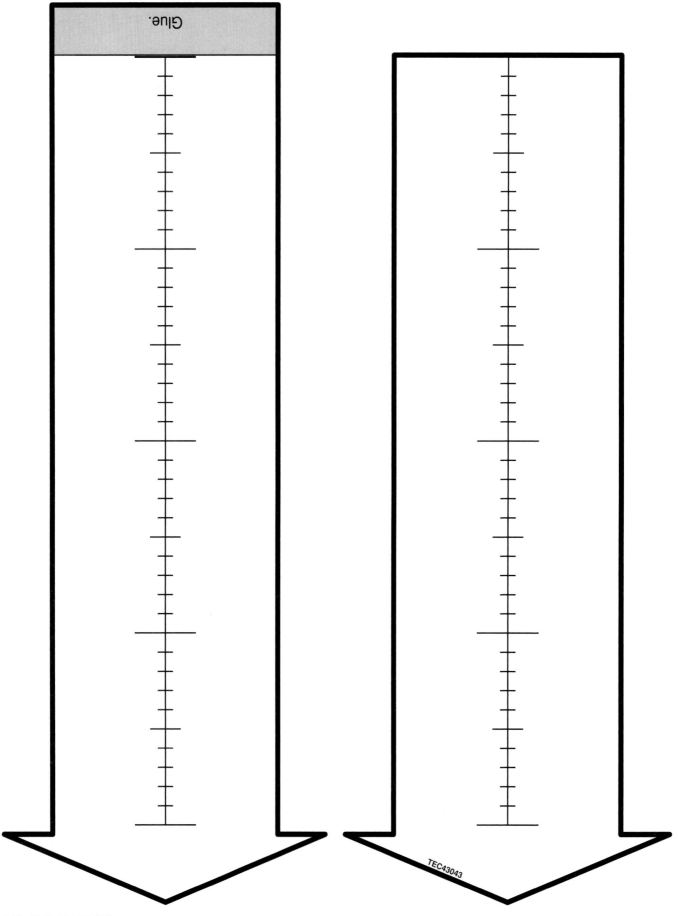

Glue.

TEC43043

Player 1

Player 2

Race to the Finish

| $\frac{4}{100}$ | 0.4 | 0.05 |
| 0.04 | $\frac{4}{10}$ | $\frac{5}{100}$ |

PIT PASS

NEED FUEL

| $\frac{3}{10}$ | 0.03 | 0.2 | $\frac{2}{100}$ | $\frac{1}{10}$ | 0.01 |
| 0.3 | $\frac{3}{100}$ | $\frac{2}{10}$ | 0.02 | 0.1 | $\frac{1}{100}$ |

| | 0.5 | 0.06 | 0.6 | 0.07 | 0.7 | 0.08 |
| | $\frac{5}{10}$ | $\frac{6}{100}$ | $\frac{6}{10}$ | $\frac{7}{100}$ | $\frac{7}{10}$ | $\frac{8}{100}$ |

64

Place Cards Here

34

Directions for two players:

1. Stack the game cards facedown on the gameboard.
2. When it's your turn, draw a card and read it. If the card names a decimal or fraction, point to the matching number in your lane. Have your partner check the key.
   - If your answer is correct, color the space and return the card to the bottom of the stack.
   - If your answer is incorrect, leave the space blank and return the card to the bottom of the stack.
   - If you draw a Lose a Turn card, return the card to the bottom of the stack; your turn is over.
3. The first player to color all the spaces in his or her lane wins.

| Player 1 | Player 2 |
| **Start** | |

Finish

| | 0.9 | 0.09 | $\frac{8}{10}$ |
| | $\frac{9}{10}$ | $\frac{9}{100}$ | 0.8 |

CHANGE A TIRE

©The Mailbox® • TEC43042 • April/May 2009

Note to the teacher: Use with "Decimal Derby" on page 137.

Game and Answer Key Cards

Use with "Decimal Derby" on page 137.

one hundredth	one tenth	two hundredths	two tenths
TEC43042	TEC43042	TEC43042	TEC43042

three hundredths	three tenths	four hundredths	four tenths
TEC43042	TEC43042	TEC43042	TEC43042

five hundredths	five tenths	six hundredths	six tenths
TEC43042	TEC43042	TEC43042	TEC43042

seven hundredths	seven tenths	eight hundredths	eight tenths
TEC43042	TEC43042	TEC43042	TEC43042

nine hundredths	nine tenths	**Pit Pass** Lose a turn.	**Change a Tire** Lose a turn.
TEC43042	TEC43042	TEC43042	TEC43042

Need Fuel Lose a turn.	**Pit Pass** Lose a turn.	**Change a Tire** Lose a turn.	**Need Fuel** Lose a turn.
TEC43042	TEC43042	TEC43042	TEC43042

Race to the Finish Answer Key

one hundredth = 0.01, $\frac{1}{100}$

one tenth = 0.1, $\frac{1}{10}$

two hundredths = 0.02, $\frac{2}{100}$

two tenths = 0.2, $\frac{2}{10}$

three hundredths = 0.03, $\frac{3}{100}$

three tenths = 0.3, $\frac{3}{10}$

four hundredths = 0.04, $\frac{4}{100}$

four tenths = 0.4, $\frac{4}{10}$

five hundredths = 0.05, $\frac{5}{100}$

five tenths = 0.5, $\frac{5}{10}$

six hundredths = 0.06, $\frac{6}{100}$

six tenths = 0.6, $\frac{6}{10}$

seven hundredths = 0.07, $\frac{7}{100}$

seven tenths = 0.7, $\frac{7}{10}$

eight hundredths = 0.08, $\frac{8}{100}$

eight tenths = 0.8, $\frac{8}{10}$

nine hundredths = 0.09, $\frac{9}{100}$

nine tenths = 0.9, $\frac{9}{10}$

TEC43042

✚ = **Math Mission** ✗ = ✚

Complete each task.
Put a ✓ in each box after the task is complete.

Start time ____:____   End time ____:____

☐ Write the digits of a friend's phone number. What is the sum of the digits?	☐ Look at this month's calendar. What is the date of the third Wednesday?
☐ Compare the number of girls and boys in the room. _____ girls ◯ _____ boys Write a sentence about these numbers. _____ _____	☐ Choose any three books. How many pages does each book have? Book 1 ____ Book 2 ____ Book 3 ____ What is the total number of pages of the three books? ____ pages
☐ Look around the room. What objects are cubes, spheres, and cylinders?	☐ Use a ruler to measure three objects in the room. Name each object. one inch _____ one foot _____ one yard _____
☐ Count the number of desks in the room. Multiply that number by the number of legs on a desk. ____ desks ____ legs on a desk What is the total number of desk legs in the room? ____	☐ How much time did it take you to complete this page? ____ minutes

©The Mailbox® • TEC43043 • June/July 2009

Mini and Max Cards

Use with "Series of Numbers" on page 140.

TEC43043

TEC43043

Name _____ Capacity

Pour More

• •

Containers	Prediction	Conclusion

Note to the teacher: Use with "Pour More" on page 139.

Name_____

Working in the Garden

Write <, >, or = to make a true number sentence.
To find the path to the garden, color each section that shows an equality (=).

		3 + 4 __ 11 − 4	12 − 6 __ 5 + 8	4 + 6 __ 7 + 2
8 + 7 __ 9 + 4	14 − 7 __ 13 − 9	6 + 5 __ 9 + 2	18 − 9 __ 15 − 6	11 − 1 __ 3 + 7
15 − 5 __ 18 − 6	3 + 8 __ 4 + 5	13 − 5 __ 9 + 9	6 − 5 __ 4 − 4	2 + 6 __ 16 − 8
6 + 12 __ 8 + 10	8 − 5 __ 12 − 9	7 + 6 __ 16 − 3	12 − 4 __ 17 − 9	7 + 7 __ 6 + 8
11 − 5 __ 10 − 4	9 − 6 __ 7 − 3	5 + 9 __ 12 − 2	8 + 1 __ 14 − 6	16 − 9 __ 5 + 3
6 + 9 __ 17 − 2	12 − 8 __ 10 − 6	14 − 8 __ 15 − 9		

Ski Cap Sort

Read the clues. Fill in the chart.
Draw a ✓ if the cap matches the snowpal.
Draw an X if the cap does not match the snowpal.
Cut apart the cap cards. Glue each one on the matching snowpal.

Blizzard   Chilly   Frosty   Icy   Snowy

Clues

- Blizzard does not want a white cap.

- Frosty wants a cap that matches his scarf.

- Snowy does not want a polka dot or white cap.

- Chilly does not want a cap with polka dots.

- Icy wants a plaid cap.

	striped	polka dot	white	plaid	black
Icy					
Chilly					
Frosty					
Blizzard					
Snowy					

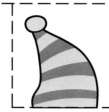   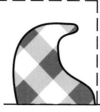 

Time to Strut

Draw clock hands or write the time to match each time given.

| 8:35 |

| 11:45 |

| 2:10 |

| 1:25 |

| 4:00 |

©The Mailbox® • TEC43041 • Feb./Mar. 2009 • written by Laura Wagner, Austin, TX • Key p. 310

Bonus Box: Choose two clocks. On the back of this page, write each time in words.

Name _____

Weight and volume

Tip the Scale

Cut apart the cards.
Match each item with its unit of measure.
Glue.

pounds

ounces

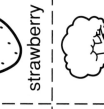

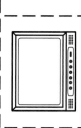
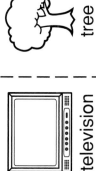
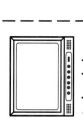
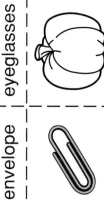

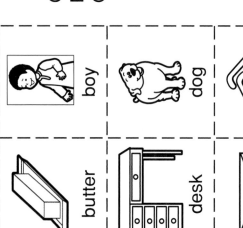

Bonus Box: On the back of this page, write an estimated weight for each item above.

©The Mailbox® · TEC43043 · June/July 2009 · Key p. 311 · Laura Wagner · Austin, TX

butter	boy
desk	dog
envelope	eyeglasses
paper clip	pumpkin
shell	strawberry
television	tree

Secret Numbers

Solve each problem in its matching box.
Hint: Start at the end of the problem and
    do the opposite of each task listed.
Write the answer on the line.
Cross off the matching number.

12
3
29
4
25
6̶
33
9

A. Double the number and add 12 to get 24.
What is the secret number?

SECRET NUMBER
6

B. Add 10 to the number and subtract 7 to get 15.
What is the secret number?

SECRET NUMBER

C. Subtract 10 from the number and add 14 to get 33.
What is the secret number?

SECRET NUMBER

D. Subtract 5 from the number and add 10 to get 30.
What is the secret number?

SECRET NUMBER

E. Double the number and subtract 6 to get 12.
What is the secret number?

SECRET NUMBER

F. Add 20 to the number and subtract 13 to get 40.
What is the secret number?

SECRET NUMBER

G. Find $\frac{1}{2}$ of the number and add 7 to get 9.
What is the secret number?

SECRET NUMBER

H. Double the number, subtract 2, and add 16 to get 20.
What is the secret number?

SECRET NUMBER

A. $\begin{array}{r} 24 \\ -12 \\ \hline 12 \end{array}$ = 6	B.	C.	D.
E.	F.	G.	H.

Say Cheese!

Multiply.
Color the matching answer in each row.
Follow the path to show the mouse's favorite cheese.

80 x 4	320	324	120	124
11 x 7	88	77	87	78
33 x 2	65	55	66	56
62 x 3	185	186	96	95
22 x 4	88	66	86	68
40 x 6	246	240	100	106
71 x 5	126	356	355	125
52 x 4	96	98	206	208
31 x 8	249	118	248	119
20 x 3	50	63	60	53

American   Swiss   Cheddar   Mozzarella

©The Mailbox® • TEC43041 • Feb./Mar. 2009 • Key p. 311

OUR READERS WRITE

Our Readers Write

I scored a goal in gym class.

Name: Emilia
Grade: 2
Year: 2008-9
Teacher: Ms. Jake
School: Saltsburg Elementary

Emilia's School Memories

Memory Books

To start a keepsake of school memories, I give each student three paper lunch bags and guide her to stack the bags with alternating open ends. Next, I have her fold the stack in half and staple the bags along the fold. Then I have the student decorate her book with ribbons and stickers. Throughout the year, I guide each student to use the pages to write about special events and accomplishments. I also have her place photographs, certificates of achievement, and other memorabilia inside the bag openings.

Stephanie Jake, Saltsburg Elementary, Saltsburg, PA

Awesome Apples

On Back-to-School Night, I have each parent or guardian write a note to his child on an apple cutout and then tape it to a tree display. The next morning, students pick their apples from the tree and read the words of praise and encouragement.

Rosemarie Giovinazzo, Harrington Park Elementary
Harrington Park, NJ

To: Marcus
From: Dad

I am so proud of you! I like the way you keep your desk organized. It's going to be a great year! Keep up the good work! I love you!

Timesaver Buckets

This colorful organization tip helps me save instructional time. I purchase a different-colored bucket for each of my student groups. Before my students' daily arrival, I put in each bucket sets of worksheets, manipulatives, and other materials needed for the day's lessons. I also sort each set of worksheets with different-colored paper clips so I can signal to my group captains which set to hand out. At the end of the day, the buckets are returned to me so I can replenish supplies for the next day.

Kassie Witt, W. D. Munson Primary, Mulvane, KS

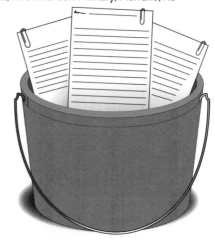

Give Them a Break

I give my students' parents or guardians two parent homework passes at Back-to-School Night. I explain that each pass provides them with a break from two homework nights, but it cannot be used for projects or studying for tests. To redeem the homework pass, the parent signs the pass and returns it to school with her child.

Tara Rooney, Stokes Elementary, Levittown, NY

★ **Parent Homework Pass** ★
Enjoy one night free of homework!

Student name: _____
Date: _____

_____
parent signature

Bedazzling Displays

To spruce up my bulletin boards, I use wrapping paper instead of butcher paper. I also die-cut my letters from printed scrapbook paper that I purchase from discount stores. My bulletin boards are always seasonally bright and cheery!

Sara Miller, All Saints Episcopal School, Lubbock, TX

Reference Cubes

I use plastic photo cubes to display classroom rules, procedures, and other handy tips. The cubes are easy to set up and require very little space. I place the cubes around the classroom for easy student access.

Melissa Axner, Campbell Park Elementary, St. Petersburg, FL

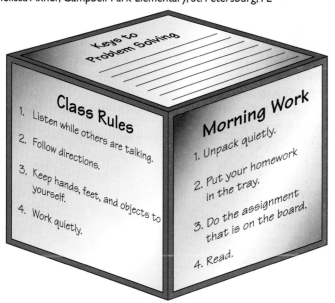

Keys to Problem Solving

Class Rules
1. Listen while others are talking.
2. Follow directions.
3. Keep hands, feet, and objects to yourself.
4. Work quietly.

Morning Work
1. Unpack quietly.
2. Put your homework in the tray.
3. Do the assignment that is on the board.
4. Read.

Birthday Bags

On the first day of school, I have each student decorate her own birthday bag. I give her a white paper bag and guide her to personalize both sides with her name, her birthday, and pictures that tell about her. I collect the bags and keep them until each birthday arrives. On the morning of a birthday, I invite the class to write on a birthday-themed reproducible something special about the celebrated student. When everyone has signed it, I fold the paper and place it in the bag along with a pencil, bookmark, or special treat. For students with summer birthdays, I set aside the last week of school to celebrate.

Mitzi Mayfield, Melissa Ridge Elementary, Melissa, TX

Today's my birthday!
Monica
September 5, 2008

Happy Birthday Monica!
Very helpful Tony
Super nice! Hannah
Great gymnast! Alexa
My best friend! Pat

Recorded Readings

Here's how I keep track of my students' reading progress throughout the year. At the beginning of the school year, each student brings a blank cassette tape to school. I have him begin a recording by stating the date, book title, and author. Then I have the student record himself reading a short story. Every month, my students record stories that are progressively more advanced. I use the recordings to assess my students and discuss their progress at parent conferences. At the end of the year, I send the cassettes home.

Linda B. West, Jefferson Elementary, Winston-Salem, NC

Learning Cursive Letters

To familiarize my students with the cursive alphabet, I use the letters on my cursive alphabet display as the column headings for my word wall. I place new vocabulary words under the cursive letters so my students can make an association between the printed and cursive letters.

Emily Stump, Summit Elementary, Ashland, KY

Our Readers Write

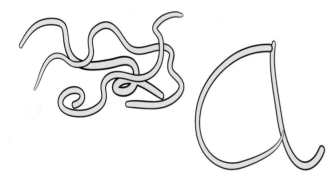

Neat Noodles

Here's a fun way to teach cursive writing. The night before a cursive lesson, I boil spaghetti and add olive oil to prevent it from sticking. The next day, I model the proper way to shape the spaghetti into cursive letters. Then I give each student a handful of pasta and have him practice on his own.

Rebecca McGrath, Liberty Christian School
Owings Mills, MD

Spelling Solutions

I give each student a mini memo book to make a personal spelling dictionary. My students label each page with a different letter of the alphabet. Throughout the year, they add new vocabulary words to their dictionaries. During a writing assignment, each student refers to his dictionary to help with his spelling. If a word is not in his dictionary, I help the student add it to his book.

Jo Ann Kiefer, Apache Elementary, Albuquerque, NM

Learning Charts

To help my students reflect on the different units they study, I tape a large sheet of bulletin board paper to a closet door. I divide the paper into sections labeled with the units we're studying. During free time, I invite my students to write on the paper their ideas about the topic or new skills they learned that day. When we finish a unit, I display the paper in another location as a reminder of our learning.

Christina Bainbridge, Centreville, MI

Teacher Keepsake

I keep a scrapbook of my students' drawings and letters. It's a three-ring binder filled with plastic sheet protectors. When a student gives me a picture or letter, I immediately file it away inside my binder where it is safely stored and easy to view.

Andrea Leverton
Alpac Elementary
Pacific, WA

Scientific Fashion Sense

I get my students excited about science by wearing lab coats. I ask my parents to donate adult size, long-sleeve, white button-up shirts, and I purchase extra shirts at a thrift store. Then, when we conduct a science experiment, I have each student wear a shirt as a lab coat.

April Parker, St. Pius X School
Greensboro, NC

Sweet Snowball Recipe

1. Cut a one-inch slice of banana.
2. Pick up the slice with a toothpick and dip the banana into orange juice.
3. Roll the slice in powdered sugar until the slice is covered.
4. Set the slice aside and let it dry.

Snack Center

My students practice following directions with this tasty idea. I place a step-by-step "no bake" recipe and all the ingredients at a center. I observe students as they make the snack and then I give them time to eat it.

Julie Lewis, J. O. Davis Elementary, Irving, TX

A Straight Verse

To help my students remember the difference between horizontal and vertical lines, I teach them this chant.

When I stand up and have a straight spine,	*(Lay arms on top of each other and then slowly lift one arm to make a 90 degree angle.)*
Then I make a vertical line.	*(Point arm straight up to the ceiling.)*
When I lay flat upon my spine,	*(Slowly lower arm back on top of other arm.)*
Then I make a horizontal line.	*(Lay arms flat together.)*

Becky Cooke, Bonham Elementary, San Angelo, TX

A Great Hiding Place

I store plastic shopping bags in a balloon valance that hangs in my room. Whenever one of my students needs an extra bag to take something home in, I always have a bag on hand. It's a useful and decorative way to store bags.

Vona Harper, Dieck Elementary, Swartz Creek, MI

The Final Product

To help my students learn the steps for two-digit by two-digit multiplication, I have them use two different-colored pencils—one color for multiplying the ones and another for multiplying the tens. It makes the steps less confusing, and my students multiply more accurately with this colorful idea.

Lynsey Smith, Cecil D. Andrus Elementary, Boise, ID

$$\begin{array}{r} 52 \\ \times\ 48 \\ \hline 416 \\ +\ 2080 \\ \hline 2{,}496 \end{array}$$

Our Readers Write

Favorite Winter Activity

Sledding	Daniela	Nadia	
Ice-Skating	Jeffrey	Joel	Finn
Skiing	Faith	Cassie	
Sledding	Will	Ava	

Dividing Digit by Digit

When teaching long division, I give each student a sheet of graph paper and an index card. I show my students how to write a division problem on the paper and cover all but the first digit of the dividend with an index card. Then I lead each student to slide the index card to reveal one number at a time as she works the problem. The index card also guides my students to write the quotient in the correct place.

Susan Durgavich, St. Michael School, Annandale, VA

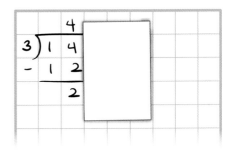

Graph It

For a quick and easy way to practice **graphing skills** with my students, I use sticky notes. Once a week I make a graph on the board. I have each student write his name or draw a picture on a note and then place it on the graph. My students also use sticky notes to make bar graphs. It's that simple!

Melanie Guido, St. Francis–St. Stephens School, Geneva, NY

Deck the Halls

I use decorative seasonal garland to give my classroom displays a three-dimensional look. The garland is easy to hang and even easier to store because it's so flexible.

Stephanie Allen, Berlin Memorial School, Berlin, MA

Multiples of five, line up!

Moving by Multiples

Whether we're lining up for lunch or moving to the carpet, my students use their student numbers to practice identifying multiples. When we're ready to move, I have each student think about his assigned number. First, I ask for a specific group to move, such as those students whose numbers are multiples of five. Then the whole class counts aloud by fives as these students situate themselves. I continue this way, calling for other groups of multiples and the group of prime numbers, until everyone is with the group.

Nancy Fountain, John Greene School, Warwick, RI

Portable Center

Here is a simple way to address limited classroom center space. I preload clipboards with center activities. I also tie a pencil to a piece of yarn and tie the yarn to the clipboard. Each clipboard gives students a sturdy place to work, and students have the materials they need in one spot.

Emily Dearstyne, Pleasant Valley School, Schenectady, NY

Post-Reading Quiz

To help my students reinforce main ideas and details, I have them pretend to be the teacher. After they read a story or passage, it is their job to write a five-question quiz. Sometimes I have them provide their own answers, and other times I have each student switch papers with a partner. Either way, this activity makes students think about what they've read.

Meredith Black, Augusta Christian Schools, Augusta, GA

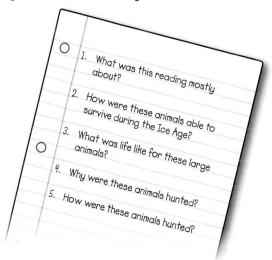

1. What was this reading mostly about?
2. How were these animals able to survive during the Ice Age?
3. What was life like for these large animals?
4. Why were these animals hunted?
5. How were these animals hunted?

A Laugh a Minute

I give my students practice with public speaking by designating a time once a week as joke time. Each student comes to school with an age-appropriate joke or riddle to tell in front of the class. Some students write their own, and others find ones to share from a joke book. Either way, students look forward to sharing their jokes and riddles. Plus they gain confidence in speaking in front of the class.

Christa Burnette, Patrick Springs Primary
Patrick Springs, VA

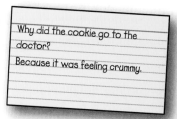

Why did the cookie go to the doctor?
Because it was feeling crummy.

Our Readers Write

Quiet Preparation

When I help my students prepare for standardized testing, I give each child four index cards. I direct the students to letter the cards A–D. Then I display practice test questions on the overhead and have each student hold up the appropriate letter card to show the answer. This is a great way to keep the room quiet as I assess how well each child understands the questions.

April Fowler, Hunterdale Elementary, Franklin, VA

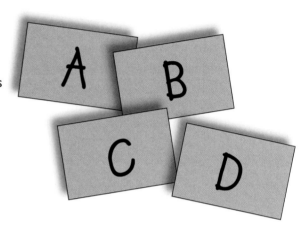

Mystery Numbers

When we have a couple of minutes to spare between activities, I play a guessing game with my students. I think of a number and give clues aloud, such as "My number is larger than 20 but smaller than 40. The sum of the digits is nine. What's my number?" When I can, I try to provide clues that lead to more than one correct answer. It's a great way for students to apply math vocabulary!

Angie Ulrich, Millersport Elementary, Millersport, OH

36!

Or 27!

Special Delivery

To incorporate Valentine's Day into a classroom lesson, I lead students in a discussion of the most efficient way to deliver their valentines. I record their ideas on the board, and then I help students understand that mail is sorted by zip codes and street addresses before it is delivered. We compare this information to their initial ideas for delivering their valentines; then I have students vote for the most efficient delivery method. I've found that when they agree to sort them, it's easiest to have the students sort them by student name in small groups, combine the cards with the other groups' cards, and then have each student deliver a supply of cards. What an interesting way to bring a real-world practice into the classroom!

Melissa Marks, Pittsburgh, PA

Beautiful Borders

Adding color to your bulletin board is a snap with brightly colored duct tape. I use colors that reflect the season or holiday and place the tape on the outer edge of my bulletin board. When it is time to change colors, the tape lifts right off!

Veronica Abii, Vivian Elementary, Vivian, LA

Recycling Picture Books

To give my well-read and well-loved picture books new life, I make them into folder covers, bookmarks, and vocabulary visual aids. Simply tear out pictures and text that you would like to reuse, trim with pinking shears, and laminate. With this tip, you still have pieces of your old picture books saved for years to come.

Madeline M. Spurck, Neil A. Armstrong Elementary
Richton Park, IL

Polar bears' fur **camouflages** them in the snow.

Lions live in groups called **prides.**

Sing a Song!

For a harmonious way to help my students remember cause and effect, I teach them a song. To add movement, we pantomime playing the banjo at the end of each verse!

Lana Stewart, Earnest Woods Intermediate
Wills Point, TX

The Cause and Effect Song
(sung to the tune of "I've Been Working on the Railroad")

A cause is the reason something happens.
A cause is the reason, I know.
A cause is the reason something happens.
Play that on your old banjo!

An effect is what happens later.
An effect is later, I know.
An effect is what happens later.
Play that on your old banjo!

Check the Ones!

Here's a great way to show students how to rule out multiple-choice answers on math tests. I teach my students to work the ones place in the problem and then stop. Then I tell them to cross out all answer choices that do not have the same ones digit. At this point, my students narrow down their choices before they continue, and they have a better chance of choosing the correct answer.

Mary Ferrell
Oak Grove Lower Elementary
Hattiesburg, MS

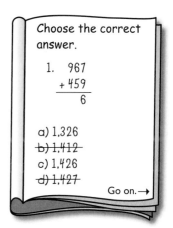

Choose the correct answer.

1.   967
    + 459
    ——————
          6

a) 1,326
b) 1,412
c) 1,426
d) 1,427

Go on. →

Freeze-Frame!

I use a simple command to transition students to or from a special class. When it's time to stop an activity and line up, I simply call out, "Freeze-frame!" Students freeze exactly where they are, make a mental note of their position, and then line up. When they return to the classroom, I tell students to get back into freeze mode. Then I say, "Unfreeze!" and students continue working as though they had never left.

Amanda Osterhart, Coopersville West Elementary, Coopersville, MI

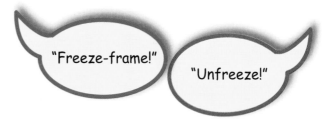

"Freeze-frame!"

"Unfreeze!"

Get Your Groove On!

Dance time has become a favorite activity in my classroom. At the end of each day I put on an energetic, upbeat song. Then my students and I boogie down. They love to play air guitar and practice their best dance moves. Sometimes I teach them some of my favorite steps. Dance time is a fun way to help my students get out their wiggles and engage in a class bonding activity.

Lora Townsend, Carver Elementary Academy, Amarillo, TX

Our Readers Write

Science in an Album

For a unique science report, I have students use 4" x 6" photo albums to display their research about animals. A student alternates each page with either a photo or a drawing of her animal and a specific fact written or typed on an index card. When students have filled their albums, I challenge them to creatively display their animals on the front covers. As students share their albums, they read each fact and show the corresponding picture. These inexpensive projects make great keepsakes.

Leanne Baur, Our Lady of Mount Carmel School, Baltimore, MD

Coyotes are part of the dog family. They live in the wild.

Shower the Student-Teacher

I use this shower idea to send my student-teacher off well-prepared for the future. I ask parents and students to help me fill a basket with items such as markers, pens, stickers, sticky notes, books, games, and a subscription to *The Mailbox* magazine. It's fun to invite other staff members to participate too!

Kelly Nestler, Pecatonica Elementary, Pecatonica, IL

Self-Checking Activities

To make any matching activity self-checking, I write part of a compound word on the back of one card and the other part of the word on its corresponding card. Students match the cards and then flip them over to see if they make a word. This way my students practice two skills at once!

Brooke Beverly, Dudley Elementary, Dudley, MA

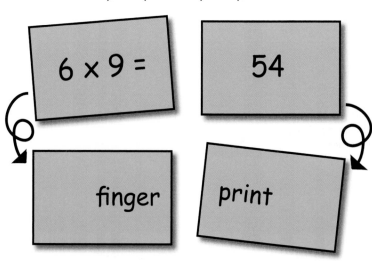

Size Check

To help my students know when their pencils are too short, I post a reminder above the pencil sharpener. Then I have students check the lengths of their pencils before they sharpen them. That way we don't lose any tiny pencils in the sharpener!

Sara Hanberg, Richardson Elementary, Central Point, OR

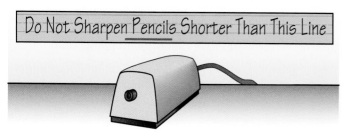

Who's Gone?

Instead of having my kids carry germy bathroom passes, I use two bottles of hand sanitizer, one labeled for boys and the other for girls. If a boy needs to go to the bathroom, he puts the appropriate bottle of sanitizer on his desk before he leaves. When he returns, he uses the sanitizer and puts the bottle back on the shelf. This works the same way for the girls. Now I know at a glance who is missing, and the amount of germs in my classroom is reduced.

Tina Perruna
West Haverstraw Elementary
West Haverstraw, NY

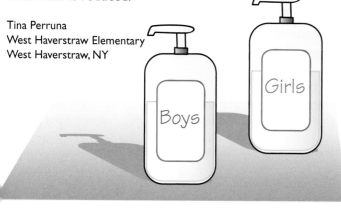

Safekeeping

Keeping up with my USB drives can be difficult. To solve that problem, I store them in a brightly colored, hard eyeglasses case. The case is easy to spot in my purse or on my desk, and my drives stay protected.

Barb Witteman
Concordia College
Moorhead, MN

Flashlight Fridays

To spice up our silent reading time, I have each student bring an inexpensive flashlight and spare batteries to keep at school. On Fridays, I turn out the lights and let the kids curl up with their books and flashlights.

Christy Gergits
Whittier Elementary
Downers Grove, IL

Save and Swap

Here's an idea to help teachers review content in the fall. Toward the end of the school year, each teacher on my grade level places in her own box leftover worksheets and unused portions of student workbooks. At the end of the year, we each pass our box to a different teacher in the next grade up. In the same manner, teachers from the grade level below us send us their leftovers. This save-and-swap provides free materials we can use to review skills during the first weeks of the new school year.

Mary Davis
Keokuk Christian Academy
Keokuk, IA

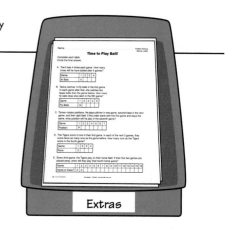

Our Readers Write

The Right Mark

To ensure that my students use the correct markers on the whiteboard, I wrap white electrical tape around the end of each wipe-off marker. This easy indicator helps students select a marker that will wipe off the board!

Julie Rains
Tri-County R-VII
Jamesport, MO

Wall of Fame

Have you ever wondered what to do with all those school pictures of past and current students? I make a wall of fame! I display these photos on a bulletin board to show my students that they are special people in my life. Students enjoy seeing their older siblings and friends I've also taught!

John Blake, Woodlake Elementary, Mandeville, LA

Mr. Blake's Wall of Fame

Know, Show, Go!

I use this easy technique to teach my students a valuable test-taking strategy. First, students underline what the question wants to *know*. Then they find the answer or pertinent information in the passage and highlight it—that's the *show* part. Finally, students *go* to the answer space and fill it in.

H. Wagner
South Harrison Township Elementary
Harrisonville, NJ

Sidewalk Painting

To combat spring fever, I jazz up my spelling, math, and writing practice by letting my students write their work on the sidewalk.

Sharon Asman, Read Elementary, Oshkosh, WI

To make sidewalk paint, I add a little food coloring to equal parts of water and cornstarch. The paint is quick and easy to make and it doesn't stain clothing.

Melanie Guido, St. Francis-St. Stephens School, Geneva, NY

Something

READING

READING

Alike and Different
Character analysis

A child folds a sheet of paper in half vertically. Then he makes two equally spaced cuts in the top layer. On each of the first two resulting flaps, he writes the name of a different character from a familiar book. Under each flap, he writes phrases that describe the character. On the last flap, he writes both characters' names. Then he lifts the flap and writes sentences that explain how the characters are alike and how they are different. Finally, he draws an illustration on each flap.

Piper R. Porter, Mountain Way Elementary, Granite Falls, WA

Think and Swat
Syllabication

To prepare for this whole-class game, enlarge the fly cards from the top of page 187 and post them on the board. Divide the class into two teams and give each team a clean flyswatter. To play, select a child to go to the board; then read aloud a vocabulary word. If the child swats the fly with the correct number of syllables, award one point to his team. Then choose a child from the other team and have her take a turn in the same manner. Continue playing as time allows. The team with more points wins.

Lynn Sanders, Sope Creek Elementary, Marietta, GA

Becoming an Illustrator
Reading comprehension

After students have completed a narrative-writing assignment, collect their edited stories. Give each story to a child other than the author and tell her she will illustrate it. The child reads the story and divides it into sections by marking the key events with her pencil. She makes a book by copying each section onto a 6" x 9" page and then illustrating each page. Invite each illustrator to meet with her book's author to share her work. Provide time for the pair to make a cover for the book. Then invite each pair to share its book with the class.

Rita Skavinsky, Minersville Elementary Center, Minersville, PA

Cover Your Bases
Reading unfamiliar words

To make sense of unfamiliar words, have each child keep a tagboard copy of the baseball field pattern on page 187 in his reading folder. When he's reading and finds a word he doesn't know, the child takes out the manipulative and follows the steps to determine the unknown word. Then he stores the manipulative in his folder until he needs it again.

Amanda Smith, Birmingham Elementary, Toledo, OH

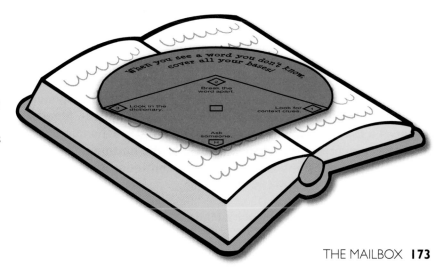

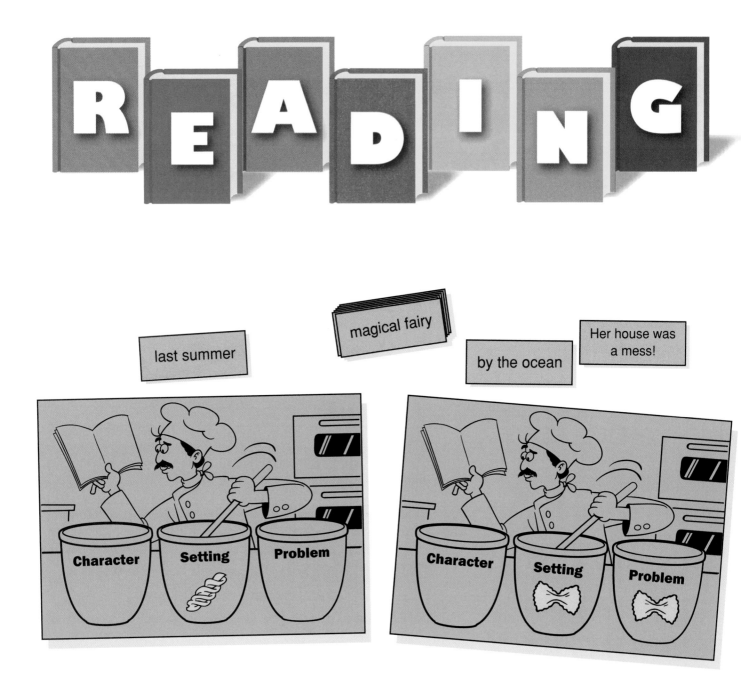

Important Ingredients

Story elements

For this partner game, make two copies of the gameboard from the
top of page 188 and one copy of the game cards at the bottom of the
same page. Cut apart the game cards, program the back of each one
with the corresponding story element, and stack them faceup. To play,
Player 1 draws a card, reads it aloud, and names the corresponding story
element. Then he turns the card over to check his answer. If correct, Player
1 places a marker, such as dried pasta, on the corresponding pot and keeps
the card. If incorrect, he returns the card to the bottom of the stack. Player 2
takes a turn in the same manner and play continues until all cards have been
read. The player with more markers wins.

Sheila Ziegler, Red Rock Elementary, Mattawa, WA

Simple Reminder
Author's purpose

Here's a mnemonic device students are sure to use! Simply tell students that naming an author's purpose is as easy as *PIE*—the author writes to *persuade, inform,* or *entertain.* Encourage them to use the letters and their meanings when they need to determine an author's purpose.

Betsy Leatherman, Urbandale Elementary, Battle Creek, MI

Question Cutouts
Comprehension

This idea works great with small groups! Program paper cutouts with different questions, such as those shown. Place the cutouts in a container, and direct each child to choose a cutout before reading a selection. After reading, encourage each child to share her question and its answer with the rest of the group. Then have students return the cutouts to the container so you can use them again with another group.

Becky Shelley, Grove, OK

Peer Reviews
Evaluating books, motivation

To set up this book-review system, have the class determine a rating scale for the books they read. Display a copy of the rating system in the classroom library by a supply of notecards and a recipe box filled with alphabetized divider cards. To review a book, a child writes on a notecard the title, author, and illustrator of a recently read book. Next, she labels the card with her rating of the book, adds a brief explanation of her rating, and signs her name. Then she uses the book's title to file the completed notecard in the recipe box. As more students file their reviews in the box, students will have more recommended books to read!

Kari M. Wood, Becker Elementary, Austin, TX

If I could give you any gift in the world, I would give you a role in an action movie. I think you have a great imagination and you like pretending. Being in an action movie would be just the thing to make you happy and add a little excitement to your life!

Wrap It Up
Analyzing characters

After reading a fiction story, a child chooses a character. He brainstorms gifts that would be appropriate for the character, considering ones that are not store-bought. The student chooses a gift and draws it on a sheet of story paper. Next, he writes a brief description of the gift, telling why he chose it. Then he places an 8½" x 11" piece of gift wrap atop the story paper and staples it in place. After that, the student trims a gift tag from a paper scrap, labels it, and tapes it to the gift wrap. If desired, he wraps up his project by adding a decorative bow.

Kristin Riley, Helen Mae Sauter School, Gardner, MA

Words in a Flash
Reading high-frequency words

Use a slide show computer program to engage students in a high-frequency word review. Type one word per slide and set each frame to display for about four seconds. Display the program where students can see it, and have students read each word as it appears onscreen.

Phyllis Sprangel, Northeast Elementary, Jackson, MI

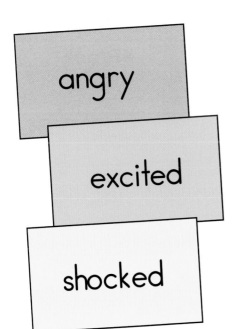

A Flair for Reading
Reading expressively

Here's a practice activity that will give students a reason to be dramatic! In advance, label index cards with adjectives that describe emotions. Direct a student pair to choose a card and take turns reading a short book or poem, using the emotion on the card as a guide for how to read. Encourage students to choose a different card and read the same selection again, this time using the newly selected emotion. It won't take long for students to apply these skills to other reading activities!

Tracie Sipe, Trevilians Elementary, Louisa, VA

Picturing Read-Alouds
Visualizing text, vivid vocabulary

This idea works great when chapter books are read aloud. Before starting a book, have each child write the title on a copy of page 189 and number the boxes to correspond to the book's chapters. (Make additional copies if the book has more than six chapters.) Explain to students that, as you read a chapter aloud, they should draw in the corresponding box images to show what they visualize. Also instruct students to write in the same box examples of the author's good word choices. Provide time for each student to share her images with a partner; then use students' drawings to assess their understanding of each chapter.

Christina Bainbridge, Central Elementary, White Pigeon, MI

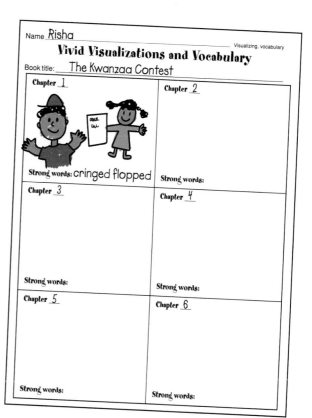

READING

Sweet Sentences
Cause and effect

To prepare this matching activity, a child cuts the cards from a copy of page 190 and stacks the cause cards facedown. He lays the effect cards faceup in three rows. The student draws a cause card, reads it, and then finds the matching effect card. He glues the cards to a 12" x 18" sheet of paper and continues until he has matched each pair of cards.

Michelle Bayless, Ruther Glen, VA

Cause
Tim had some extra candy.

Effect
He shared it with his brother.

Here's the Difference
Nonfiction text

Help students compare and contrast genres with this simple activity. Direct each child to open a textbook that contains nonfiction passages, such as a social studies or science book. Lead students in a discussion of the similarities and differences between this book and a reading textbook or a chapter book. Guide them to point out features—such as headings, subheadings, boldfaced words, maps, and diagrams—that are in the nonfiction textbook but not the fiction book.

Pam Girgenti, Marlton, NJ

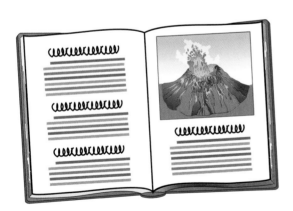

Call Me!
Motivation

This portable prop encourages students to read aloud. During guided reading time, have a child imagine that she's talking to a friend as she softly reads the book's text into a deactivated cell phone.

Beth Sine, Dr. Brown Elementary, Waldorf, MD

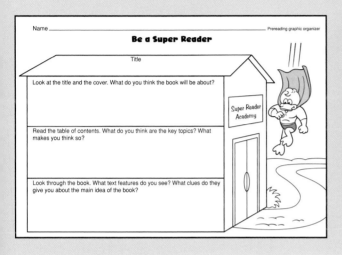

Building Super Readers
Setting a purpose for reading

Use this graphic organizer to introduce a nonfiction book. First, review with students the text features found in nonfiction books. Provide each student pair with a copy of the book; then direct the duo to use the cover, table of contents, and text features to complete a copy of page 191. Provide time for students to share their responses with the class.

adapted from an idea by Jean Erickson, Grace Christian Academy, West Allis, WI

A Happening Hut
Retelling a story

After a child reads a fiction story, have him list its six main events on a sheet of paper. Then have him follow the directions below to make a three-dimensional hut to display information about the story.

Materials for each student:
6" x 18" white construction paper strip crayons
9" construction paper circle tape
scissors

Steps:
1. Fold the paper strip into six equal sections and number the sections from 1 to 6. Write about and illustrate one event in each section, ordering the events from beginning to end.
2. To create the walls, tape the ends of the strip together so the words and illustrations face outward.
3. To create the roof, draw a point in the center of the circle. Draw a straight line from the point to the outer edge and then cut along the line. Write the book's title on the outer edge of the circle. Overlap and tape the two cut edges to form a cone.
4. Put the roof on the walls.

Lou Smeja, Emerson School, Elmhurst, IL

READING

Name That Genre
Common forms of literature

In advance, gather grade-level books that represent different types of literature and label the books with numbered sticky dots. Make an answer key by recording the books' numbers and genres on a sheet of paper. Place the books and a genre list, like the one shown, at a center. A student selects a book, writes the book's number and title on a sheet of paper, and skims through the book. Then he writes the book's genre next to the number on his paper. After the student finishes looking through all the books and identifying each form of literature, he uses the key to check his answers.

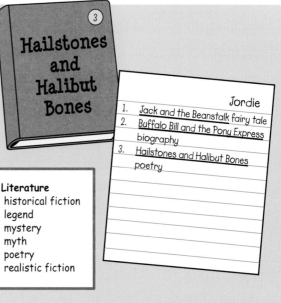

Types of Literature	
autobiography	historical fiction
biography	legend
expository	mystery
fairy tale	myth
fantasy	poetry
folk tale	realistic fiction

Jordie
1. Jack and the Beanstalk fairy tale
2. Buffalo Bill and the Pony Express biography
3. Hailstones and Halibut Bones poetry

Leonardo da Vinci

- born in Italy on April 15, 1452
- designed machines and drew plans for other inventions
- painted the <u>Mona Lisa</u>

"Bear-y" Famous People
Biographies

Here's a great way for students to share what they read about famous people. After reading a biography, have each child write three related facts on an index card and the name of the subject of the biography on another card. If desired, have the student use the booklet on page 193 as a guide to gather information. Then have each student cut out and decorate a copy of the bear pattern on page 192 so it resembles the person whom her biography is about. Have her create at least one relevant accessory for her bear. Display each child's bear and fact card on a board titled "Guess Who." Place the name cards nearby and encourage students to visit the board, read each fact card, and match the names to the facts.

Christine Lincoln, Calvary Baptist Christian School, Watertown, WI

The Power of Punctuation
Reading with inflection

ABC. DE! FGHI? JKL? MNO! PQRS. TU? VW? XY. Z!

To encourage students to read with fluency, write the alphabet on the board, randomly inserting endmarks into the sequence. Read the series aloud, modeling the intonation for the class. After several students have read the series aloud, change the endmarks and have other student volunteers read the series. Discuss with the class how the intonation changes when the endmarks change. Next, have each student write the alphabet on a sentence strip, adding endmarks as desired. Have each child read his strip aloud to a partner and then read his partner's strip aloud before assigning new pairs and repeating the activity.

Amanda Acosta, Scott Libby Elementary, Litchfield, AZ

Today's Word Category
Compound Words

Password, Please
Reviewing vocabulary

For a quick oral assessment, laminate a sign that says Today's Word Category and post it outside the classroom door. Each day, use a dry-erase marker to program the sign with a different category, such as compound words, verbs, or contractions. As each student walks into the room, she names a word that matches the listed category. Throughout the day, remind students of the category and encourage them to locate examples while reading.

adapted from an idea by Cheryl Latil, Magnolia Park Elementary, Ocean Spring, MS

Reading Detectives
Signaling text evidence

This idea quickly assesses students' comprehension. After reading a nonfiction passage, ask the class a recall question and direct each child to skim the text until he finds the answer. Then have him flag the answer by placing a sticky note next to the text evidence. A simple scan of the room will reveal the students who need further instruction.

Elizabeth Noble, North Dover Elementary, Dover, NJ

READING

Campfire Songs
Fluency

This classroom campfire is the place to read and recite popular children's campfire songs. To make a campfire, roll three or more sheets of brown paper into logs and stack them as shown. Next, crumple gray paper into balls so they resemble rocks and set them in a circle around the logs. Cut pieces of red, yellow, and orange paper (flames) and glue them to the logs. Then provide students with copies of songs to read, chant, or sing together.

Amy McAllister, Grassy Waters Elementary, West Palm Beach, FL

"The Bear Went Over the Mountain"

"The Ants Go Marching"

"Do Your Ears Hang Low?"

Words That Crunch
Contractions

COULDN'T
could not

I'LL
I will

THEY'RE
they are

IT'S
it is

GLUE

To prepare this hands-on center, set out a bowl of alphabet cereal, several paper strips, and glue. A student uses the cereal to spell a contraction on a paper strip and then glues the pieces down. To make the apostrophe, she glues a broken cereal piece between the two letters that form the contraction. The child shows the meaning of the contraction by writing on the strip the two words that form it. She makes more contractions as time allows.

Melanie Guido, St. Francis-St. Stephens School
Geneva, NY

One Word at a Time
High-frequency words

Want to take down your word wall and provide a learning opportunity at the same time? Try this! Assign a letter to each pair of students and direct them to secretly choose a word from the word wall that begins with that letter. Have each duo write on an index card three clues about its word. Collect the index cards and read aloud a set of clues. When the correct answer is given, select a student to remove the word from the wall. Continue reading clues until all the words are removed from the wall or all sets have been read.

Nancy Fountain, John Greene School, Warwick, RI

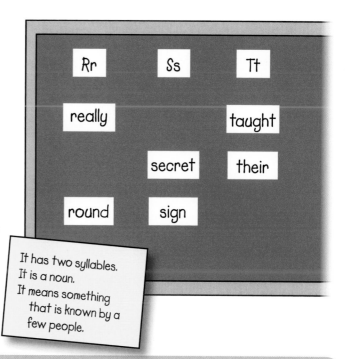

It has two syllables.
It is a noun.
It means something that is known by a few people.

Math Curse
by Jon Scieszka
Gavin

Reading Garden
Independent reading

Motivate students to read by decorating a corner of your room so it resembles a garden. Place crisscrossed paper strips on the wall to form a lattice. Then add artificial ivy garland to the lattice and around the bookcases. If desired, place potted plants on the floor. Put crayons, paper, and scissors in plastic flowerpots. Each time a student finishes a book, have him cut out a flower, write the book's title and author on it, and display it on the lattice.

adapted from an idea by Michelle Nuckols, Community Christian School, Woodstock, VA

Suggested Tasks
Read a how-to book.
Read one chapter a day.
Read about your favorite animal.
Read a book of poems.
Read about a state you want to visit.
Read two different versions of the same fairy tale.
Read a book with at least 100 pages.
Read a mystery.

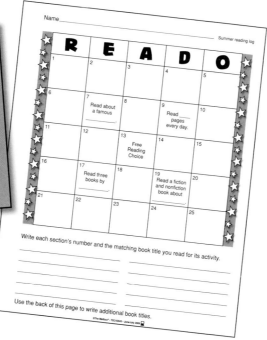

Summer Is for Reading
Literary genres

Add variety to students' summer reading list with this fun activity. Program a copy of the gameboard on page 194 with tasks like the ones shown. Give each child a copy of the gameboard and an envelope labeled with your return address. Direct each student to mark every activity he completes with an X and have his parent initial the box. Encourage the student to mail the gameboard to you when he completes five activities in a horizontal, vertical, or diagonal row.

Kim Hintze, Show Low, AZ

READING

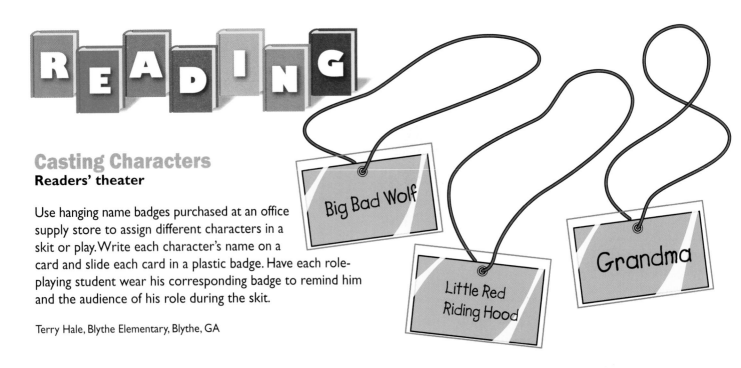

Casting Characters
Readers' theater

Use hanging name badges purchased at an office supply store to assign different characters in a skit or play. Write each character's name on a card and slide each card in a plastic badge. Have each role-playing student wear his corresponding badge to remind him and the audience of his role during the skit.

Terry Hale, Blythe Elementary, Blythe, GA

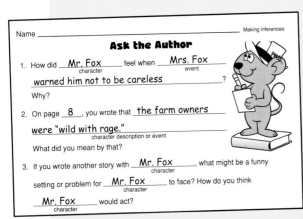

Interview the Author
Making inferences

Before reading a fiction selection, program a copy of the bottom of page 195 with corresponding character names and events. After students read the selection, give each pair of students a copy of the programmed page. Have one child in each pair pretend to be the author of the story while the other acts as an interviewer. Direct each interviewer to ask the questions and write the author's responses on another sheet of paper. If desired, instruct students to reverse roles. If time permits, have students reenact their interviews in front of an audience.

Jennifer L. Kohnke, Saint Charles, IL

Seeing Is Believing
Fact and opinion

Display eight to ten interesting pictures of people or animals. Point to a picture and state a fact about it. Direct students to stand if they think the statement is a fact or remain seated if they think the statement is an opinion. Choose a student to point to the evidence in the picture that supports the fact. Next, state an opinion about a different picture and repeat the process, calling on a different child to explain what makes the statement an opinion. Continue the activity with several other pictures. Then ask students to make their own fact and opinion statements about the pictures.

Lynn Sanders, Sope Creek Elementary, Marietta, GA

Train of Thought
Making connections

Students share text-to-self, text-to-text, or text-to-world connections with this decorative idea. After reading, have a student write on an index card the type of connection he made and an explanation of his connection. Next, direct him to write the book's title and author on a copy of the train engine pattern from page 195. Guide the student to color the pattern, cut it out, and post his engine and card on a wall as shown. Encourage other students who read the same book to add cards to the train.

The Salamander Room
by Anne Mazer

text-to-self
When Brian found a salamander and took it home, it reminded me of the time I found a woolly caterpillar in my backyard. I put it in a jar, poked holes in the lid, and put fresh grass and a stick in the jar.

Luke

Poetry Chart
Elements of poetry

Poem	Theme	Rhythm	Rhyme	Alliteration	Repetition	Simile or metaphor
"At the Seaside"	Digging in the sand	✓	✓			✓

In advance, gather several children's poetry books that contain different forms of poetry. Also copy on the board the chart shown. Choose four short poems that have some or all of the elements listed on the chart. Read a poem aloud, write the poem's title on the chart, and have students identify the poem's theme. Write the theme on the chart. Then have students tell you which elements on the chart are present in the poem, and place a check under each appropriate heading. Continue with the other three poems. Then have partners work together to find a poem to share with the class that has most of the elements listed on the chart.

Laura Johnson, South Decatur Elementary, Greensburg, IN

Soaring Vocabulary
Using a dictionary

To prepare this center, cut out a tagboard copy of the kite bow pattern on page 195. Place the bow template at a center along with a dictionary, construction paper, and a list of directions like the one shown. To make a kite, a child folds a sheet of paper in half vertically and then horizontally and cuts the paper as shown. Next, the student unfolds her paper and writes a current vocabulary word on the kite. She also writes the word in a sentence and illustrates the sentence. Then she traces the bow template five times on construction paper scraps and cuts out the bows. The student finds the word in the dictionary and labels each bow according to the directions. Finally, she cuts a thin strip of paper, glues it to the back of her kite, and glues each bow in order on the strip. Display the kites around the room.

Janice Ferguson, Longfellow Elementary, Idaho Falls, ID

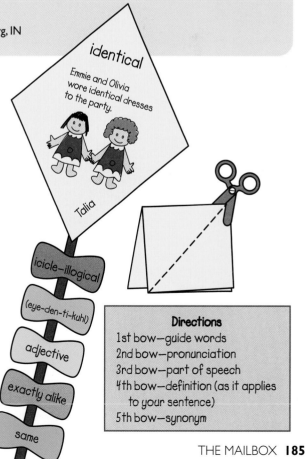

identical

Emmie and Olivia wore identical dresses to the party.

Talia

icicle–illogical

(eye-den-ti-kuhl)

adjective

exactly alike

same

Directions
1st bow—guide words
2nd bow—pronunciation
3rd bow—part of speech
4th bow—definition (as it applies to your sentence)
5th bow—synonym

Comprehension Cabins
Make, revise, and confirm predictions

Build students' reading skills with this handy learning log. To make one, a student cuts out the log cabin patterns from a brown copy of page 196. Next, he tapes four index cards side by side to form a horizontal row. Then he writes the book's title and author on the first card and records on each of the remaining cards his predictions before, during, and after reading. The child glues the first and last index card onto each log cabin. Finally, he folds the index cards into a booklet and decorates the front and back covers if desired.

adapted from an idea by Barclay Marcell
Theodore Roosevelt Elementary, Park Ridge, IL

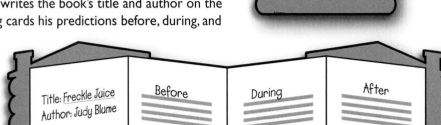

Title: Freckle Juice
Author: Judy Blume

Before

During

After

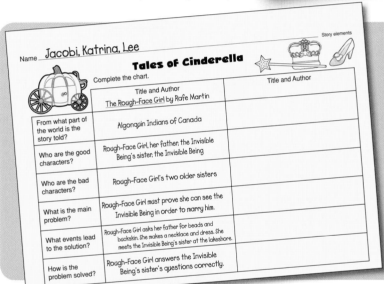

Name ___Jacobi, Katrina, Lee___

Tales of Cinderella

Complete the chart.

Story elements

Title and Author The Rough-Face Girl by Rafe Martin	Title and Author
From what part of the world is the story told? Algonquin Indians of Canada	
Who are the good characters? Rough-Face Girl, her father, the Invisible Being's sister, the Invisible Being	
Who are the bad characters? Rough-Face Girl's two older sisters	
What is the main problem? Rough-Face Girl must prove she can see the Invisible Being in order to marry him.	
What events lead to the solution? Rough-Face Girl asks her father for beads and buckskin. She makes a necklace and dress. She meets the Invisible Being's sister at the lakeshore.	
How is the problem solved? Rough-Face Girl answers the Invisible Being's sister's questions correctly.	

"Cinder-who"?
Comparing story elements

Assign each small group a different version of a Cinderella fairy tale and give them a copy of the chart on page 197. Have the students use their story to complete the first column. At another time, have groups switch tales and complete the second column of the chart. Provide time for students to compare and discuss their findings.

Laura Johnson, South Decatur Elementary, Greensburg, IN

Dear Ms. Goldman,
You should visit Mr. Zuckerman's farm. You wouldn't believe all the good food that I find in the pig's trough. My favorite time of the day is in the morning. I climb over the edge of the trough and help myself to the slops. I love the warm milk and potato skins. It's a rat's delight! Please come for a visit soon. You won't regret it!

Your friend,
Templeton

Ms. Goldman
Brown Street School
10 Brown St.
Cheltenham, PA 00000

Postcard Perspectives
Point of view, setting

Students express a character's viewpoint with this creative-writing activity. First, a student chooses a character and a setting from a recently read story. Considering the character's point of view, he writes on a large index card a postcard that describes the setting to his teacher or principal. He signs the postcard with the character's name and then draws the setting on the card's other side.

Jennifer Goldman, Cheltenham, PA

Check out the reading skill sheets on page 198–202!

TEC43038   TEC43038   TEC43038

Baseball Field Pattern
Use with "Cover Your Bases" on page 173.

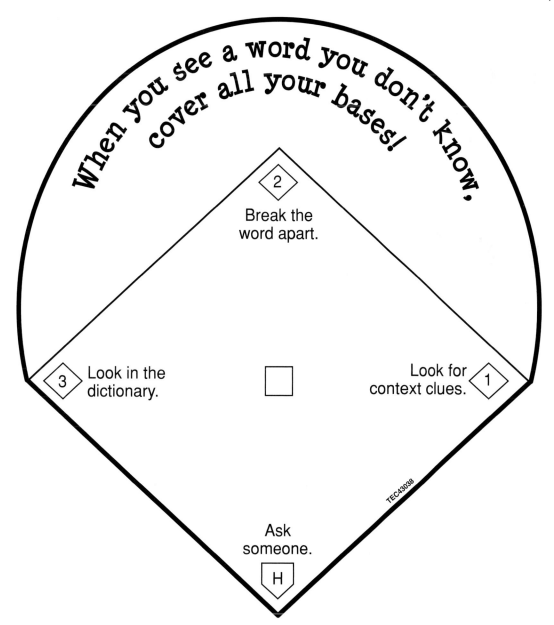

When you see a word you don't know, cover all your bases!

2 — Break the word apart.

3 — Look in the dictionary.

1 — Look for context clues.

H — Ask someone.

TEC43038

Gameboard and Game Cards

Use with "Important Ingredients" on page 174.

Character **Setting** **Problem**

©The Mailbox® • TEC43039 • Oct./Nov. 2008

Character	Setting	Problem
magical fairy TEC43039	by the ocean TEC43039	A bird lost its way. TEC43039
Willy TEC43039	last summer TEC43039	A spell was cast on a prince. TEC43039
Principal Jones TEC43039	in a far-off land TEC43039	A cat was stuck in a tree. TEC43039
Officer Neal TEC43039	on the playground TEC43039	They were out of money. TEC43039
Mrs. Frog TEC43039	in a dark forest TEC43039	Her house was a mess! TEC43039

©The Mailbox® • TEC43039 • Oct./Nov. 2008

Vivid Visualizations and Vocabulary

Book title: _____

Chapter ___ **Strong words:**	**Chapter** ___ **Strong words:**
Chapter ___ **Strong words:**	**Chapter** ___ **Strong words:**
Chapter ___ **Strong words:**	**Chapter** ___ **Strong words:**

Note to the teacher: Use with "Picturing Read-Alouds" on page 177.

Cause and Effect Cards

Use with "Sweet Sentences" on page 178.

Cause Billy wanted to give his mother some candy for Valentine's Day. TEC43041	**Cause** Brad saw a candy wrapper on the ground.	**Cause** Kelly ate a grape-flavored lollipop.
Cause Tim had some extra candy.	**Cause** Sarah left a chocolate bar in her backpack.	**Cause** There was no more taffy in the store.
Cause Zack blew a large bubble, and it popped.	**Cause** Tina lost the valentine she made for her teacher.	**Cause** Ken and Susan both wanted the last cupcake.
Effect It made her teeth purple.	**Effect** He shared it with his brother.	**Effect** They cut it in half.
Effect The gum was stuck on his nose.	**Effect** The chocolate bar broke into pieces.	**Effect** He bought some for her at the store.
Effect She made a new one out of pink paper.	**Effect** He picked it up and threw it in the trash.	**Effect** Lily bought jelly beans instead.

Be a Super Reader

Title _____

Super Reader Academy

Look at the title and the cover. What do you think the book will be about?

Read the table of contents. What do you think are the key topics? What makes you think so?

Look through the book. What text features do you see? What clues do they give you about the main idea of the book?

Note to the teacher: Use with "Building Super Readers" on page 179.

THE MAILBOX 191

Bear Pattern
Use with "'Bear-y' Famous People" on page 180.

TEC43042

Your Opinion

- What do you like most about the person?
- What has this person taught you?
- In what ways would you like to be like this person?

Fun Facts

- Is the person still living?
- What are some facts people might not know about the person?
- In what ways have people honored the person?

A Guide to Writing a Biography Book Report

Name _____

©The Mailbox® • TEC43042 • April/May 2009

A Success Story

- How did the person become a success?
- How have the person's actions changed other people's lives?
- What awards or honors has the person received?

How to Fold

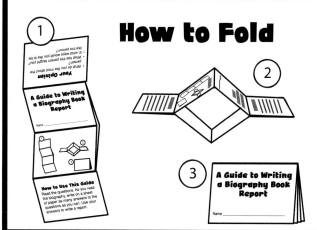

① Your Opinion
- What do you like most about the person?
- What has this person taught you?
- In what ways would you like to be like this person?

A Guide to Writing a Biography Book Report

Name _____

How to Use This Guide
Read the questions. As you read the biography, write on a sheet of paper as many answers to the questions as you can. Use your answers to write a report.

②

③ A Guide to Writing a Biography Book Report

Name _____

Early Life

- How was the person's life before he or she was famous?
- Where did the person learn the skills he or she needed to be a success?
- Did anything make the person's success hard to achieve? If so, tell about it.

How to Use This Guide

Read the questions. As you read the biography, write on a sheet of paper as many answers to the questions as you can. Use your answers to write a report.

The Beginning

- What is the full name of the person?
- When and where was this person born?
- Describe the person's life as he or she grew up.

Note to the teacher: To use with "'Bear-y' Famous People" on page 180, have each student cut out a copy of the pattern on this page. The child folds the pattern in half vertically, cuts along the bold line, and folds the paper on each fold line. Then the child holds the ends of the paper, pushes the ends towards the center, and folds the pages to make a booklet.

Name____

R	E	A	D	O
1	2	3	4	5
6	7 Read about a famous ________.	8	9 Read ____ pages every day.	10
11	12	13 Free Reading Choice	14	15
16	17 Read three books by ________.	18	19 Read a fiction and nonfiction book about ________.	20
21	22	23	24	25

Write each section's number and the matching book title you read for its activity.

________________________________ ________________________________

________________________________ ________________________________

________________________________ ________________________________

________________________________ ________________________________

________________________________ ________________________________

Use the back of this page to write additional book titles.

 Note to the teacher: Use with "Summer Is for Reading" on page 183.

Kite Bow Pattern
Use with "Soaring Vocabulary" on page 185.

Train Engine Pattern
Use with "Train of Thought" on page 185.

TEC43042

TEC43042

Name_____   Making inferences

Ask the Author

1. How did _____ feel when _____
                  character   event

   _____?

   Why?

2. On page _____, you wrote that _____

   _____.
                    character description or event

   What did you mean by that?

3. If you wrote another story with _____, what might be a funny
                                        character

   setting or problem for _____ to face? How do you think
                           character

   _____ would act?
        character

Log Cabin Patterns
Use with "Comprehension Cabins" on page 186.

Name _____

TEC43043

Story elements

Tales of Cinderella

Complete the chart.

	Title and Author	Title and Author
From what part of the world is the story told?		
Who are the good characters?		
Who are the bad characters?		
What is the main problem?		
What events lead to the solution?		
How is the problem solved?		

©The Mailbox® · TEC43043 · June/July 2009

Note to the teacher: Use with "'Cinder-who'?" on page 186.

Name

A Pizza Problem

Write the word for each clue.
Use the word bank.

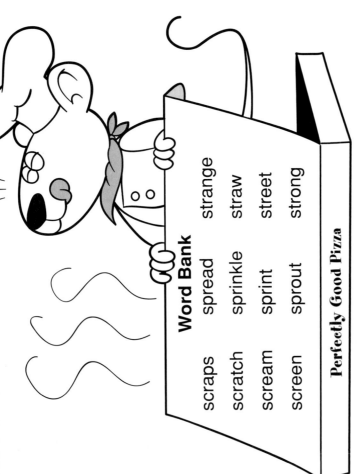

1. a thin tube used for drinking ☐ _ _ _

2. a light rain _ _ ☐ _ _ _

3. to run at top speed _ _ _ ☐ _

4. to rub to stop itching _ _ _ _ ☐ _

5. a road in a town or city _ _ _ _ ☐ _

6. a young plant growth _ _ ☐ _ _ _

7. a long, loud yell _ _ _ ☐ _ _

8. unusual _ _ ☐ _ _ _ _

9. having a lot of power _ _ _ _ ☐ _

10. leftover bits of food _ _ _ _ ☐ _

11. to push or move apart _ _ _ ☐ _ _

12. a flat surface on which movies are shown _ _ _ ☐ _ _

Word Bank

scraps	spread	strange
scratch	sprinkle	straw
scream	sprint	street
screen	sprout	strong

Perfectly Good Pizza

How do you fix a broken pizza?
Write each boxed letter from the right
in order on the lines below.

_ _ _ _ _ O

S T _ _

©The Mailbox® • TEC43041 • Feb./Mar. 2009 • Key p. 311

Sorting Shells

Add *ful* or *less* to each base word.
Write each new word on its matching pail.
Color the shells by the code.

Color Code
yellow = *ful*
orange = *less*

-less

-ful

bowl

bottom

flaw

belly

spoon

wire

spot

forget

wish

price

end

fright

Doctor's Orders

Read the story.
Circle the best word to complete each sentence.

Last week I had the <u>flew/flu</u>. My dad took me <u>to/two</u> the doctor. It felt like <u>hours/ours</u> before they were able to see me. When the nurse took me back, he had to <u>way/weigh</u> me. Then he said I had to <u>wear/where</u> a gown. I changed into the gown. Then the nurse had to ask me <u>some/sum</u> questions. I was glad my dad was <u>their/there</u> to help me answer them. Soon the doctor came <u>in/inn</u>. She told me I <u>wood/would</u> not need a shot. She <u>made/maid</u> me agree to drink a lot of juice. She said it would help me <u>heal/he'll</u> faster. The doctor also told my dad I would <u>knead/need</u> plenty of rest to get over the flu. I am happy to report that we followed the doctor's orders and I got better <u>right/write</u> away. Now I feel <u>great/grate</u>!

Bonus Box: Copy the words you did not circle onto another sheet of paper. Write a story using as many of the words as you can. Underline each word you use.

Royal Research

Read the dictionary entry.

king (kĭng) *noun* **1.** A man who rules a country. *[George Washington did not want to be called our king.]* **2.** The person or thing thought to be the most powerful in a certain setting. *[The lion is known as the king of the jungle.]* **3.** A game piece in checkers and chess. *[It is important to protect the king when playing chess.]* plural **kings**

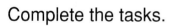

Complete the tasks.

1. Draw a star above the entry word.

2. Draw a line under the entry word's part of speech.

3. Draw a rectangle around the part that shows how to say the entry word.

4. Circle the numbers that show the different meanings of the entry word.

Answer the questions.

5. What part of speech is the word *king?* _____

6. How many meanings of the word *king* are shown? _____

7. How do you spell the plural form of the word *king?* _____

8. Which meaning relates to games? _____

9. Which meaning might be found in a social studies book? _____

10. Would the word *kind* or *kingdom* come after *king* in the dictionary? _____
    How do you know? _____

    _____

Name ______________________________

Graphic Organizer
Supporting details

Topic: ______________________

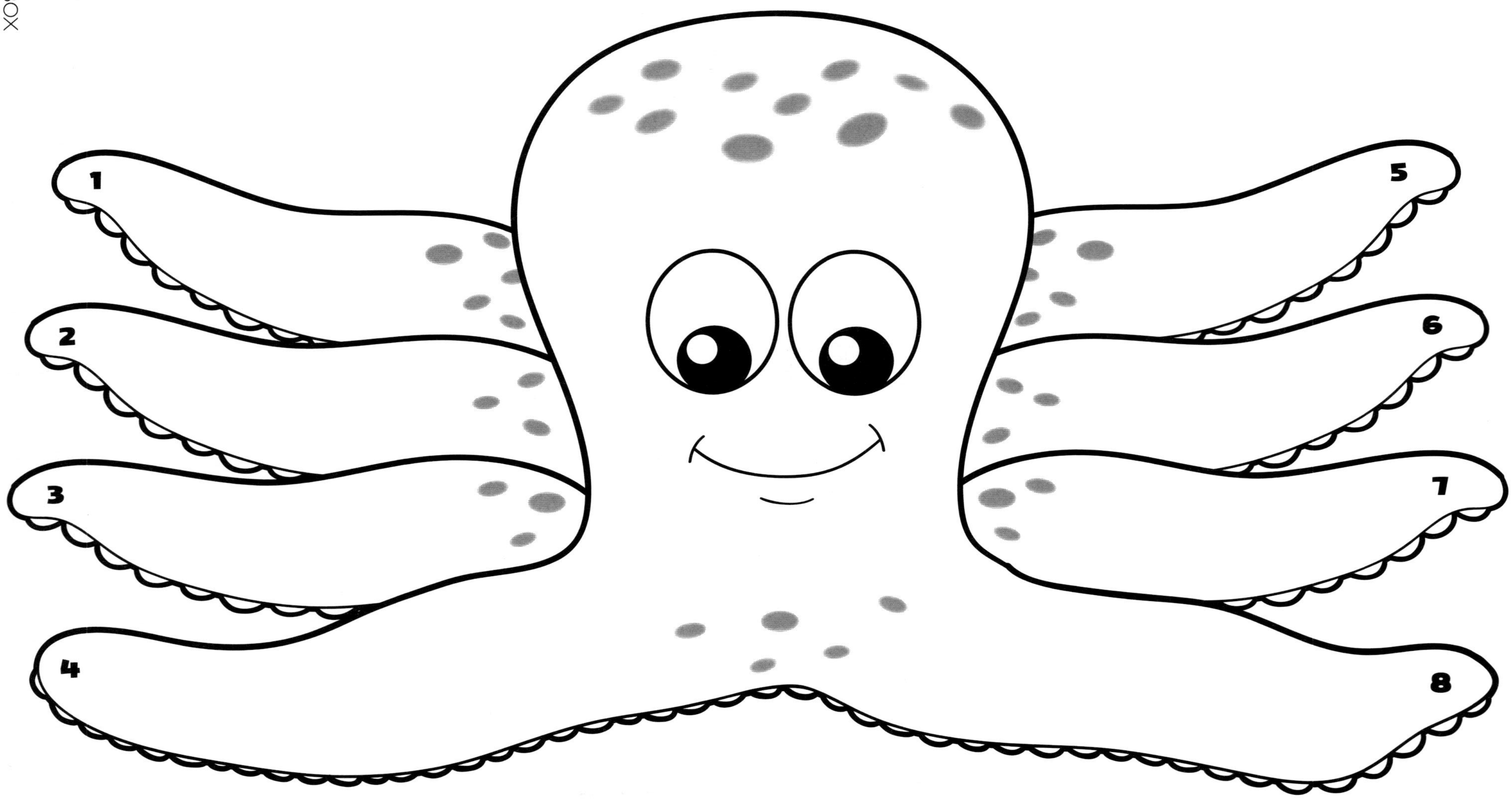

Note to the teacher: After reading a nonfiction passage, provide each student with a copy of this page. Have the student write the topic at the top of the page and eight supporting details on the octopus's legs.

SIMPLY SCIENCE

Tropical Rain Forest

macaw

sloth

poison arrow frog

anaconda

Home, Sweet Home

Animal habitats

Use this small-group activity to review different animal habitats. In advance, place a large sheet of drawing paper, resource books, and drawing supplies in each of several different areas around the room. Label each area with a specific habitat, such as "desert," "woodlands," "arctic tundra" or "tropical rain forest." Then program for each habitat four or five cards, each with the name of a different animal found there. To begin the activity, give each student a card. On your signal, guide each student to locate his animal's habitat. Then lead the students in each group to draw a background of their habitat, draw the animals on their cards, and tape the cards to the background. Display the projects on a wall titled "Home, Sweet Home: Where Animals Belong."

Proof in the Pudding
Changes in matter

To provide a better understanding of the terms *dissolve, solution,* and *mixture,* have each student make pudding! First, a student scoops one tablespoon of instant pudding mix into a resealable plastic bag and observes the powder's properties. Next, she measures and pours into her bag 2½ tablespoons of milk, seals the bag, and gently squeezes the bag until the powder dissolves in the milk. The student observes the resulting solution. Then she adds a small amount of cookie crumbs to her solution to make a mixture and predicts if the crumbs will dissolve in the pudding. Finally, the student uses a permanent marker to write her name on the bag and places the bag in a refrigerator. Later in the day, the student removes her bag from the refrigerator to confirm or reject her prediction. Then she uses a spoon to taste her scientific treat.

Kelly Hanover, Jane Vernon Elementary, Kenosha, WI

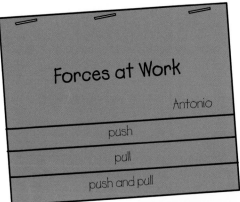

How Does That Move?
Forces and motion

After introducing the concepts of push and pull, have students make a simple booklet that shows examples of these forces at work. Direct each student to layer two sheets of paper so the edges are about one inch apart. Then have him fold the papers and staple them along the fold. Guide each student to label his booklet pages as shown and have him draw an illustration or glue a magazine photo cutout on each page. Next, guide him to write on each page a brief description that tells how the force is applied in the picture. Then provide time for each student to present his booklet to a partner.

adapted from an idea by Laurie Moore
Roland Russom Elementary
Dallas, GA

Simply Science

Good Vibrations
Sound

To prepare this demonstration, cut the bottom off an empty cylinder, such as an oatmeal or bread crumb container. Tightly stretch a piece of plastic wrap over one end of the container and secure it in place with a rubber band. To start the demonstration, ask a volunteer to lie on the floor while the rest of the class gathers around him. Have the child hold the container above his mouth so the covered end is at the top. Place some rice atop the plastic wrap and instruct the child to speak normally into the container; then have him shout. Direct the child to share what he observed from his perspective as he completed each task. Then lead the class in a discussion of the demonstration and the relationship between vibrations and sound. Afterward, have students cut out and assemble the booklet from a copy of page 210.

Malinda Pryor, Pine Ridge Elementary, Ellerslie, GA

Singing About the Stages
Water cycle

Here's a song that's sure to help students understand the stages of the water cycle. If desired, encourage students to create motions as they sing the lyrics.

Brandee Orgeron, Gonzales Primary School, Gonzales, LA

I'm a Little Raindrop
(sung to the tune of "I'm a Little Teapot")
I'm a little raindrop, small and round.
Watch me as I fall to the ground.
When the sun comes out and starts to glow,
I'll evaporate and up I'll go.

In the sky so high, I will cool down
And join other drops to form a cloud.
When the cloud gets heavy, watch me go.
I'll fall again as rain or snow.

Make It Work
Air

For this investigation, give each student a plastic sandwich bag, a rubber band, and an inexpensive party blower. Challenge each student to make the blower unroll without putting the blower in his mouth. Provide guidance as needed to help students determine that they need to blow up the bag, put the blower in a small opening in the bag, seal the opening with the rubber band, and then push on the bag to make the blower unroll. Then lead students in a discussion of the power of air.

Cyndi Stumpf, Ellen T. Briggs School, Lake Hopatcong, NJ

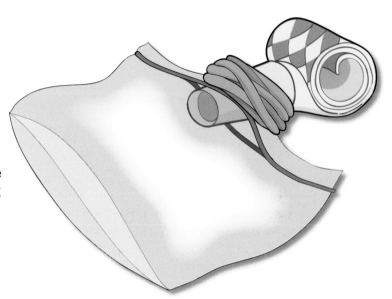

Quick Catch and Release
Observing rocks

To practice observation skills while studying rocks, take students outside to locate interesting rocks. After each child has "caught" a rock, return to the classroom and direct each child to sketch the rock on a sheet of paper. Then have her use her observation skills to write a descriptive paragraph about the rock. Provide time for each student to share her rock and observations with a small group. Then journey back outside to "release" the rocks into the wild.

Joy West, Cross Creek Elementary, Thomasville, GA

Confection Comparison
Properties of matter

In this small-group activity, students compare the physical properties of three different candies. First, have the whole class name physical properties of matter—such as color, shape, hardness, and buoyancy—and list the characteristics on the board. Next, provide each small group with three different candies and a copy of the Venn diagram on page 211. Guide students to work together to examine the candies and complete the diagram.

Michelle Bayless, Ruther Glen, VA

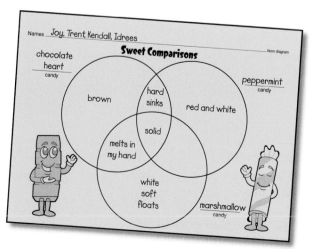

Simply Science

Funny Facts
Life cycles

Give each child a copy of the frog or butterfly comic strip cards from page 212. A child cuts apart the cards and places them in order. He writes a sentence from the animal's point of view to describe each phase. Next, the child colors the cards and glues them in order on a sentence strip. He trims the excess strip and then writes a title and his name.

Julie Hamilton, The DaVinci Academy, Colorado Springs, CO

Insect or Imposter?
- ☐ six legs
- ☐ three main body parts
- ☐ wings
- ☐ antennae
- ☐ hard outer shell

Insect or Imposter?
Physical characteristics

In this partner activity, students pretend to be entomologists as they separate insects from imposters. To prepare, place in a container several pictures of insects and noninsects. Have each pair of students take one picture from the container and copy the checklist shown onto a sheet of paper. For each characteristic the animal has, guide the duo to mark the list; then have each pair share its picture and results. Keep a list on the board of which are insects and which are imposters.

April Lewis, Warsaw Elementary, Warsaw, NC

Soak Up the Sun
Plant adaptations

First, have each small group soak four paper towels in water. Direct students to gently wring out each towel, arrange it according to the chart, and place it on a cookie sheet. Instruct each group to put the cookie sheet in a sunny location and then check the wetness of each towel throughout the day. Lead the class to understand that dry-climate plants, such as cacti, have thick stems. These stems, like the fourth towel, retain water in hot conditions, which helps the plants survive. Conclude the activity by having each student write a summary of what she observed and learned.

Carolyn Burant, St. John Vianney School, Brookfield, WI

towel 1 = lay flat with no folds
towel 2 = fold in half one time
towel 3 = fold in half three times
towel 4 = fold in half six times

Animals on Parade
Habitats

As a class, choose a habitat to study. After learning about its characteristics, plants, and animals, have each child choose a different animal to research in depth. In addition to preparing a written project about the animal, such as a report or poster, direct each child to fashion a simple costume to represent the animal. On a designated day, lead students in a parade of animals for other classes at your grade level to enjoy. After the parade, have each child share his written project with his classmates.

Jennifer McClure, Steiner Ranch Elementary, Austin, TX

S'more Sun
Solar energy

Get cooking with this edible activity! First, have each child break half a graham cracker into two pieces. Direct her to place a large marshmallow and a snack-size chocolate bar between the graham cracker pieces. Next, guide the child to wrap the treat in foil and place it in direct sunlight. Periodically check to see whether the chocolate and marshmallow have melted; once they have, lead students in a discussion of the sun's energy and its effects on the treat and other objects on Earth.

Marjorie Archer, Nova Blanche Forman Elementary, Davie, FL

Examine and Question
Observations, science journals

When students record activity learnings and experiment observations in their science journals, also have them generate a related question. Encourage students to start the question with *how, why,* or *what if.* Not only will students challenge their understanding of the topic, but you can also use the questions to plan follow-up activities or provide independent learning experiences.

April Parker, St. Pius X School, Greensboro, NC

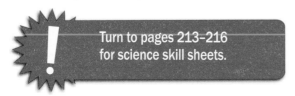

Turn to pages 213–216 for science skill sheets.

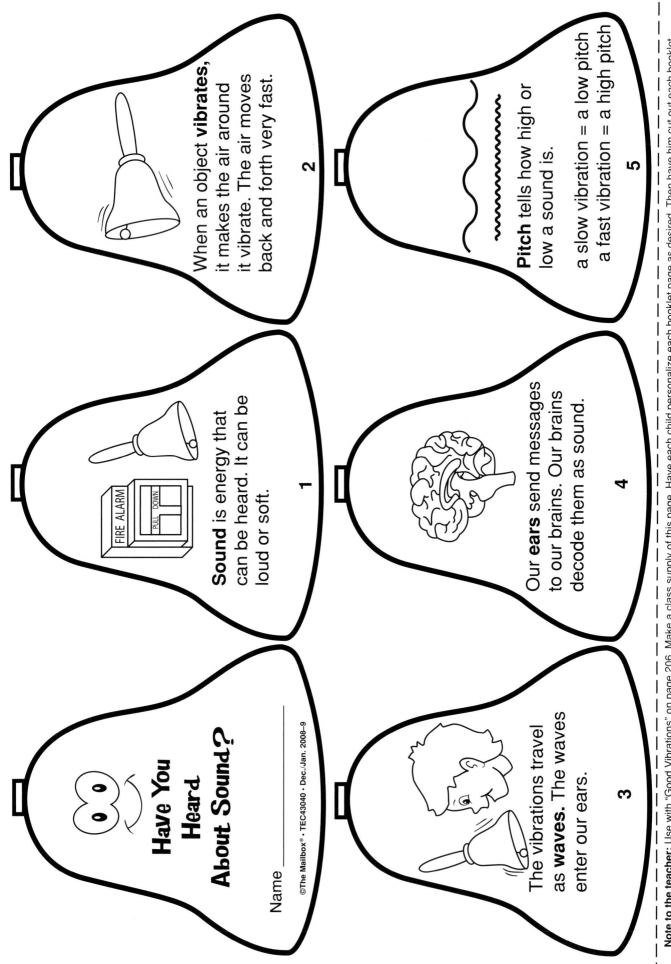

Have You Heard About Sound?

Name _____

©The Mailbox® • TEC43040 • Dec./Jan. 2008-9

2

When an object **vibrates**, it makes the air around it vibrate. The air moves back and forth very fast.

5

Pitch tells how high or low a sound is.

a slow vibration = a low pitch
a fast vibration = a high pitch

1

Sound is energy that can be heard. It can be loud or soft.

FIRE ALARM
PULL DOWN

4

Our **ears** send messages to our brains. Our brains decode them as sound.

3

The vibrations travel as **waves**. The waves enter our ears.

Note to the teacher: Use with "Good Vibrations" on page 206. Make a class supply of this page. Have each child personalize each booklet page as desired. Then have him cut out each booklet page, stack the pages in order, and staple them together.

Venn diagram

Sweet Comparisons

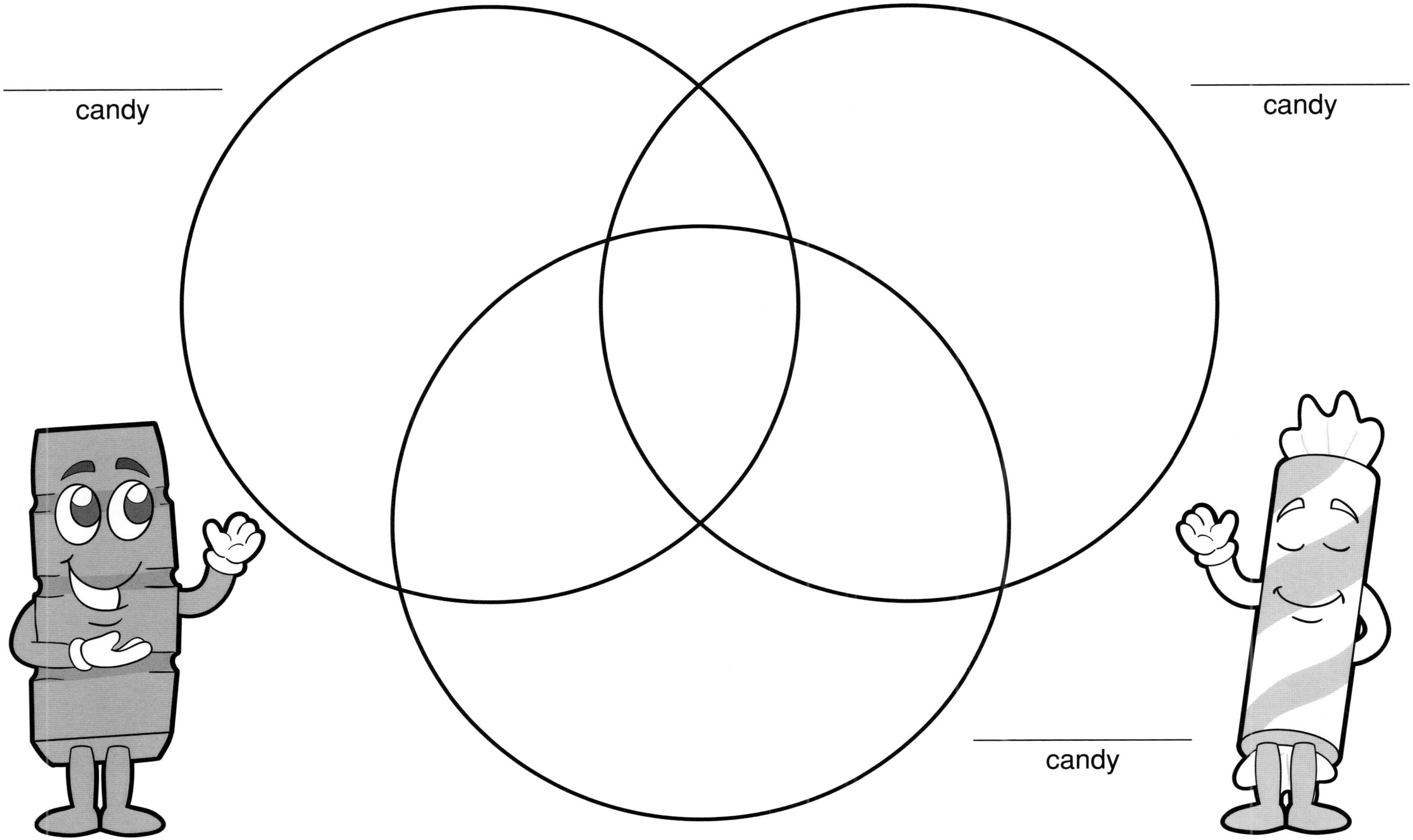

candy _____

candy _____

candy _____

©The Mailbox® • TEC43041 • Feb./Mar. 2009

Note to the teacher: Use with "Confection Comparison" on page 207.

Comic Strip Cards

Use with "Funny Facts" on page 208.

Frog

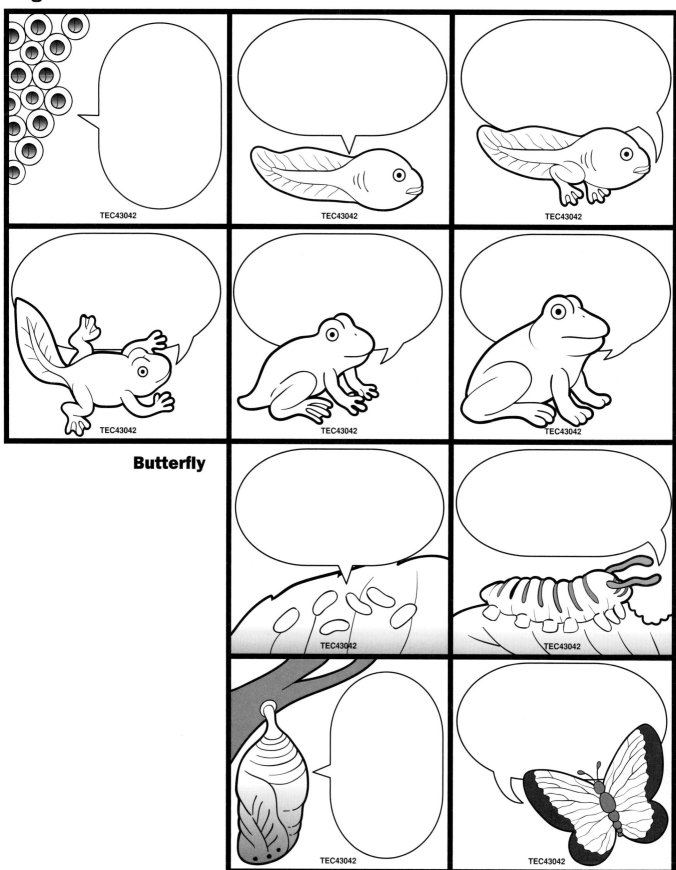

Butterfly

Name That Change

Draw or write to complete the chart.
In the last column, circle the matching change.

Picture	Description	Type of Change
1.	change of <u>shape</u> caused by <u>folding or cutting</u>	physical or chemical
2.	change from _____ to _____ caused by _____	physical or chemical
3.	change from <u>strong metal</u> to <u>weak metal</u> caused by <u>rusting</u>	physical or chemical
4.	change from _____ to _____ caused by _____	physical or chemical
5.	change from a <u>solid</u> to <u>a liquid</u> caused by <u>melting</u>	physical or chemical
6.	change from _____ to _____ caused by _____	physical or chemical

Toothless Grin

Cows do not have top front teeth.

When you smile, do you have a gap where your top front teeth should be? Cows do! Instead of front teeth, a cow has a pad of skin just under its top lip. So how does it chew? A cow uses its bottom and back teeth. An adult cow has 32 teeth in all. But it also has a gap where there are no teeth. The gap helps the cow take in a large amount of grass. Here's how: First, a cow uses its long tongue to pull on a big batch of grass. Next, it shoves the grass through the gap in its mouth. It pinches the grass between its bottom front teeth and pad of skin. Then the cow swings its head to tear the grass. When the torn grass is in the cow's mouth, the cow swallows it.

pad of skin

bottom teeth

Make each sentence true.
Cross out the word that does not belong.
Write the correct word. Use the word bank.

Word Bank
above
grab
head
tongue
top

1. A cow has a pad of skin under its lower lip.

2. A cow uses its teeth to pull on grass.

3. The gap in a cow's mouth helps it mow grass.

4. The gap in a cow's mouth is found below the bottom teeth.

5. A cow swings its tail to tear the grass.

 ©The Mailbox® • TEC43041 • Feb./Mar. 2009 • Key p. 312

Long Live the Land Turtle

A tortoise can live more than 100 years!

A **tortoise** (`tor-təs) is a kind of turtle that only lives on land. Most have high, domed shells.

A female tortoise lays her eggs in a hole in the ground. She covers the eggs with soil. Then she leaves them underground to develop on their own. When it has grown inside the egg, each young tortoise uses an egg tooth to break its egg, hatch, and dig out of the hole. Many of these **hatchlings** do not live longer than ten years. They might become a meal for a raccoon or fox. Some do not make it because people have destroyed their habitats.

Those that do **survive** can live a long life. One such tortoise was given to the royal family of Tonga in the 1770s. Many people think it was about 188 years old when it died in 1965. Another tortoise was thought to be 255 years old when it died in a zoo in India.

Write a meaning for each word.
Use the passage to help you.

1. tortoise _____

_____

2. hatchlings _____

_____

3. survive _____

_____

Bonus Box: Draw a diagram to show the life cycle of a tortoise. Draw pictures and use words from the passage to label each picture.

Living in the Rain Forest

More than half the world's plant and animal species can be found in tropical rain forests.

Many plants and animals live in tropical rain forests. The plants depend on the animals to help them live and grow. The animals depend on the plants to help them live and grow. If a plant dies, the animals that depend on it may die. If an animal dies, the plants that depend on it may die.

The fig tree depends on animals to help it live and grow. The fig tree grows a large supply of fruit. Each fruit is filled with seeds. During the day, animals like monkeys and toucans feed on the fig fruit. At night, bats stop by for a meal. The fruit's seeds are passed in the animals' waste. This helps spread the seeds.

The cocoa tree is another plant that needs animals. It makes large pods of seeds. The seeds make more trees. But the pods do not often fall off the tree or open when they are ripe. Animals like monkeys need the pods for food. They open the pods to eat the pulp inside. This allows seeds to fall to the ground. The animals help the cocoa tree continue its life cycle.

Complete the chart.
Use the passage.

Cause	Effect
1.	The plants that depend on it may die.
2. Fig trees grow fruit.	
3. The fruit's seeds are passed in the animals' waste.	
4.	The cocoa seeds fall to the ground.

 ©The Mailbox® • TEC43043 • June/July 2009 • Key p. 312

WHAT WORKS FOR YOU?

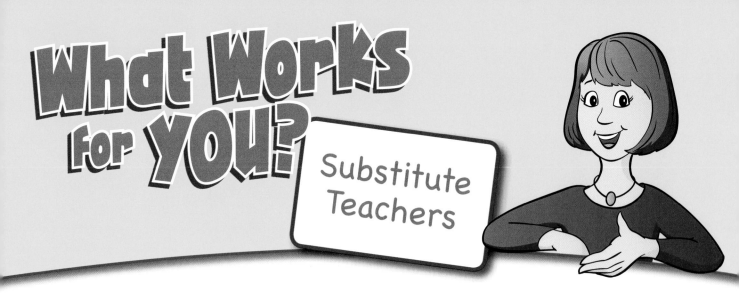

What Works for YOU?

Substitute Teachers

I leave student copies of a **questionnaire** for my substitute teacher. At the end of the day, each student rates how his day went and how the class did as a whole. Each child also writes a letter on the back of the form telling me about his day. It's a great way to make students accountable for their actions. (Look on page 221 for a reproducible questionnaire that works great with this idea.)

Piper Porter, Trent Elementary, Spokane, WA

I created a **seating chart** that can be used by any teacher who works with my students. I place my seating chart inside a plastic sheet protector and use a dry-erase marker to star the names of students who might require additional attention. I keep the chart at the front of the room so it's easily accessible. The substitute can use the chart to learn students' names and to keep track of students she's called on during lessons. When I'm back in the classroom, all I need to do is wipe away her marks and use the seating chart as my own student tracking sheet.

Amanda Acosta, Scott Libby Elementary, Litchfield Park, AZ

When I know I'm going to need a substitute, I leave a **token of my appreciation** with my plans and materials. I tape onto a bag of popcorn a note that reads "Thanks for popping in!" It's an easy way to show the substitute that I am thankful for his help.

Colleen Dabney, Williamsburg, VA

My weekly **organizational system** ensures that our flow of learning does not change, even when I'm absent. I stack five bins, each labeled with a day of the school week. Each Friday, I gather materials for the following week's lessons and place them in the appropriate bins. On top of each set of materials, I include a laminated schedule. That way, if I should unexpectedly be absent, a substitute will have all the things she needs in one place and she'll know exactly when to use them.

Melissa Fletcher, DuBois Area Catholic Schools, DuBois, PA

What Works for You?

Student Disagreements

I give students a piece of paper and a few minutes to **write about their disagreement.** Before I read each child's paper aloud for discussion, I remind students that we will only discuss what is written on the papers. This helps my students focus on the important details and forces them to let the little things go.

Laura Johnson, South Decatur Elementary, Greensburg, IN

No hurt feelings!
INSULT-FREE ZONE

I set up my classroom as an **insult-free zone** in order to avoid student disagreements and hurt feelings. After I explain that insults and put-downs are hurtful, I post a sign as a reminder to students. What happens if I overhear one student insulting another? I say, "Ouch!" and direct the child to compliment the classmate he insulted.

Mary F. Harding, Thomas J. Pappas School, Phoenix, AZ

To keep little problems from escalating into bigger ones, I have my students **role-play.** At periodic class meetings, I have students name general issues that they see happening among their peers. I list the issues on the board and then divide students into groups. Each group is assigned an issue and students work together to determine a solution. I provide time for each group to discuss the issue and role-play one possible solution for the class.

Michelle Zakula, Saint Roman School, Milwaukee, WI

To end a disagreement, I encourage each student involved to **write at least one solution** on a sheet of paper. I collect the students' papers and then meet with them together. We examine all the solutions and look for ideas that are similar. From these similar ideas, I lead students to a solution that makes the students happy. If the students' ideas are too different, I lead them in a discussion to reveal a solution that works.

Elaine Norton, Hiddenite, NC

There's a reproducible on page 222 that works great with this idea. Check it out!

What Works for You?

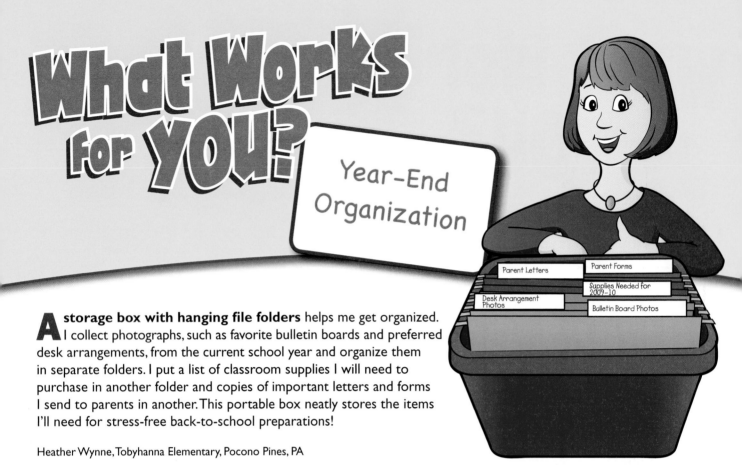

Year-End Organization

A storage box with hanging file folders helps me get organized. I collect photographs, such as favorite bulletin boards and preferred desk arrangements, from the current school year and organize them in separate folders. I put a list of classroom supplies I will need to purchase in another folder and copies of important letters and forms I send to parents in another. This portable box neatly stores the items I'll need for stress-free back-to-school preparations!

Heather Wynne, Tobyhanna Elementary, Pocono Pines, PA

To save prep time later, I **prepare manipulatives now.** For example, I fill a class supply of film canisters or resealable plastic bags with bingo chips. Students use these ready-to-go manipulatives in the fall for bingo-style games, math problems, or center activities.

Katherine Boldt, McKinley Elementary, Appleton, WI

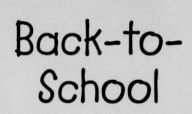

Back-to-School

I make **storage envelopes** to hold my classroom decorations and teaching tools. I take a large sheet of poster board, fold it in half from top to bottom, and tape the sides together. Then I slide my decorations inside and label the envelope with its contents. Since the envelope is made of poster board, the items inside don't get bent!

Laura Johnson, South Decatur Elementary, Greensburg, IN

I keep a file folder wish list. When I see an item in a magazine that I'd like or I need for my classroom, I cut out the picture and tape it inside a file folder. I have the folder handy when I complete my supply order or when I shop garage sales over the summer. It's an easy way to keep up with the things I'll need in the fall.

Jean Hiller, Canton Charter Academy, Canton, MI

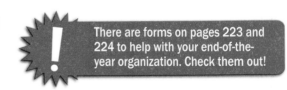

There are forms on pages 223 and 224 to help with your end-of-the-year organization. Check them out!

My Report

Think about today.
Color your answers to complete the chart.

I followed the rules.	all day	sometimes	never
I worked hard to do my best.	all day	sometimes	never
I am proud of my actions.	all day	sometimes	never
My classmates followed the rules.	all day	sometimes	never
My classmates worked hard to do their best.	all day	sometimes	never
My classmates can be proud of their actions.	all day	sometimes	never

©The Mailbox® • TEC43041 • Feb./Mar. 2009

Name _____ Questionnaire

My Report

Think about today.
Color your answers to complete the chart.

I followed the rules.	all day	sometimes	never
I worked hard to do my best.	all day	sometimes	never
I am proud of my actions.	all day	sometimes	never
My classmates followed the rules.	all day	sometimes	never
My classmates worked hard to do their best.	all day	sometimes	never
My classmates can be proud of their actions.	all day	sometimes	never

©The Mailbox® • TEC43041 • Feb./Mar. 2009

Note to the teacher: Use with the first idea on page 218.

Student Solutions

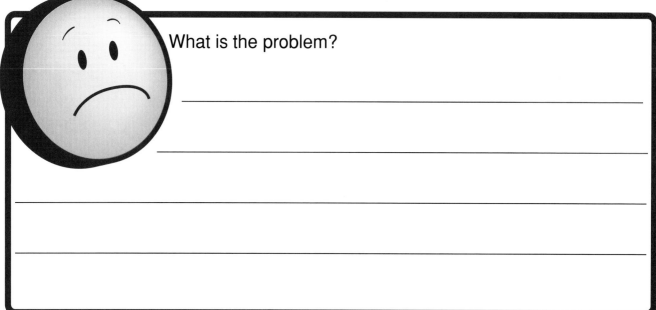

What is the problem?

_____

_____

_____

_____

Who is involved?

How would you solve this problem?

1. _____

_____

2. _____

_____

3. _____

_____

©The Mailbox® • TEC43042 • April/May 2009

Note to the teacher: Use with the fourth idea on page 219. Keep copies of this form on hand. When a disagreement occurs, have each child involved complete the form. Then place the completed forms side by side as you discuss solutions with the students. Keep the students' forms as a record of your discussion.

Things to Remember

Items Thrown Away

(R) = replace

Other Items
Needed for Next Year:

Items to Unpack First in the Fall

Item: Where It's Stored:

Teacher _____   Room _____

Note to the teacher: Complete a copy of this form as you clean and pack up at the end of the school year. Then post or file the form in a safe location. Use the form as a reference when you return for the next school year.

Teamwork Works!

Reward: _____

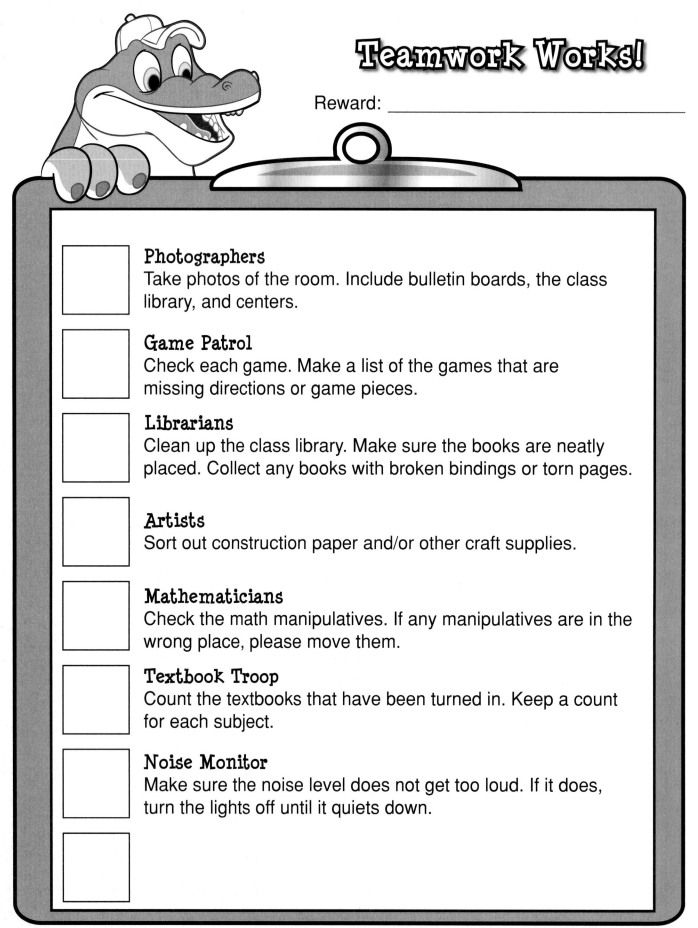

- [ ] **Photographers**
  Take photos of the room. Include bulletin boards, the class library, and centers.

- [ ] **Game Patrol**
  Check each game. Make a list of the games that are missing directions or game pieces.

- [ ] **Librarians**
  Clean up the class library. Make sure the books are neatly placed. Collect any books with broken bindings or torn pages.

- [ ] **Artists**
  Sort out construction paper and/or other craft supplies.

- [ ] **Mathematicians**
  Check the math manipulatives. If any manipulatives are in the wrong place, please move them.

- [ ] **Textbook Troop**
  Count the textbooks that have been turned in. Keep a count for each subject.

- [ ] **Noise Monitor**
  Make sure the noise level does not get too loud. If it does, turn the lights off until it quiets down.

- [ ]

Note to the teacher: Program the blank space at the bottom of this form with a task unique to your classroom; then make an overhead transparency and share it with the class. Explain that you need students' help to complete these tasks. Write a reward on the transparency. Assign groups of students to complete each task. As each group finishes, have the students check off their task. When all the tasks are completed, treat students to the reward.

WRITING & GRAMMAR

Write On!

Fall is here
Leaves will begin to change to
color. they will be orage, red, and
yellow. my mom will take lots of
pictures of them. i will collect them
and glue them on paper. Fall leaves
are beutiful!

Name Troy	Yes	No
Are capitalization rules followed?		✓
Are punctuation rules followed?	✓	
Is there a main idea?	✓	
Does each detail support the main idea?	✓	
Is grade-appropriate spelling used?	✓	

Seasonal Subjects

Assessment

Have each child write on a sheet of paper the title "Fall Is Here" and then guide him to write a paragraph that matches the title. Assess the paragraph based on a simple rubric like the one shown and then tuck them into the child's portfolio. When winter arrives, have the child write a paragraph titled "Winter Is Here." Assess the paragraph according to the same rubric and then store it with the child's fall writing. Repeat the steps in the spring and summer for a yearlong look at the development of each child's writing.

Carol Bradfield, Irving Elementary, Waterloo, IA

Colorful Possibilities
Writing sentences

In advance, program four decks of colored cards as listed. To complete the activity, a student stacks the like-colored decks facedown in a row as shown. She turns over one card in each deck and then reads the words on the cards. If the words make a complete sentence, she writes the sentence on a sheet of paper and then sets the cards aside. If the words do not make a complete sentence, she places the cards in a discard pile. She continues in this manner until she has turned over all of the cards.

Jean Erickson, Grace Christian Academy, West Allis, WI

Blue Cards	Red Cards	Green Cards	Yellow Cards
Sam	ran	to	hill.
We	jumped	behind	the bench.
They	walked	around	my house.
You	are	under	forest.
Someone	skipped	into	zoo.
Jill	was	by the	tree.
Bobby	tripped	over	a pencil.
Sally	jogged	in	the park.
Many people	rested	on	the bed.
I	sang	out of	the garden.

We   jumped   behind   the bench.

Hats Off to Writing
Motivation

When introducing a writing lesson, put on an interesting hat, such as a sombrero or a top hat. Explain to students that this special hat helps you focus on a topic and form good ideas when you're writing. Further explain that wearing your hat makes you feel like writing! Then start writing and invite your students to do the same. To spread the excitement, invite each child to bring his own hat to school and then have him wear it during writing lessons.

adapted from an idea by April Lewis, Warsaw Elementary, Warsaw, NC

Timely Prompts
Journal writing

- Which school supply is the most important: crayons, scissors, or glue? Tell why you think so.
- A backpack spends a lot of time just hanging around. But how does it feel about going to school on the first day? Pretend you're a backpack going back to school. Write about the things you're excited about and the things you may be worried about.
- Imagine that you have been asked to teach a younger student how to get ready for the first day of school. Write instructions that tell the child what he needs to know.

October 11, 2008

Dear Mom,
I had a good day today.
My friends and I made
Letter Ladies. The Letter
Lady will help me remember
how to write friendly
letters. I can't wait to
show mine to you!

Love,
Tucker

Heading

Greeting

Body

Closing

Signature

The Letter Lady

Writing friendly letters

This quick project provides students with a visual reminder of the parts of a friendly letter. To make a letter lady, a child cuts out the patterns from a copy of page 241 and glues them together as shown. When it's time to write a letter, the child refers to his Letter Lady to ensure that his writing includes each part. After each assignment, he tucks his Letter Lady into his writing journal where it will be easy to find the next time he needs it.

Kelly J. Smith, Cranberry Township, PA

Sweet Story Starters
Writing motivation

In advance, label a paper lunch bag with a code like the one shown; then put several purple, yellow, and orange paper lollipops inside. To complete the activity, a child writes a story topic. Next, she takes a lollipop out of the bag and refers to the color code to write a story starter that matches the color she has drawn. Then she returns the lollipop to the bag and writes her story.

Stacie Stone Davis, Livonia Primary, Livonia, NY

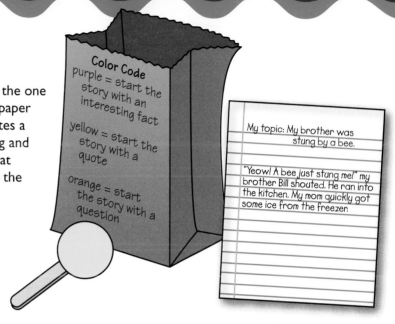

Color Code
purple = start the story with an interesting fact

yellow = start the story with a quote

orange = start the story with a question

My topic: My brother was stung by a bee.

"Yeow! A bee just stung me!" my brother Bill shouted. He ran into the kitchen. My mom quickly got some ice from the freezer.

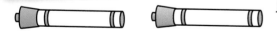

My mother likes to work in her garden. She plants lots of vege-tables. My brother likes to help her pull the weeds. I like to water the tiny plants. Soon, we will make vegetable soup!

Stop and Go
Capitalization and punctuation

Get students focused on editing with this easy idea. After writing a draft, a child uses a green highlighter to mark the beginning letter of each sentence. As he marks each letter, he checks for capitalization and makes corrections as needed. Next, the child rereads the piece and uses a pink highlighter to mark the end of each sentence. As he makes each mark, he checks for ending punctuation. If the punctuation is not there or is incorrect, the child adds or corrects it. Soon, self-editing will be as automatic as stop and go!

John Hughes, Book Cliff Elementary, Green River, UT

Timely Prompts
Journal writing

- Football teams play in the fall. What does it take to win a football game? Teamwork! Write an adver-tisement listing what it takes to be a good team member.
- Imagine you're a scarecrow and you want to come to school for the day. Write a letter to a teacher explaining why you'd like to come to school.
- On Thanksgiving, people enjoy eating lots of good food. Write a poem describing your favorite Thanksgiving foods.

Can you play for the Bears?
Good team members should be

positive
helpful
determined
proud
fun

Join our team!

Write On!

Nouns	Verbs	Adjectives
playground	swing	fun
teachers	scream	noisy
students	play	busy
trees	jump	crowded
slides	run	quick

Lewis

Three-Part Plan

Prewriting, parts of speech

To help students organize strong vocabulary for their writing, try this simple idea, which involves three parts of speech. Have each child divide a sheet of paper into three equal sections and label each section as shown. Direct each student to choose a setting for a story, such as a playground. Then have him list nouns he might see there in the first column, verbs associated with it in the second column, and adjectives associated with it in the last column. Instruct students to use their completed lists as they create their stories. For added interest, give the three parts of speech a catchy name like "Parts of Speech Trio" to help students remember this writing plan.

Siobhan Swiger, Bugg Elementary, Raleigh, NC

Get Aboard!
Parts of a paragraph

New Year's Eve is a fun night!

In advance, have each child write a topic sentence on scrap paper and collect the sentences. Next, select a student to start a paragraph train and serve as its engine. Have the child come to the front of the room, choose a sentence from the collection, and read it aloud. Then choose another student to stand behind the first student and put his hands on her shoulders. Direct him to add a sentence that supports the topic sentence. Continue with three more students, guiding two to add detail sentences and the last student, or caboose, to give a conclusion sentence. When the students successfully complete their paragraph, encourage them to repeat it as they take a short trip around the room. Repeat the process at a later date, providing time for each child to be part of a paragraph train.

Cindy Hetzel, Meadows Elementary, Valencia, CA

Christmas Must Go On
written and illustrated by everyone in Room 111

Santa and Mrs. Claus received an invitation to a holiday party. An elf had sent the invitation. It said "A Christmas Party will be held on Blizzard Lane on December 24." Santa and Mrs. Claus decided to go to the party. It sounded like fun. Santa decided to wear his red suit. Mrs. Claus wanted to wear her long red dress. They arrived on a shiny sleigh with eight reindeer. Santa was ready to party!

When they stepped off the sleigh, someone hit Santa with a snowball! Immediately, a snowball fight broke out.

All Together Now
Writing process, shared writing

The time invested in this activity is worth the result! To start, suggest a short list of possible story elements for a shared story and have the class vote on the ones they want to include. Call on each child to contribute a sentence to the story, and write each sentence on the overhead. Engage students in editing the draft for punctuation, capitalization, and details. Then write (or get an adult volunteer to write) the final draft of the story on large sheets of bulletin board paper and have students illustrate the story. Review the steps of the writing process followed to complete the activity. Then display the story and illustrations together. Not only will students be proud to show off their collaborative work, but they also will have a better understanding of the writing process and be ready to write more.

Amanda Johnson, Weigel Elementary, Cincinnati, OH

Timely Prompts
Journal writing

- Pretend Jack Frost is real. Write him a letter to learn more about his job.
- If a big winter storm were on its way, what words might a newsperson use to describe it? Make a list.
- Describe one thing you got better at during the year 2008. Name something you'd like to get better at in 2009 and tell why.

December 22, 2008

Dear Jack Frost,
I learned that you are very busy in the winter. It is your job to put the frost on windows during the cold winter months. How do you do it? Were you born with special skills, or did you have to get training? Do you get cold while you are doing your job, or do you have a uniform that keeps you warm? Please write to me and tell me all you can about your job! I can't wait to hear from you.

Yours truly,
Marisol

Writing & Grammar

Vivid Reminder
Editing for details

This simple reminder helps students remember to add vivid details when they revise their writing. As you review students' drafts, use a brightly colored highlighter or marker to draw attention to phrases and sentences that lack sufficient detail. When you return the drafts, tell students to add vivid details to the highlighted areas to make them more interesting and clear.

adapted from an idea by Jennifer L. Kohnke, St. Charles, IL

Last week I saw something really neat. My mom and I went to visit my grandpa Bob. He lives in a special home for older people. He was eating lunch when we got there, so we waited in the waiting room. That's when I saw a lady bring a dog into the home. I didn't know dogs were allowed there. The dog was cute! I like dogs, so I watched it. It wore a vest. The lady said it is a therapy dog. She brought her dog to the home to help the people who are sick. Some of these people had strokes. Many of them want to pet the dog, and that helps them practice moving their hands again. I thought that was cool!

Punctuation Patrol

Name ___Amir___

Date ___3/11/09___

The above-named student correctly used the following punctuation:

- [✓] periods
- [✓] question marks
- [✓] exclamation points
- [ ] commas
- [ ] quotation marks
- [✓] apostrophes

Signed ___Officer Sine___

Comments:
Thanks for remembering the rules! ☺

Patrolling for Positives
Punctuation

In advance, make a class supply of the patrol tickets on page 242. Cut out the tickets and attach them to a clipboard. While students are working on a writing assignment, grab your clipboard and a pen; then begin your patrol. Choose a few students and spot-check their work. For each child, complete a ticket to show the marks he used correctly and then give him the ticket to staple to his paper. Repeat the process each day until every child has received a ticket. To further motivate students, enter the name of each child who received at least two checks on his ticket in a class drawing for a silly prize.

Beth Sine, Dr. Brown Elementary, Waldorf, MD

School Day Adventures
Imaginary narrative

To set the tone for this fun, creative writing idea, read aloud *Snowmen at Night* by Caralyn Buehner. Review with students what the snowmen do while the people sleep. Ask each child to think about a favorite stuffed animal or toy at home. List on the board students' ideas about what the toys might do while the students are at school. Then have each student refer to the list to write a story titled "[Name of stuffed animal or toy] by Day." For added interest, encourage each child to bring the stuffed animal or toy to school on the day she shares the final draft of her story.

Jodi Doescher, William C. Munn Elementary, Spencerport, NY

One Place to Another
Prewriting

Help students plan a story from beginning to end. Direct each child to review a copy of any reproducible map; then have him write on his copy the name of a character and a problem that incorporates places on the map. Next, have the student mark the location where the story begins with a *B*, the middle location with an *M*, and the end location with an *E*. Guide the student to refer to the labeled map as he plans his story's settings and the events that will happen at each location.

Make a Better Picture
Adding details

To guide students toward more detailed writing, direct each child to silently read a copy of the passage on page 243, noting the underlined words and phrases as she reads. Point out to students that the passage lacks details. Next, have each student complete the tasks at the bottom of the page, reminding her that her responses should relate to the passage. Then have her rewrite the passage on another sheet of paper, replacing each underlined word or phrase with her response to the matching numbered task. Provide time for students to share their revised passages and discuss the importance of adding details to create a clear mental picture for the reader.

Writing & Grammar

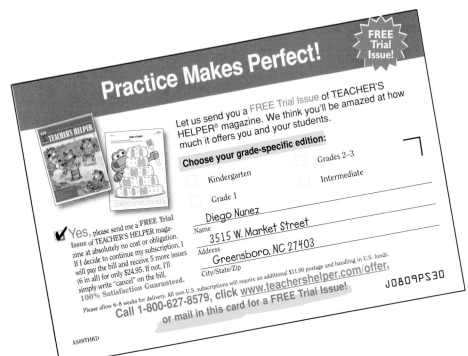

Replying to the Rules
Capitalization

Provide quick practice with capitalizing names and places in a realistic format. Give each child a magazine subscription card or other business reply card and direct her to draw a large X over the return mailing information. Then have the student use capitalization rules to complete the card with real or fictitious information.

Litsa Jackson, Covington Integrated Arts Academy, Covington, TN

Reuse and Rewrite
Poetry

Here's an easy way to expose students to a variety of poetry styles. Gather an assortment of new or used greeting cards. Have each student pair read a poem from a card and identify rhyme schemes, couplets, or stanzas found in the poem. Then challenge students to rewrite the poem and provide time for students to share their revisions aloud.

Colleen Dabney, Williamsburg, VA

It's your day!
I hope it's the best.
Get in some play.
And then have some rest.

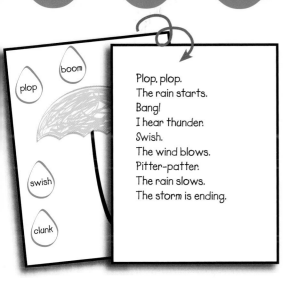

plop
boom
swish
clunk

Plop, plop.
The rain starts.
Bang!
I hear thunder.
Swish.
The wind blows.
Pitter-patter.
The rain slows.
The storm is ending.

Make a Splash
Onomatopoeia

Whether rain is part of your winter weather or a fixture during spring, here's an activity students can relate to! First, direct each child to draw an umbrella shape on a sheet of paper. Next, have students write above the umbrella words that describe sounds heard during rainstorms. Explain to students that some words are named by the way they sound, which is known as onomatopoeia. Guide each child to draw a raindrop around each such word. Then have each child write on the back of her paper a poem about the rain, being sure to include examples of onomatopoeia.

adapted from an idea by Christina Bainbridge, Centreville, MI

Writing Prompts

February

- Pretend that your dentist has given you the Best Smile Award. Write a thank-you speech. Thank your dentist and everyone who has helped you have such a great smile.

- Think about someone or something that you love. Write a riddle about your choice. Include at least three clues in your riddle.

- Pretend that Cupid will come to your school just before Valentine's Day. He wants to blend in, so he needs new clothes. Draw a picture showing how he might dress to blend in that day. Then write about his new outfit.

- Make a list of words that describe winter. Then write a paragraph about winter. Use at least five words from your list.

- Is it good or bad that February is the shortest month of the year? Tell why you think so.

March

- March is Music in Our Schools Month. What instrument do you like to play or listen to most? Write about the instrument. Convince the reader that it is the best instrument of all.

- March is Women's History Month. Write a letter to a woman who you think has done important work in her life. Tell her why you think her work is important.

- Alexander Graham Bell was born on March 3, 1847. He invented the telephone. Pretend you are on the phone with a friend. Write what each of you will say. Use quotation marks.

- Write about a time you felt lucky.

- Think about the many meanings of the word *spring*. Use each meaning of *spring* in a different sentence.

Writing & Grammar

A Ready Review
Spelling

Incorporate spelling practice into transition times. Tell students that they will spell three spelling words aloud as they prepare for the next activity. As students transition, say the word and use it in a sentence; then direct students to spell the word aloud. Repeat with two more words.

Carolyn Burant, St. John Vianney School, Brookfield, WI

> As you're getting out your math books, let's spell three words. *Nickel.* "I lost a nickel on the bus." Spell *nickel.*

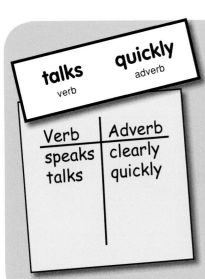

talks verb

quickly adverb

Verb	Adverb
speaks	clearly
talks	quickly

Acting Secretly
Verbs and adverbs

To prepare this whole-class activity, copy and cut apart the cards on page 244. Stack them facedown at the front of the room. To begin, select a student to come forward and choose a card. Guide the child to silently read the phrase on the card and then act it out for her classmates. Call on another student to determine the action, or verb, being demonstrated. Then encourage students to determine how the action is being carried out, or what adverb was on the card. After the word pair has been determined, record it on a chart like the one shown and select another child to have a turn. To encourage a shy student to participate in this activity, allow her to work with a partner.

Patricia Rigueira, Southern Cross School, Beccar, Buenos Aires, Argentina

Ask for Improvements
Revising drafts

Display the acronym shown and review it with the class. As each student completes a rough draft, invite him to read it aloud for the class. Before he begins, tell students to think about how the writer can improve his work as they listen to the draft. Encourage each student to write on an index card a question that might clarify the writing's details and events or a suggestion on how to improve the piece, all while keeping a positive tone. When the writer has read his draft, provide time for him to call on his classmates to share their questions and suggestions; then have those students pass the writer their cards. Direct the writer to use the questions and suggestions to revise his draft.

Sugar Thiessan, Grace Abbott Elementary, Omaha, NE

Ask questions and
Suggest improvements while
Keeping your words positive!

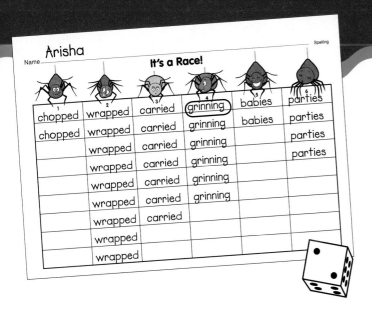

It's a Race!
Spelling

Here's an independent activity that works like a game. Give each child a copy of page 245. The child writes a different spelling word at the top of each column. Next, she circles the word she thinks she will write most often (the projected winner). She rolls a die and writes the corresponding word in its column. The first word to reach the bottom of the paper is the winner. To ensure practice with all the spelling words from her list, the student plays again at another time with another set of six words.

Shannon Stanton, West Elementary, Alton, IL

Writing Prompts

April

- April 1 is April Fools' Day. Write about a time you or someone you know was tricked.

- April 22 is Earth Day. Write at least one paragraph telling how to take care of the earth.

- If you were asked to make a new jelly bean flavor, what would you choose? Describe how your new jelly bean tastes and how it looks.

- It is said that April showers bring May flowers. What else can a rainy day bring?

- Pretend that you have been given a special egg to care for. Tell why it is special, how you care for it, and what happens when it hatches.

- Think of a classroom activity that would be fun to do outdoors. Write to convince your teacher to have the activity outside.

May

- May 10 is Mother's Day. Think of a mom from a story you have read. Write to tell what makes this character a good mom.

- Memorial Day is May 25. This is a day to think about soldiers who gave their lives for our freedom. If you could plan an event to honor them, what kind of event would you have? Tell what you would do and why.

- Write a thank-you letter to someone who has helped you at school this year. You might write to a teacher, another adult, or even another student.

- List as many words as you can think of that rhyme with *May*. Then use the words to write a rhyming poem.

- Pretend that you have been put in charge of field day for your class. Make a schedule to show all the games for that day. Include a time and a short description for each game.

Writing & Grammar

I love when the ice cream truck drives down my street.

It always plays a happy tune to get my attention.

When it stops in front of my house, it is full of my favorite frozen treats.

A visit from the ice cream truck can make a boring day exciting.

The best summer days are those that have a visit from the ice cream truck!

Sweet Prep Work
Paragraph organization

To help students organize a paragraph, give each child four paper circles (ice cream scoops) and a brown paper triangle (cone). The child writes a topic sentence on one scoop and then writes a supporting sentence on each of the other scoops. She writes a conclusion sentence on the cone. Next, the student checks the order of her scoops to confirm that they make sense. Then she glues her scoops together and glues the bottom scoop to the cone.

Barb Olszewski, Elmer Knopf Learning Center, Flint, MI

Catch the Bug
Capitalization

Enlarge the bug jar cards on page 246, cut them out, and place them around the room. Also cut apart a copy of the firefly cards on page 247 and give a card to each child. Review with students the location of each bug jar and its corresponding capitalization rule. Direct each student to determine which rule the word, phrase, or sentence on his card should follow; then, on your signal, have the child place his card on the bug jar with the matching rule. Confirm the card placements and then guide students to move from jar to jar, copying each rule number and rewriting the words, phrases, or sentences correctly.

adapted from an idea by Virginia Conrad, Bunker R-3 Elementary Bunker, MO

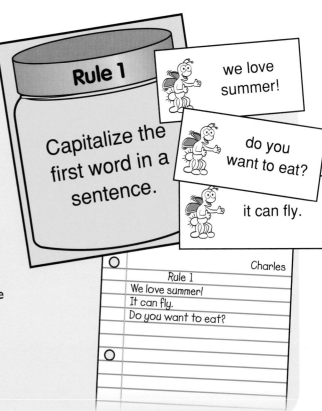

Rule 1

Capitalize the first word in a sentence.

we love summer!

do you want to eat?

it can fly.

Charles

Rule 1
We love summer!
It can fly.
Do you want to eat?

Fill Your Bags
Compound subjects and predicates

Direct each child to fold a piece of 4" x 6" paper in half, unfold the paper, and glue along two sides to make a pocket. Then have the student repeat the steps to make a second pocket. Next, instruct him to personalize a copy of the golf bag cards on page 248, cut them out, and glue one on each pocket. The child cuts apart the golf club cards and places each card in its corresponding pocket.

by Ciarra

Verb Day was such a fun day. We had extra recess that day. Ms. Bond had us do many actions. Then we wrote about them. How cool is that?

Picture This!
Motivation

Choose a photo from a fun class activity. Place the photo on the top half of a sheet of lined paper; then copy a class supply. Encourage students to reflect on the activity and write a detailed paragraph about the event. **As an alternative,** copy a variety of pictures each onto lined paper and place the papers at a center. Have each student select an interesting photo and write her paragraph on the lines below it.

Heidi Bond, Eliza Hart Spalding Elementary, Boise, ID

A Global Journey
Imaginary narrative

What better way to spend the summer than to take a trip around the world? Have students consider what transportation would make their trips unique and fun, such as roller skates, scooters, or skateboards. Then have each child plan his trip by listing a basic itinerary. Direct each student to use his itinerary to write a news story as though he has completed the trip. Encourage him to elaborate with details from his itinerary; problems or dangers he encountered; or how he ate, drank, and slept on his trip. Remind students to include an attention-grabbing title that sums up the trip.

Linda Masternak Justice, Kansas City, MO

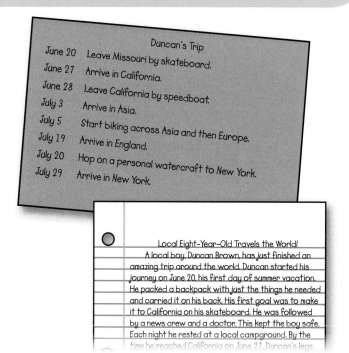

Duncan's Trip

June 20	Leave Missouri by skateboard.
June 27	Arrive in California.
June 28	Leave California by speedboat.
July 3	Arrive in Asia.
July 5	Start biking across Asia and then Europe.
July 19	Arrive in England.
July 20	Hop on a personal watercraft to New York.
July 29	Arrive in New York.

Local Eight-Year-Old Travels the World!
A local boy, Duncan Brown, has just finished an amazing trip around the world. Duncan started his journey on June 20, his first day of summer vacation. He packed a backpack with just the things he needed and carried it on his back. His first goal was to make it to California on his skateboard. He was followed by a news crew and a doctor. This kept the boy safe. Each night he rested at a local campground. By the time he reached California on June 27, Duncan's legs

Writing & Grammar

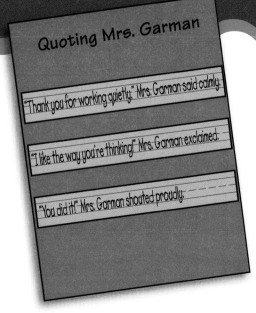

Quoting Mrs. Garman

"Thank you for working quietly," Mrs. Garman said calmly.

"I like the way you're thinking!" Mrs. Garman exclaimed.

"You did it!" Mrs. Garman shouted proudly.

Quote the Teacher
Quotation marks

Challenge each student to recall a statement you've made during the year and to think about how you said it. Direct each child to write the statement on a sentence strip, add quotation marks, and include a descriptor to tell how you made the statement. Display the strips on a piece of bulletin board paper programmed with the title "Quoting [your name]." If desired, add a photo of yourself as well. Keep the display posted for incoming students to read in the fall.

Kelly Garman, Lake Elementary, Millbury, OH

 Turn to pages 249–254 for writing organizers and skill-based practice pages.

Writing Prompts

June

- June 14 is Flag Day. Make a list of all the places you see the American flag. Then sort the places into two or more groups. Label each group.

- Summer begins on June 21. Describe your favorite summer game, activity, or event.

- What would you like to learn more about this summer? Make a list of topics. Then tell how you might learn more about each one.

- Pretend you are an insect. Write a letter to your class to tell about your good traits.

- Make a newspaper ad for a new line of beach towels. Draw a picture of one of the towels and use strong words to sell your product.

- Plan a healthy picnic lunch for you and a friend.

July

- July 4 is Independence Day. Many cities and towns have parades. Plan a parade route through part of your city or town. Include when and where the parade will start, the names of local places it will pass, and where it will end.

- Write a list of tips for keeping cool on hot summer days.

- If you were invited to visit a pool or water park with a friend, what safety rules would you need to follow? Name three or more safety rules and tell why they need to be followed.

- Summer is great for stargazing. Pretend you have been chosen to name a star. Tell what you would name it and why you would give it that name.

- Tell what you think "the dog days of summer" means.

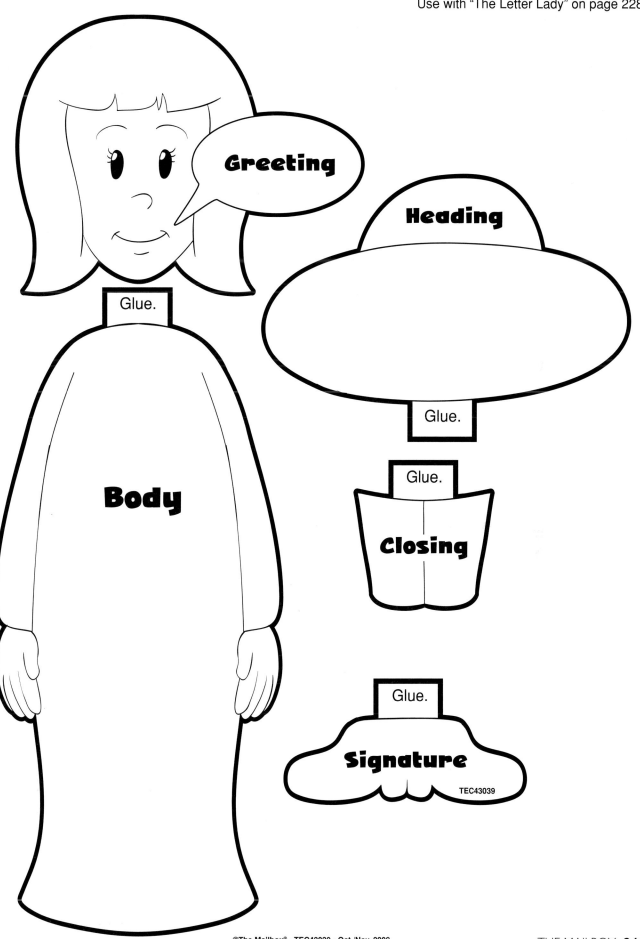

Patrol Ticket Patterns

Use with "Patrolling for Positives" on page 232.

Punctuation Patrol

Name _____

Date _____

The above-named student correctly used the following punctuation:

☐ periods

☐ question marks

☐ exclamation points

☐ commas

☐ quotation marks

☐ apostrophes

Signed _____

Comments:

TEC43041

Punctuation Patrol

Name _____

Date _____

The above-named student correctly used the following punctuation:

☐ periods

☐ question marks

☐ exclamation points

☐ commas

☐ quotation marks

☐ apostrophes

Signed _____

Comments:

TEC43041

Family Picture Day

Read the passage.

It started out like any other Saturday. First, I got up and had <u>breakfast</u>.[1]
Next, I played <u>a game</u>.[2] Then the phone rang. It was the photo studio.
They were calling to remind us that it was our family picture day. Everyone
scrambled to get ready. I put on my <u>favorite clothes</u>.[3] I barely had time to
run a comb through my <u>hair</u>[4] before my parents rushed me to the car. As
soon as I stepped outside, I felt the wind. It nearly knocked me down!
I forced my way to our <u>car</u>,[5] and soon we were on our way.

When we got inside the studio, I saw my hair for the first time. It looked
<u>bad</u>.[6] I wasn't the only one who was attacked by the wind. My whole family
had been too! The <u>man</u>[7] who would take our picture tried not to laugh at us.
Soon we got settled in front of the camera. It wasn't hard to make us smile
for the picture. We all looked so <u>bad</u>[8] that we got the giggles. After about
an hour, we were done. We couldn't wait to see our photo. We knew this
was a family picture we'd never forget!

Complete each task.

1. Write a detailed list of foods you ate for breakfast. _____
   _____

2. Name the game you played, and tell with whom you played it. _____
   _____

3. Tell about your favorite outfit. Include colors. _____
   _____

4. Describe your hair. _____

5. Describe a family car. _____

6. Compare your bad hair to something else that looks bad. _____
   _____

7. Describe the man. _____

8. Write a better word to tell how bad you and your family looked. _____

Verb and Adverb Cards

Use with "Acting Secretly" on page 236.

cries — verb	loudly — adverb	walks — verb	slowly — adverb
talks — verb	quickly — adverb	drives — verb	badly — adverb
speaks — verb	clearly — adverb	answers — verb	correctly — adverb
asks — verb	politely — adverb	whispers — verb	softly — adverb
dresses — verb	warmly — adverb	writes — verb	neatly — adverb
safely — adverb	crosses — verb	loudly — adverb	claps — verb
gently — adverb	washes — verb	kindly — adverb	helps — verb
loosely — adverb	ties — verb	tightly — adverb	holds — verb

TEC43042

Name _____

Spelling _____

It's a Race!

	1	2	3	4	5	6

Note to the teacher: Use with "It's a Race!" on page 237.

Bug Jar Cards

Use with "Catch the Bug" on page 238.

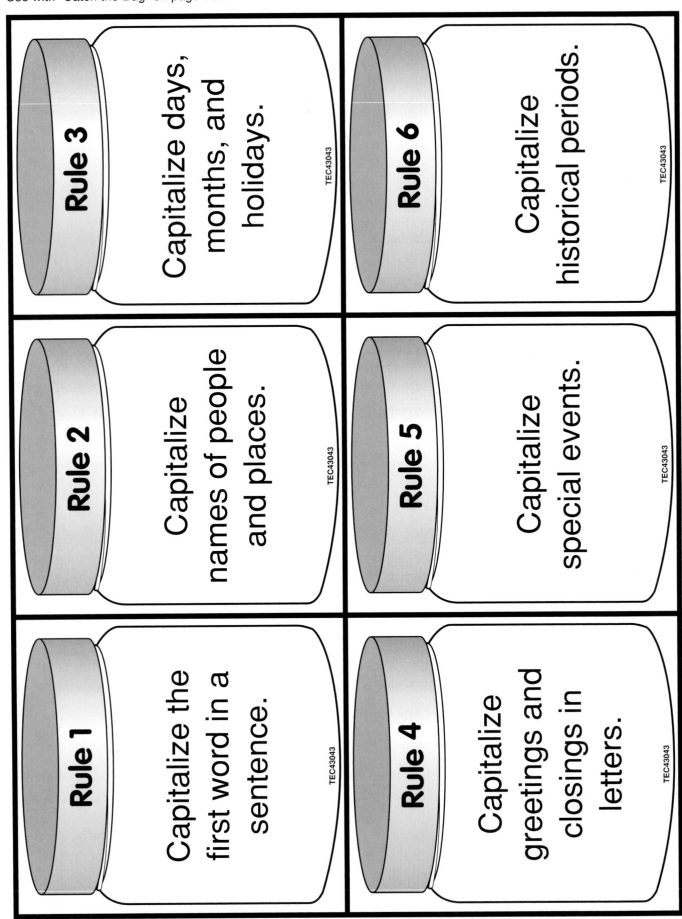

Rule 3
Capitalize days, months, and holidays.

TEC43043

Rule 6
Capitalize historical periods.

TEC43043

Rule 2
Capitalize names of people and places.

TEC43043

Rule 5
Capitalize special events.

TEC43043

Rule 1
Capitalize the first word in a sentence.

TEC43043

Rule 4
Capitalize greetings and closings in letters.

TEC43043

it can fly. TEC43043	we love summer! TEC43043	do you want to eat? TEC43043
mr. bug TEC43043	dr. bright TEC43043	ms. night TEC43043
airville TEC43043	pine city TEC43043	palm beach TEC43043
friday TEC43043	tuesday TEC43043	june TEC43043
july TEC43043	flag day TEC43043	father's day TEC43043
dear Fred, TEC43043	love, TEC43043	sincerely, TEC43043
bugville parade TEC43043	wingtown music festival TEC43043	insectland air show TEC43043
stone age TEC43043	space age TEC43043	middle ages TEC43043

Golf Bag and Club Cards

Use with "Fill Your Bags" on page 239.

Compound Subject

Name

Compound Predicate

Name

1	Many men, women, and children play golf.
2	A golf course is grassy and often has sand traps.
3	A golfer swings a club and hits the golf ball.
4	Woods and irons are two types of golf clubs.
5	Chris and Joy play golf every Friday.
6	Sometimes they play with Anna and invite Ryan too.
7	These golfers spend hours talking and playing the course.
8	Joy and Anna always have very good scores.
9	Chris and Ryan do not play so well.
10	They all like the fresh air and enjoy the exercise.

TEC43043

©The Mailbox® • TEC43043 • June/July 2009 • Key p. 312

Buddy Up?

⭐**1** **Prompt**

Your teacher is planning to move desks around. Should you be allowed to choose who you sit next to in class?

⭐**2** **Plan**

Write your answer as a complete sentence.

_____

_____

Give three good reasons that support your answer.

1. _____

_____

_____

2. _____

_____

_____

3. _____

_____

_____

⭐**3** **Write**

Write a complete response to the prompt. Get the reader's attention and support your ideas. Convince your teacher to do what you want her or him to do!

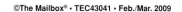

Note to the teacher: Give each child a copy of this page to reinforce persuasive writing skills.

THE MAILBOX **249**

Heads-Up to a New Group

 Prompt
Think about what next year's students will need to know about your grade in order to have a great year.

2 Plan
What is one thing they should know about their class work?

What is one thing they should know about their homework?

What is one other thing they should know?

 Write
Write a letter to next year's class. Tell about your grade. Use details to support each idea you write about. Help the students understand how to do a good job in your grade next year.

©The Mailbox® • TEC43042 • April/May 2009

Finished Product

⭐**1**

Prompt
Think of a fun topic you learned about this year.

⭐**2**

Plan
List facts about the topic. Use reference books to support your facts.

Fact:

Page(s):

Reference:

Fact:

Page(s):

Reference:

Fact:

Page(s):

Reference:

⭐**3**

Write
Use the facts to write a short report about the topic you chose. Use your own words!

Note to the teacher: Give each child a copy of this page to help reinforce report-writing skills.

His and Her Hoops

Write the pronoun that can replace each underlined noun.
Color a matching basketball for each pronoun.

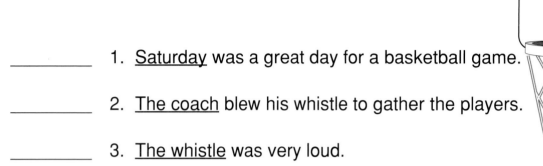

_____ 1. <u>Saturday</u> was a great day for a basketball game.

_____ 2. <u>The coach</u> blew his whistle to gather the players.

_____ 3. <u>The whistle</u> was very loud.

_____ 4. <u>The players</u> ran to the coach.

_____ 5. <u>Coach Brown</u> made his choice of team captains.

_____ 6. <u>Jim</u> stood next to Coach Brown.

_____ 7. <u>Sarah</u> stood on the coach's other side.

_____ 8. <u>Jim and Sarah</u> flipped a coin to see who would pick first.

_____ 9. <u>Sarah</u> won the coin toss.

_____ 10. Then <u>the captains</u> took turns picking who would be on their teams.

_____ 11. <u>Sarah</u> chose all the girls to be on her team.

_____ 12. <u>The game</u> was played with the boys against the girls.

He   It   He   It   He   It

She   They   She   They   She   they

©The Mailbox® • TEC43041 • Feb./Mar. 2009 • Key p. 312

Life at the Pond

Circle the nouns on each lily pad.
For each noun pair, write a phrase that shows ownership.

1. (tongue) of a (frog)

   a frog's tongue

2. rays of the sun

   _____

3. bill of a duck

   _____

4. edge of the water

   _____

5. shell of a turtle

   _____

6. egg of a tadpole

   _____

7. wings of a heron

   _____

8. leaves of a tree

   _____

9. fins of a fish

   _____

10. stem of a plant

    _____

Name _____

Ready to Burst

Underline each adjective in the passage.
Find each underlined word in the puzzle.

Did you find
12 adjectives?

d	i	f	f	e	r	e	n	t	u
s	b	a	u	g	o	l	d	k	u
w	l	v	r	o	l	o	w	d	n
i	c	o	l	o	r	f	u	l	s
l	g	r	e	d	t	o	n	o	a
l	f	i	r	s	t	c	e	u	f
o	u	t	j	b	a	n	k	d	e
w	n	e	x	c	i	t	i	n	g
s	i	l	v	e	r	a	j	f	o

Did you know that the first time the Fourth of

July was celebrated, back in 1777, fireworks were

used? That's what my good friend Poppy told me.

He knows all about these exciting displays. Poppy's

favorite pastime is watching fireworks. He loves to

hear the loud noises they make. He also enjoys

their colorful sparks. Poppy told me that fireworks

have different names, such as spider, cake, and

willow. A willow has silver or gold sparks. The

sparks fan out like a willow tree. Poppy always

reminds me that fireworks are fun to watch but that

they can be unsafe. He says they should only be

used by experts.

©The Mailbox® • TEC43043 • June/July 2009 • Key p. 312

LANGUAGE ARTS UNITS

Working With Fiction

Jean Erickson, Grace Christian Academy, West Allis, WI

SECRET MESSAGES
Author's theme

In advance, have your media specialist gather for you a few books with a common theme, such as friendship, persistence, or honesty. Display the books with a supply of index cards, an envelope, and a paper sign with the question "What's the Secret Message?" To introduce the activity, select another book and read it aloud. Remind students that the message the author wants to share with the readers is called the theme; then lead a discussion of the read–aloud's theme. Next, direct students to the book display and explain that these books have a common theme. Encourage each student to use his free time to read at least two of the books and determine the common theme. Then have the student write the titles of the books he read on an index card, record the theme, and place the card in the envelope. After some time, remove the cards from the envelope and award each student who wrote an appropriate theme a small prize; then replace the books with a new set.

GETTING PERSONAL
Characters

Help students consider the thoughts of fictional characters! After reading a story, have each child fold a piece of paper in half and, with the fold at the top, draw the head of one of the story's characters. Direct the child to cut out the head, leaving the fold intact. Pose a question such as "What is the character like?" or "How would the character like to spend his or her free time?" Then guide the student to lift the character's head and write or draw on the inside responses that reflect the character's personality or preferences.

adapted from an idea by Lindsey Marshall, Monroe Elementary Enid, OK

I, Amber Brown, would like to spend my free time playing with my best friend Justin.

I would like to eat unbaked brownie mix.

I would also like to try new flavors of bubble gum.

TIME AND PLACE
Setting

To make this quick visual reminder, copy onto tan paper the tepee pattern on page 258 and cut it out. Bring the ends together to form a cone shape; then staple them in place. Display the tepee and help students understand that the consonants heard in the word *tepee* (*t* and *p*) represent the two words that describe setting: *time* and *place*. When a child needs to describe a story's setting, encourage her to look at the tepee as a reminder to include time and place in her response.

PLOTTING UPS AND DOWNS
Problem and solution

Lead students to identify more than one problem and solution in their fictional texts. Share the story *Fortunately* by Remy Charlip and discuss the pattern of problems (unfortunately) and solutions (fortunately) found in it. Have students name the problems and solutions as you list the responses on the board under the appropriate headings, as shown. Later, share another story, such as *Little Grunt and the Big Egg: A Prehistoric Fairy Tale* by Tomie dePaola, and have students use the unfortunately/fortunately pattern to record the story's problems and solutions on their own papers.

Georgia Bernheim, Colonel Johnston Elementary, Ft. Huachuca, AZ

Unfortunately
The party was far away.

Fortunately
Ned's friend loaned him an airplane.

Unfortunately
The airplane's motor exploded.

Fortunately
Ned found a parachute.

Tepee Pattern

Use with "Time and Place" on page 257.

TEC43039

Name _____

Devon's Dilemma

Read the selection.
Answer the questions.

    As soon as Devon Dragon got off the school bus, he started to fly down the street. He was eager to get home! His grandparents had come for a visit. Devon loved spending time with his grandparents. They lived far away, so he did not get to see them very often. Devon didn't want to waste a minute of his time with them.

    Before he knew it, Devon was home. It sure was quiet! "Hello," he called out. No one answered. He went from room to room, looking for his family. His family wasn't there!
Devon was very disappointed. Then he noticed a large box on the kitchen table. It had his name on it! Devon jumped up and down and clapped. Then he moved closer to get a better look. The box was big! He tried to shake the box, but it was too heavy. He wanted to open it, but didn't know if he should. He didn't know who the package was from, and he didn't want to upset anyone. Devon tapped his wing on the box, wondering what to do.

1. Why was Devon eager to get home? _____

   _____

2. What do you think will happen next? _____

3. Use details from the selection to complete the sentences.

   Devon was sad because _____

   _____

   Then Devon was happy because _____

   _____

4. How can you tell this selection is fiction? _____

   _____

Word Analysis

Laura Johnson, South Decatur Elementary, Greensburg, IN

un
dis
re

order

ly
ful
able

Peter

disorder–lack of order

SPIN YOUR WHEELS
Prefixes and suffixes

In advance, cut out a copy of the affix wheels and word cards on page 262. Use brass fasteners to attach the wheels to opposite ends of a nine-inch sentence strip as shown. Place the word-making manipulative, the base-word cards, and a dictionary at a center. A student places a card on the strip and turns the prefix wheel to make a new word. He checks the dictionary to confirm his answer. If a word is made, the student writes the word and its meaning on a sheet of paper. He continues with each prefix; then he repeats the process with the suffix wheel. If time allows, the student then makes words that use both prefixes and suffixes.

NAME THAT WORD
Compound words

For this partner activity, cut out a copy of the game cards and answer key on page 263. Have one player shuffle the definition cards and stack the cards facedown while the other player arranges the word cards faceup between them. To begin, Player 1 draws a definition card and reads it aloud. She chooses two word cards to make a compound word that matches the definition. Player 2 checks the answer key. If the answer is correct, Player 1 keeps the three cards and her turn ends. If it is not correct, she returns the cards. Then Player 2 takes a turn. The game continues until all cards have been matched. The player with more cards wins.

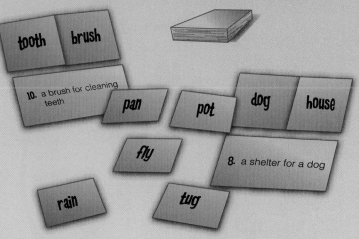

DIP OR DOUBLE DIP?
Inflectional endings

Divide the class into two teams and draw an ice cream cone on the board for each team. In turn, ask a student from each team to spell a word from the list shown. Direct the student to identify the word as either a dip word, a word whose final consonant is not doubled before an inflectional ending, or a double dip word, whose final consonant is doubled. Then have him spell the word. If the student spells a dip word correctly, have him draw one ice cream scoop on his team's cone. If the student spells a double-dip word correctly, have him draw two ice cream scoops on his team's cone. The team with more scoops at the end of the game wins.

UNDERCOVER
Base words

Students use this handy tool to determine word meaning. To make an affix wand, cut out a copy of the top of page 264. Fold the cutout in half and glue the two sides back to back with a craft stick between them. To start the activity, write a sentence on the board like the one shown. Have a student read the sentence aloud, place the wand underneath the word with an affix, and use the wand to help him explain the meaning of the sentence. Then have the student cover the affix with the wand and reread the sentence. Lead him to tell the difference between the two sentences.

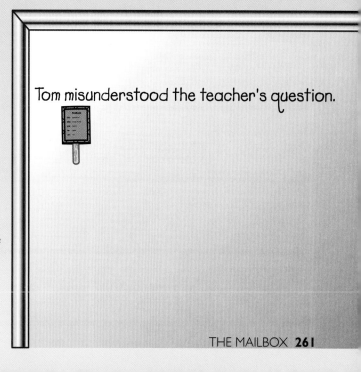

Tom misunderstood the teacher's question.

agree	certain
load	order
comfort	enjoy
pay	peace
fair	fill
respect	success
forget	like
trust	usual

1. a button found at an outside door that is pushed to ring a bell TEC43040	**2.** a poisonous snake with a rattle at the end of its tail TEC43040	**3.** an arc of colors that appears in the sky TEC43040
4. a flying insect with large, brightly colored wings TEC43040	**5.** the nail of a finger TEC43040	**6.** a pot in which to grow plants TEC43040
7. a sea creature that has five arms TEC43040	**8.** a shelter for a dog TEC43040	**9.** a flat cake made of batter and cooked in a pan TEC43040
10. a brush for cleaning teeth TEC43040	**11.** a fire built outdoors, such as at a camp TEC43040	**12.** a U-shaped band of iron that is fitted to a horse's hoof TEC43040
13. a powerful boat used for towing or pushing TEC43040	**14.** a piece of land used by children for playing TEC43040	**15.** a box that contains sand for children to play in TEC43040

pan TEC43040	**flower** TEC43040	**rain** TEC43040	**rattle** TEC43040	**star** TEC43040	**play** TEC43040	**Answer Key** 1. doorbell
camp TEC43040	**butter** TEC43040	**tooth** TEC43040	**dog** TEC43040	**finger** TEC43040	**door** TEC43040	2. rattlesnake 3. rainbow 4. butterfly
horse TEC43040	**tug** TEC43040	**sand** TEC43040	**ground** TEC43040	**shoe** TEC43040	**fire** TEC43040	5. fingernail 6. flowerpot 7. starfish
snake TEC43040	**nail** TEC43040	**pot** TEC43040	**bell** TEC43040	**bow** TEC43040	**house** TEC43040	8. doghouse 9. pancake 10. toothbrush 11. campfire 12. horseshoe
cake TEC43040	**fly** TEC43040	**fish** TEC43040	**brush** TEC43040	**box** TEC43040	**boat** TEC43040	13. tugboat 14. playground 15. sandbox TEC43040

Affix Wand Pattern

Use with "Undercover" on page 261.

Prefixes

dis- opposite of

mis- wrong or bad

pre- before

re- again

un- not

Suffixes

-able fit for or capable of

-er one that does

-ful full of

-less not having

-ly in a specific manner

TEC43040

Name_____ Base words

Circle It!

Use a yellow crayon to circle each base word.

1. misplace
2. quieter
3. kindness
4. reread
5. unsinkable

6. unequal
7. harmless
8. preheated
9. washable
10. suddenly

11. planning
12. disappear
13. flavorful
14. looked
15. preview

Bonus Box: Choose a word from the list. On the back of this page, write one sentence that uses only the base word. Then rewrite the sentence and use the base word with its affix or affixes.

©The Mailbox® • TEC43040 • Dec./Jan. 2008–9 • Key p. 312

Parts of Speech

TOUCHDOWN!
Identifying nouns and pronouns

To prepare this partner game, label a green file folder as shown and program a set of 30 cards with pronouns and nouns. To begin, each player chooses a different team: Pronouns (heads) or Nouns (tails). One player shuffles the cards and stacks them facedown. Then each player places a penny on the 50-yard line. The student on the Pronoun team selects a card and reads it. If the word is a pronoun, he moves his penny ten yards toward his goal. If the word is not a pronoun, his turn is over. Then his partner selects a card and, if the word on the card is a noun, moves ten yards toward her goal. The first player to score a touchdown is the winner.

Jean Erickson, Grace Christian Academy, West Allis, WI

A SHORT PASS
Using adjectives

For this activity, give each small group of students a copy of the graphic organizer on page 267 and a picture of an object, such as a sneaker, a car, or a cake. Designate one student in each group the team leader and have him write the object's name on the football. Signal each leader to pass the picture and organizer to the person on her right, who fills in a blank with an adjective that describes the picture. Continue in this manner until the organizer is complete. Then provide time for each student group to share its work aloud.

Barbara Saul, Pine Hill School, Eureka, CA

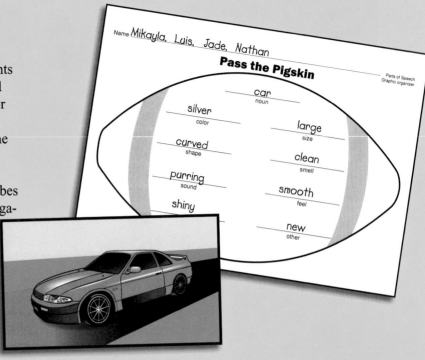

TIME MACHINE
Using verb tenses

In advance, copy and cut apart the spinner and cards on page 268. Also draw a tic-tac-toe grid on the board. Divide students into two groups: Xs and Os. To play, have one student from the X group use a pencil and paper clip to spin the spinner. Guide her to select a card; read the verb on the card; and then use the verb in a sentence, matching the tense spun on the spinner. If the student uses the verb in the correct tense, she draws an X on the grid. If she does not use the verb correctly, her turn is over. Then the other team takes a turn. The first team to connect three letters in a row is the winner.

adapted from an idea by Kathryn Davenport
Partin Elementary, Oviedo, FL

REFLECT AND LIST
Naming nouns, verbs, and adjectives

Here's a simple way to incorporate daily class activities and parts of speech. First, have each child fold a sheet of paper into fourths and unfold it. Direct the child to label the top left section with the name of a recent class activity—such as math, lunch, or P.E.—and then draw a brief sketch of the activity. Next, have each student label each of the remaining sections with a different part of speech, as shown, and have him list corresponding words related to the activity. What an easy way to review parts of speech!

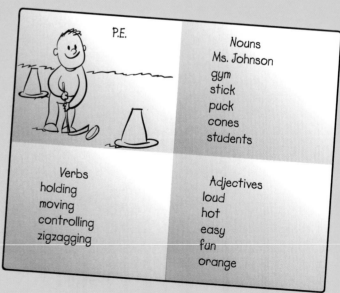

Name _____

Pass the Pigskin

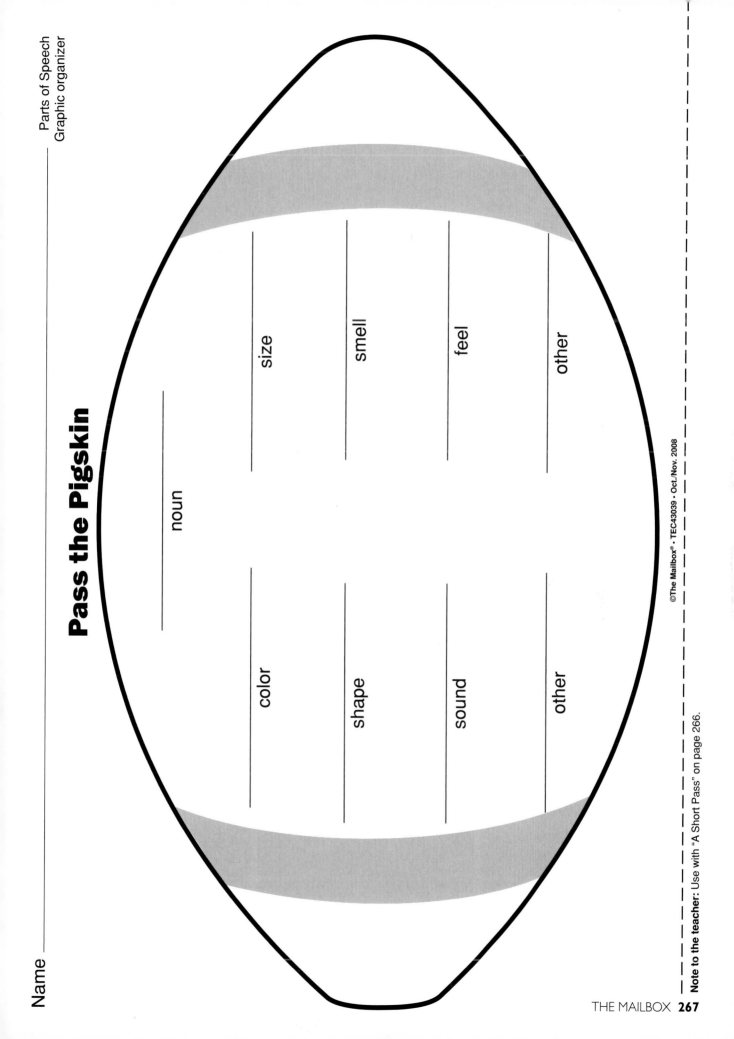

noun _____

color _____

size _____

shape _____

smell _____

sound _____

feel _____

other _____

other _____

Note to the teacher: Use with "A Short Pass" on page 266.

Verb Voyager 3000

present

past | Future

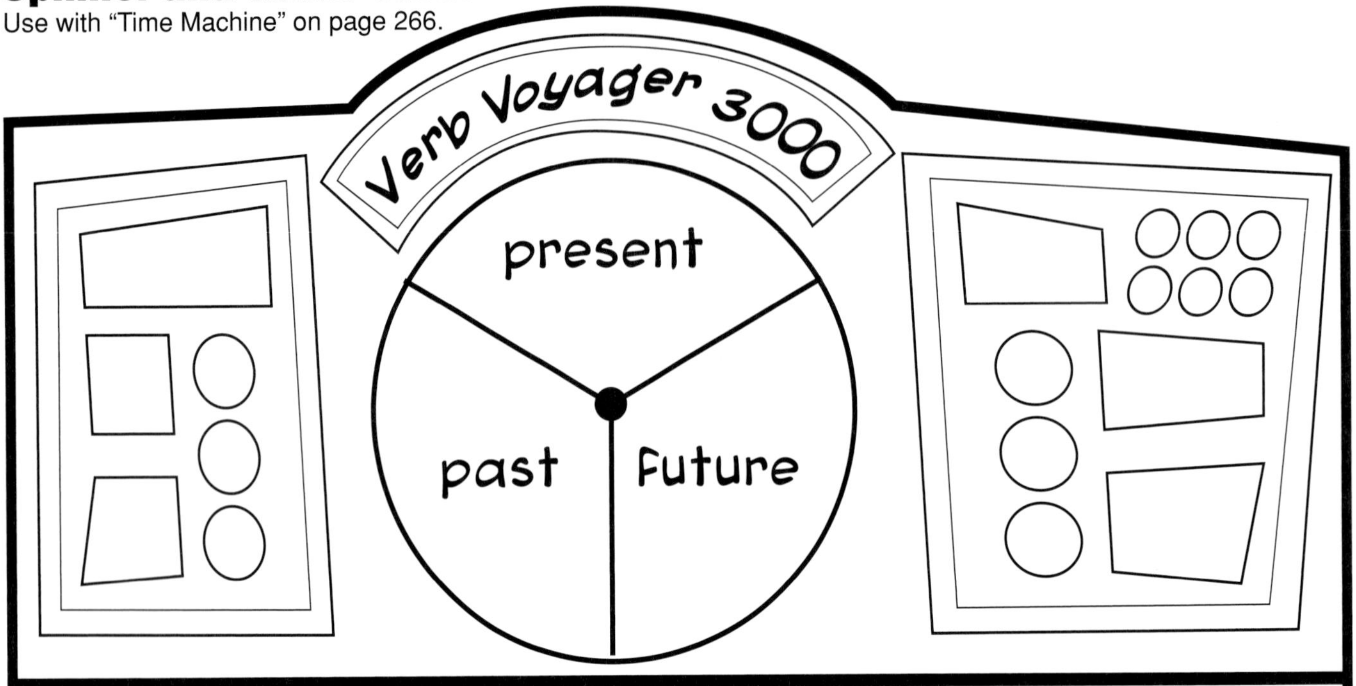

wait	clean	live
drive	write	buy
see	build	invite
run	read	fly
bring	take	speak
play	say	eat

Name_____

Tool Time

Cut apart the cards below.
Glue each picture card in the box next to its matching clues.
Use the clue words to write a sentence about each picture.
Label each word based on how you used it in the sentence.
Use the code.

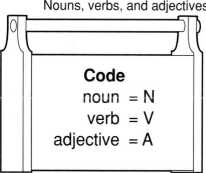

Code
noun = N
verb = V
adjective = A

1.
__ hits
__ heavy
__ nail
__ hammer
__ Mom

Sentence:

_____

_____

_____

2.
__ Ann
__ hole
__ digs
__ deep
__ shovel

Sentence:

_____

_____

_____

3.
__ log
__ cuts
__ saw
__ sharp
__ Dad

Sentence:

_____

_____

_____

4.
__ rakes
__ Tom
__ leaves
__ dry
__ yard

Sentence:

_____

_____

_____

©The Mailbox® • TEC43039 • Oct./Nov. 2008 • written by Laura Wagner, Austin, TX • Key p. 312

Prewriting

Laura Johnson, South Decatur Elementary, Greensburg, IN

Names **Jake and Jaida**

courage

Possible Settings
- ☐ first day at a new school
- ☐ going to the dentist
- ☑ in a dark bedroom during a storm

Possible Main Characters
- ☐ an eight-year-old boy named Bob
- ☐ a squirrel named Chip
- ☑ twin brothers, Tim and Jim

Possible Problems
- ☐ a toothache
- ☐ a bully on the playground
- ☑ a strange noise in the attic

Possible Outcomes
- ☐ tooth is fixed
- ☐ make new friends
- ☑ found baby birds

Setting: List three important details.
summer stormy night
no electricity
attic on the third floor

Main Character: List three important traits.
Tim is a leader.
Tim is curious.
Tim takes risks.

Problem: List three events.
A strange sound wakes Tim.
Tim and Jim gather supplies.
The noise gets louder as they climb the stairs.

Outcome: List three supporting details.
The two search the attic.
They look behind an old trunk.
They find two baby birds in a nest.

PACKING IT ALL IN
Talking with a friend, making a list

To begin this partner activity, write on the board a list of story themes, such as friendship, sportsmanship, courage, and honesty; then provide each student pair with a copy of page 272. Have the twosome cut out the suitcase pattern, select a theme, and write it on the luggage tag. Next, guide the students to use the theme to plan a story on the left side of their paper. After reviewing the plan, have them place a check mark in the box by each story element they intend to use. Then lead the students to continue brainstorming specific details for each chosen story element and write the details on the right side of their paper. At a later time, have the partners use their list to compose an original short story.

MEMORABLE EVENTS
Drawing a picture, using a story map

Read aloud the beginning of a story without showing the illustrations. Stop reading after the main character, setting, and a hint of the character's problem are clearly introduced. Tell students they will use the information from this story to plan a story of their own. Guide each student to start in the top left section on a copy of page 273. Have her draw a picture of the main character and setting. Then have her write a few words about her picture on the corresponding lines. Direct each student to then draw and write ideas for the beginning, middle, and end of the story in the sections provided. Finally, have her write a title for her future story at the top of the page. Allow time for each student to share her story ideas with a small group.

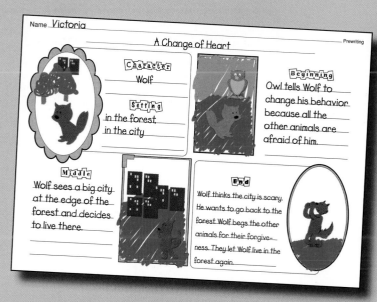

Name Victoria — Prewriting

A Change of Heart

Character
Wolf

Setting
in the forest
in the city

Beginning
Owl tells Wolf to change his behavior because all the other animals are afraid of him.

Middle
Wolf sees a big city at the edge of the forest and decides to live there.

End
Wolf thinks the city is scary. He wants to go back to the forest. Wolf begs the other animals for their forgiveness. They let Wolf live in the forest again.

Name Austin — Prewriting
Make the Connection

Nicole shows him how to play freeze tag.

She teaches him all about wall ball.

First,

Main Idea
Raj is new to America. He doesn't know how to play any American recess games.

Next,

Then

Finally,

Nicole shows him how to play four square.

Raj feels better and has fun playing with the other students.

IT'S ALL CONNECTED
Planning with a web

Make a transparency copy of a picture that shows at least one character engaged in an activity, and display it on an overhead. Direct students to study the picture and discuss possible events that might occur before, during, or after the one shown. Then have each student write on a copy of page 274 the main idea of his story, and guide him to write words or phrases in the other areas that support his main idea. Have each student share his plan with a partner and then set the plan aside to compose his first draft at another time.

DESTINATION KNOWN
Identifying audience

Read aloud the samples shown and ask students to identify whether each sample was written for a friend or for a teacher audience. Discuss the specific details that make the second sample more suitable for a teacher audience rather than a friend audience. Next, guide each student to draw on a sheet of paper a detailed picture of a special trip she has taken. After the students' drawings are complete, announce an audience for whom they are to tell a brief story about their picture. Remind each student to make proper word choices for the audience and write the words on her paper.

> Early Saturday morning, Tommy and I rode our bikes to Miller Park. We wanted the Tigers to win! So we thought we should practice before the big game.

> My best friend, Tommy, and I play on the same baseball team, the Tigers. Saturday was a big day for us. It was the Championship Game! Our team had a great chance at winning. Tommy and I thought we should practice our pitching and batting before the game. So we got up early that morning, hopped on our bikes, and rode a few blocks down Main Street to the baseball field at Miller Park.

Suitcase Pattern

Use with "Packing It All In" on page 270.

Names _____

Setting: List three important details.

Main Character: List three important traits.

Problem: List three events.

Outcome: List three supporting details.

Possible Settings
☐ ☐ ☐

Possible Main Characters
☐ ☐ ☐

Possible Problems
☐ ☐ ☐

Possible Outcomes
☐ ☐ ☐

TEC43038

Name

Beginning

End

Character

Setting

Middle

Note to the teacher: Use with "Memorable Events" on page 271.

Name

Make the Connection

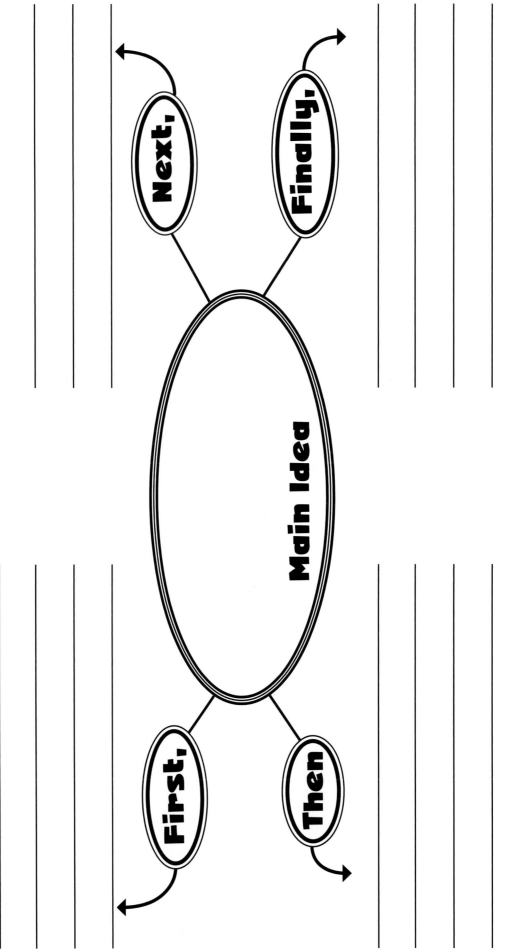

Next,

Finally,

Main Idea

First,

Then

©The Mailbox® • TEC43038 • Aug./Sept. 2008

Note to the teacher: Use with "It's All Connected" on page 271.

Writing in Sequence

Jennifer L. Kohnke, St. Charles, IL

Character and Problem

Antonio lost his world-famous pie recipe.

Event 1
He searched through all his recipe cards.

Event 2
He turned the kitchen upside down.

Event 3
He rummaged through the trash.

Event 4
He took off his baker's hat.

Event 5
Antonio found the recipe in his hat!

ONE SLICE AT A TIME
Narrative writing

Serve up some practice with ordering story events. First, each child writes on a copy of page 277 the name of his story's main character and the problem the character will face. Next, the student cuts apart the pie slices and writes on each slice a brief description of an important story event. The student organizes the slices so the events are ordered in a clockwise manner, as shown. Then he numbers each event and glues the pie to a sheet of paper. Finally, the student uses the pie organizer to write his story.

A READY REFERENCE
Transition words

Guide each child to personalize and cut out a copy of the writing reminder pattern on page 278. Direct the child to fold the pattern down the middle so the text faces outward and glue the halves together to make one shape. Encourage the child to keep the patterns with her writing materials and to refer to the reminders when writing.

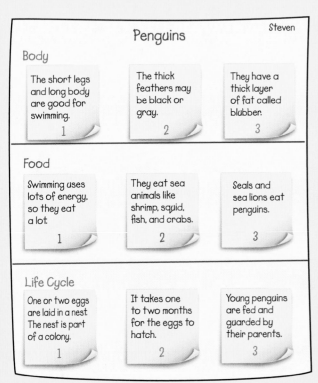

SENTENCE SORT
Expository writing

This activity helps students put their ideas in order. First, have each child divide a 12" x 18" sheet of paper into three sections, as shown, and have him write the topic of an expository writing assignment at the top of the paper. Then have the child label each row with a different main idea related to his topic. As the child records details about each main idea, have him write each fact on a separate sticky note and attach it under the matching heading. When he has at least three facts in each row, guide the child to reorder the sticky notes as needed to make the facts flow better and number each sticky note. Then have him refer to the resulting organizer to write his draft.

adapted from an idea by Susan Hass, Shields Elementary, Saginaw, MI

TIP
Help students further visually separate the main ideas by tracing each one with a different-colored marker.

COOKING UP TRANSITIONS
Writing directions

To provide practice using transition words, ask each child to bring in a favorite family recipe that lists the directions in numbered steps. Have each student rewrite her recipe, using transition words in place of the numbered steps. When the recipes have been finalized, compile them in a class cookbook and give a copy to each child.

Cali Bendel, Franklin Arts Academy, Mesa, AZ

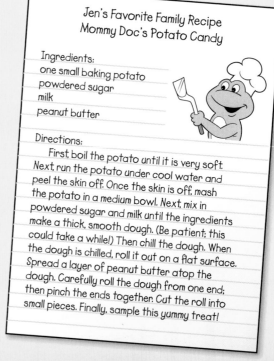

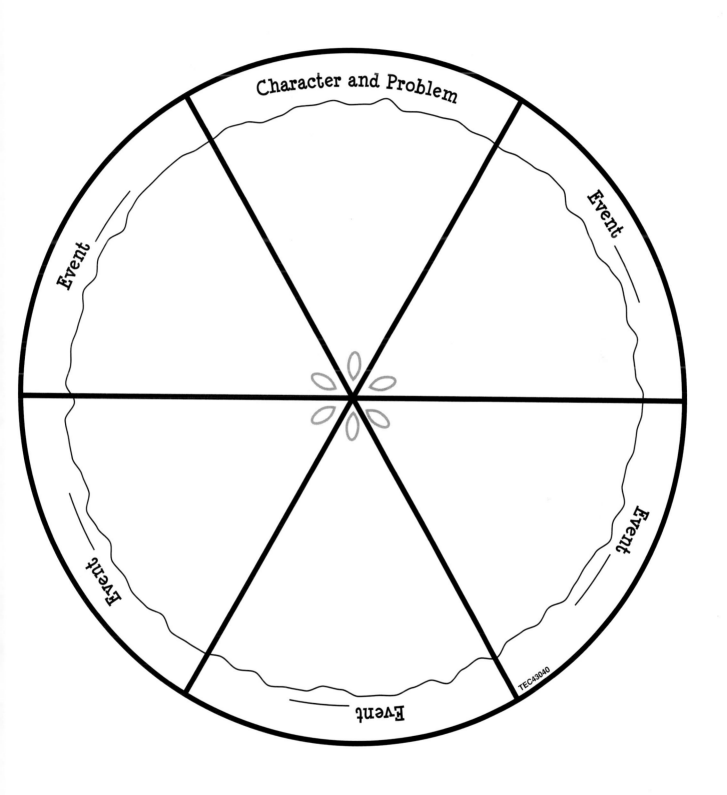

Character and Problem

Event

Event

Event

Event

Event

TEC43040

Name

Words That Show Order

Beginning
Once upon a time
In the beginning
First
To start with

Middle
Next
Then
After that
Second
Third

End
Lastly
Finally
In the end
To sum up
All in all
After

More Transition Words

Afterward

As soon as

At

Before

During

In fact

Later

Meanwhile

Now

So then

Soon

Suddenly

Until then

While

TEC43040

Listening Skills

Carolyn M. Burant, St. John Vianney School, Brookfield, WI

Scientists Find Fingles

An exciting discovery has been made in the rain forests of Brazil. While a group of scientists were studying the beautiful insects of the area, they saw creatures that no one recognized. They named the small creatures fingles.

The well-known scientists saw both male and female fingles. The males have straight green fur. The females have curly purple fur. All the fingles have large yellow eyes, and their blue ears are shaped like hearts. Fingles have six fingers on each hand.

Scientists believe that the fingles live under large fern leaves. They were seen eating berries and seeds. But they only feed at night. The bright colors of these shy creatures would attract many predators.

More scientists are flocking to Brazil to study these amazing animals. Perhaps soon we'll know more about them!

Where did the scientists find the fingles?

Do the males or the females have curly fur?

What kind of leaves do they live under?

What do fingles eat?

Why do fingles only come out at night?

THIS JUST IN
Listening for details

Breaking news from the rain forest serves as the topic of this whole-class listening activity! To prepare, write on the board the questions shown. Next, explain to students that you will read aloud a fictional article about a new animal. Remind students to listen carefully to the article's details because you will ask questions about the article afterward. Read the article from the top of page 281; then ask each question from the board and record student responses. Encourage students to check their answers as you reread the article aloud. To extend the activity, direct each student to draw a picture of a fingle based on the details in the article.

ACTIVE INSTRUCTIONS
Following multistep directions

To prepare this partner activity, place on a table a variety of objects like those listed. Next, invite each pair of students to choose three different objects from the table. Have each student write a three-step list of directions for arranging the objects. When the directions are complete, direct one student in each pair to read his directions to his partner and have her complete each step; then have him determine whether the directions were followed. Have students reverse roles and repeat the process. Follow the activity with a discussion of what listening strategies students used to achieve success.

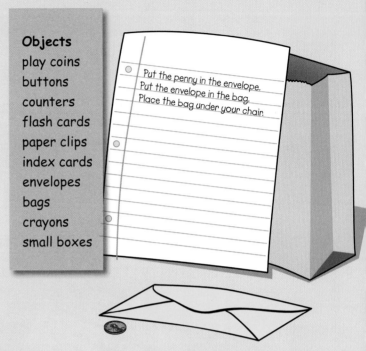

Objects

play coins
buttons
counters
flash cards
paper clips
index cards
envelopes
bags
crayons
small boxes

Put the penny in the envelope.
Put the envelope in the bag.
Place the bag under your chair.

COMMON CONNECTION
Retelling

Challenge students to listen and think with this simple time filler. Announce a list of three related items; then direct students to determine what the items have in common. Call on a student to repeat the three items aloud and then tell how they are related.

stars	aunts	books	telephone
moon	uncles	cereal boxes	microphone
airplanes	cousins	menus	ear
(Things in the sky)	(Family members)	(Things you read)	(Things you talk into)

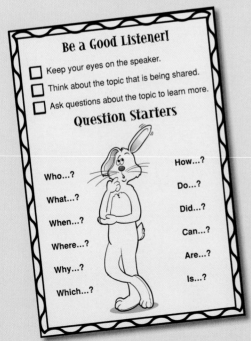

Be a Good Listener!

☐ Keep your eyes on the speaker.
☐ Think about the topic that is being shared.
☐ Ask questions about the topic to learn more.

Question Starters

Who...?   How...?
What...?   Do...?
When...?   Did...?
Where...?   Can...?
Why...?   Are...?
Which...?   Is...?

ALL EARS
Asking relevant questions

Whether it's part of a teacher-led lesson or a student presentation, this checklist helps students practice good listening skills. Guide each student to keep on her desktop a copy of the checklist from the bottom of page 281. Before a lesson or presentation, guide students to refer to the checklist to focus their listening. After the presentation, have students use the question starters to ask relevant questions, reminding students that the questions should relate to the topic presented.

Scientists Find Fingles

An exciting discovery has been made in the rain forests of Brazil. While a group of scientists were studying the beautiful insects of the area, they saw creatures that no one recognized. They named the small creatures fingles.

The well-known scientists saw both male and female fingles. The males have straight green fur. The females have curly purple fur. All the fingles have large yellow eyes, and their blue ears are shaped like hearts. Fingles have six fingers on each hand.

Scientists believe that the fingles live under large fern leaves. They were seen eating berries and seeds. But they only feed at night. The bright colors of these shy creatures would attract many predators.

More scientists are flocking to Brazil to study these amazing animals. Perhaps soon we'll know more about them!

©The Mailbox® • TEC43038 • Aug./Sept. 2008

Note to the teacher: Use with "This Just In" on page 279.

Be a Good Listener!

- [ ] Keep your eyes on the speaker.
- [ ] Think about the topic that is being shared.
- [ ] Ask questions about the topic to learn more.

Question Starters

Who…?

What…?

When…?

Where…?

Why…?

Which…?

How…?

Do…?

Did…?

Can…?

Are…?

Is…?

©The Mailbox® • TEC43038 • Aug./Sept. 2008

Note to the teacher: Use with "All Ears" on page 280.

Name_____

Listen Up!

Cut out the cards below.
Decide the purpose for listening to each speaker.
Glue each card under the matching purpose.

Listen to Learn	Listen to Follow Directions	Listen to Be Entertained

©The Mailbox® • TEC43038 • Aug./Sept. 2008 • Key p. 313

Ty recites a poem.	Joe gives a report about the moon.	Ben tells how to make a paper bird.
Sue talks about jungle animals.	Jake tells how to build a castle out of blocks.	Ms. Lee explains how to line up quietly.
Cole tells about his trip to the zoo.	Bart sings a song before the school play.	Claire tells jokes and riddles.

MATH UNITS

Place Value

Nine hundred six

Four hundred eighty

Two hundred thirty seven

FLIPPING FOR DIGITS
Modeling numbers to 999

Use this easy-to-make manipulative to help students display numbers. First, write in order each digit from 0 to 9 in each of three spiral memo notepads. Next, insert a $\frac{3}{16}$" x 12" wooden dowel rod through the bindings of the notepads. Then, to keep the notepads from sliding off the dowel, glue a decorative bead to each end of the dowel rod. To use the manipulative, present a number in word or expanded form and have a child flip the pages of the notepads to display the number.

Debbie Berris, Poinciana Day School
West Palm Beach, FL

GOT IT COVERED!
Reading numbers, identifying the value of digits

This versatile partner activity helps students work with numbers to 999 or 9,999. In advance, give each student pair two paper clips, a supply of game markers, and a copy of the spinner card on page 286 that best suits your reinforcement needs. Also guide each child to fold a sheet of paper to make 16 sections and then unfold it. Have him program each section with a different number that is less than the number on the spinner card.

To play, Player 1 uses a paper clip and pencil to spin each spinner. He looks for numbers on his gameboard that match the two clues; for example, if he spins "3" and "hundreds," he looks for numbers that have a three in the hundreds place. Player 1 reads aloud any numbers that match, then covers each one with a game marker. If no numbers match, Player 1's turn is over. Then Player 2 takes a turn in a similar manner. Students alternate play until one student has covered all of his sections.

The numbers 7,490 and 9,487 match.

HANDS-ON FUN
Modeling numbers

Students work together to demonstrate an understanding of three- or four-digit numbers. To reinforce three-digit numbers, assign each player in a team of three a place value (ones, tens, or hundreds) and direct one student to also serve as the captain. To play, write a number on the board and, on your signal, have each player place on the captain's desk her corresponding base ten blocks to build a model of that number. After a predetermined length of time, review each team's model and award a point to each team that correctly modeled the number. **To reinforce four-digit numbers,** simply group students in teams of four and assign four place values.

Marciava Harris, Flora Macdonald Academy, Red Springs, NC

A SHOWY DISPLAY
Identifying the value of digits

To start this whole-class activity, direct each student to write a number on a sheet of paper. Select two students to stand side by side at the front of the room with their papers. Next, select a third student to serve as the number expert. Each student holding a paper introduces his number. Then, with great fanfare, the number expert explains the value of each number's digits and announces which number is smaller and which number is larger. Direct the students to return to their seats. Choose three new participants and continue in this manner until each child has had a chance to go to the front of the room.

adapted from an idea by Victoria Perry, Cornish Elementary Cornish, ME

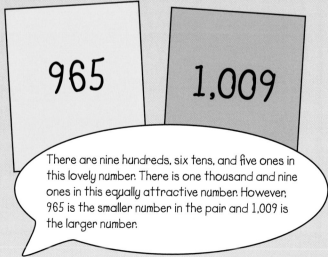

There are nine hundreds, six tens, and five ones in this lovely number. There is one thousand and nine ones in this equally attractive number. However, 965 is the smaller number in the pair and 1,009 is the larger number.

Spinner Cards

Use with "Got It Covered!" on page 285.

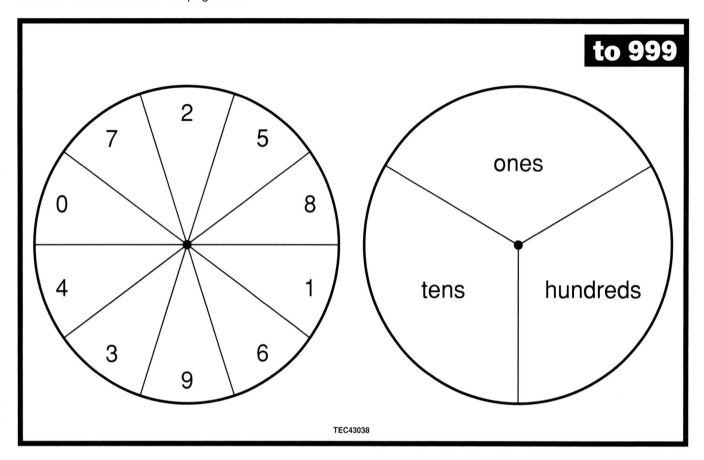

to 999

TEC43038

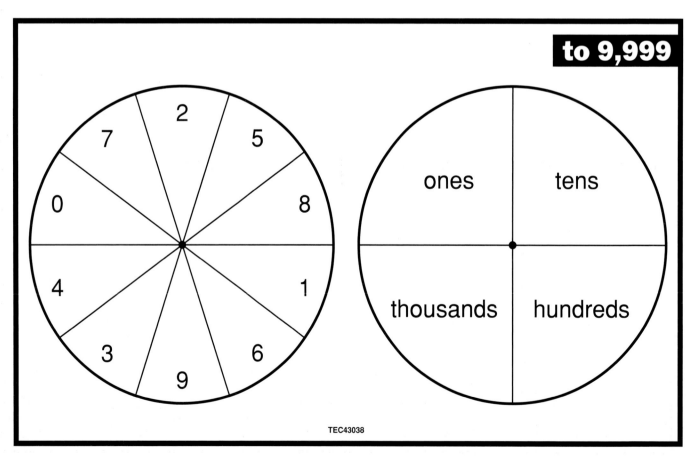

to 9,999

TEC43038

Math in the Mud

Read each clue.
Circle the three-digit number hidden in the pigpen.
   (Hint: Some of the numbers overlap.)
Write the number on the line.

A. There is a 6 in the hundreds place and a 2 in the tens place. _621_

B. There is a 1 in the hundreds place. The other two digits
   are the same. _____

C. The same digit is in the hundreds place and the tens place. _____

D. There is a 9 in the hundreds place. _____

E. There is an 8 in the ones place. _____

F. There is a 9 in the tens place. _____

G. There is a 4 in the hundreds place. The sum of the three digits is 13. _____

H. There is a 1 in the hundreds place. The sum of the other two digits is 13. _____

4 2 7 9 0 1 6 6 4 3 1 3 5 8 6 2 1 4 9

Number Patterns

Laura Wagner, Bais Menachem Hebrew Academy, Austin, Texas

FALL INTO PLACE
Small group

With this activity, each group will create a different pattern based on a common pattern rule. To start, have each group place on the floor an enlarged copy of the number grid on page 289. Announce a pattern rule, such as add three, and have each group record the rule on a sheet of paper. Then direct one member of each group to drop a paper clip on the grid. Guide students to use the number the paper clip lands on as the first number in their pattern; then have each student write on the group's paper the next number in the pattern. Provide time for groups to share their results; then announce another pattern rule and repeat the activity. **To make the activity more challenging,** do not announce a pattern rule. Instead, direct three students in each group to drop a paper clip on the grid and have the group members organize the numbers to start and label a pattern. Then have the group members extend the pattern.

TAKE YOUR PICK
Partners

To prepare this hands-on activity, cut apart the squares from a tagboard copy of a hundred chart. Place the squares numbered 1 through 10 in a bag labeled "Pattern Rule Number" and place the remaining squares in another bag. Next, program at least one paper triangle with a different operation symbol for each skill you plan to review; then place the triangles facedown on the workspace.

To complete the activity, one student establishes the pattern rule by turning over a triangle and then selecting a square from the Pattern Rule Number bag. Then the other child selects a square from the other bag to serve as the starting number. The duo writes the pattern rule and the starting number on a sheet of paper. Then students write the next four numbers in the pattern. If the pattern rule cannot be used four times with the starting number drawn, the child returns the square to the bag and selects another. After the pattern is recorded, the students return the materials to the starting locations, switch roles, and repeat the process with a new set of numbers.

Laura Wagner and Mary Burgess, Howell Valley Elementary, West Plains, MO

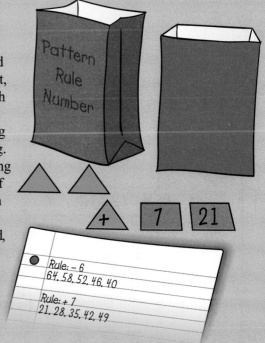

Rule: – 6
64, 58, 52, 46, 40

Rule: + 7
21, 28, 35, 42, 49

ALL OR NOTHING
Whole class

95, 91, 87, 83, 79

Subtract 4

Here's a game that will get everyone thinking about number relationships. First, direct each child to write a number pattern on a paper strip. Then have him fold back the last number in the pattern. Instruct each student to write the corresponding pattern rule on the back of his strip. Check each student's pattern and rule; then divide the class into several teams. To play, choose a student (Player 1) to share his pattern with the class. Then select a player from another team (Player 2) to name the next number in the pattern and the pattern rule. If both answers are correct, Player 1 unfolds the strip to reveal the number, turns the strip around to reveal the pattern rule, and then gives his strip to Player 2's team. If either or both answers are incorrect, allow a player from a different team to provide the answers. Continue playing in this manner until every student has shared his pattern. The team with the most strips wins.

Number Grid

Use with "Fall Into Place" on page 288.

1	2	3	4	5	6
7	8	9	10	11	12
13	14	15	16	17	18
19	20	21	22	23	24
25	26	27	28	29	30

TEC43039

Name _____

What Comes Next?

Write the rule for each pattern.
Cut apart the cards.
Glue the card that shows the next number in each pattern.

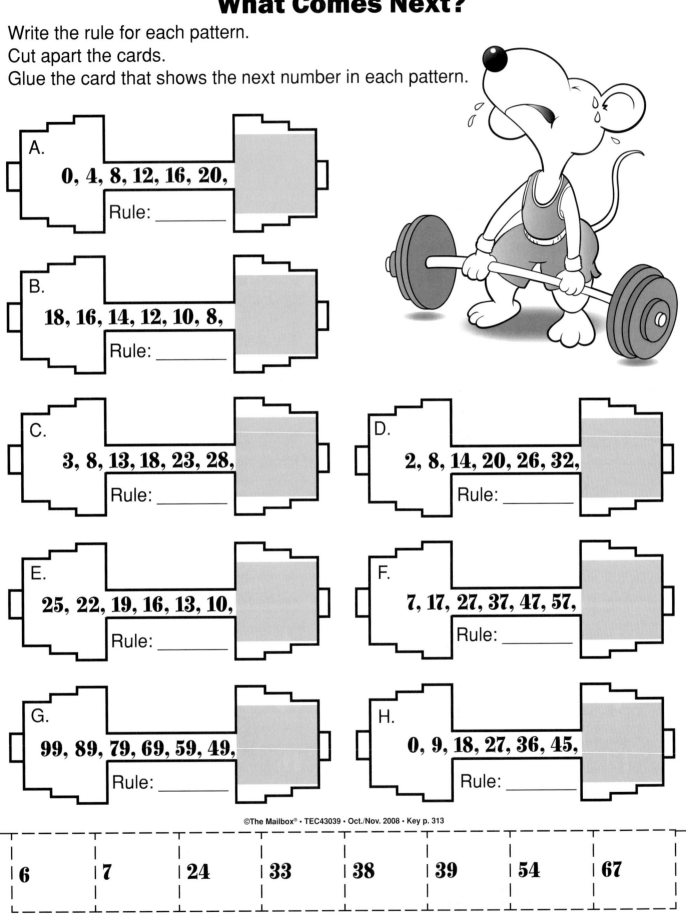

A. 0, 4, 8, 12, 16, 20,

Rule: _____

B. 18, 16, 14, 12, 10, 8,

Rule: _____

C. 3, 8, 13, 18, 23, 28,

Rule: _____

D. 2, 8, 14, 20, 26, 32,

Rule: _____

E. 25, 22, 19, 16, 13, 10,

Rule: _____

F. 7, 17, 27, 37, 47, 57,

Rule: _____

G. 99, 89, 79, 69, 59, 49,

Rule: _____

H. 0, 9, 18, 27, 36, 45,

Rule: _____

©The Mailbox® • TEC43039 • Oct./Nov. 2008 • Key p. 313

6   7   24   33   38   39   54   67

Name _____

Healthy Routines

Read each problem.
Make a pattern to solve.
Write the final answer.
Cross off the matching answer on the ball.

A. Mo did 3 push-ups on Sunday.
    Each day after that, Mo did 4 more
    push-ups than the day before. How
    many push-ups did Mo do on the
    following Saturday?

    Pattern:

    ____, ____, ____, ____, ____, ____, ____

    Answer:

    _____

B. The first week he went running, Matt
    ran 4 miles in 36 minutes. Each
    week after that, he ran 2 minutes
    faster. On the sixth week, how long
    did it take Matt to run 4 miles?

    Pattern:

    ____, ____, ____, ____, ____, ____

    Answer:

    _____

C. Maria swam for 18 minutes the first
    week of practice. Each week, she
    swam five minutes longer. How
    long did she swim during the fourth
    week?

    Pattern:

    ____, ____, ____, ____

    Answer:

    _____

D. Molly did 5 sit-ups on Tuesday.
    Each day after that, she did twice
    as many sit-ups as the day before.
    How many sit-ups did Molly do on
    Friday?

    Pattern:

    ____, ____, ____, ____

    Answer:

    _____

E. Marco jumped rope 74 times in a row.
    Each time after that, Marco jumped
    6 fewer times than the time before.
    On his fifth try, how many times did
    Marco jump?

    Pattern:

    ____, ____, ____, ____, ____

    Answer:

    _____

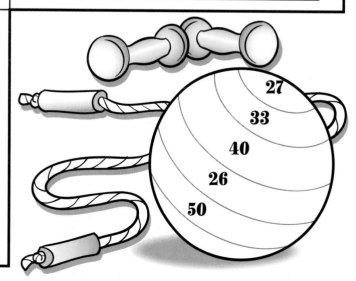

27
33
40
26
50

Computation Strategies

Laura Wagner, Bais Menachem Hebrew Academy, Austin, TX

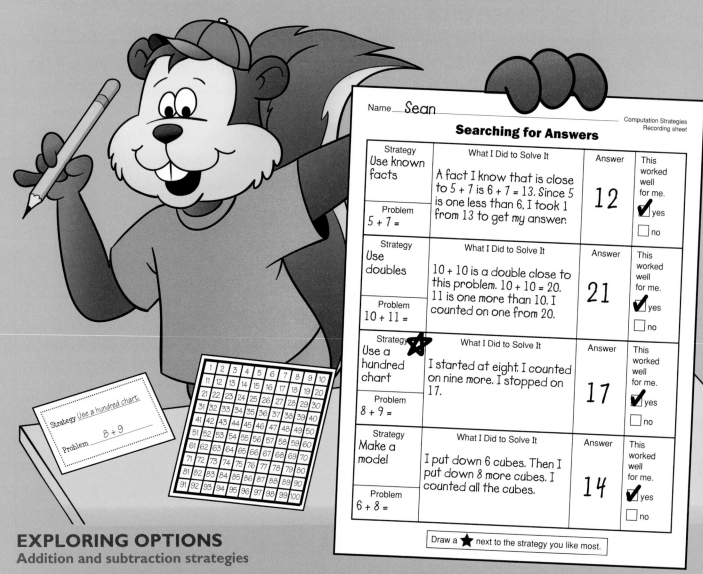

Name __Sean__

Computation Strategies
Recording sheet

Searching for Answers

Strategy	What I Did to Solve It	Answer	This worked well for me.
Use known facts **Problem** 5 + 7 =	A fact I know that is close to 5 + 7 is 6 + 7 = 13. Since 5 is one less than 6, I took 1 from 13 to get my answer.	12	☑ yes ☐ no
Use doubles **Problem** 10 + 11 =	10 + 10 is a double close to this problem. 10 + 10 = 20. 11 is one more than 10. I counted on one from 20.	21	☑ yes ☐ no
Use a hundred chart ★ **Problem** 8 + 9 =	I started at eight. I counted on nine more. I stopped on 17.	17	☑ yes ☐ no
Make a model **Problem** 6 + 8 =	I put down 6 cubes. Then I put down 8 more cubes. I counted all the cubes.	14	☑ yes ☐ no

Draw a ★ next to the strategy you like most.

Strategy __Use a hundred chart.__

Problem ____8 + 9____

EXPLORING OPTIONS
Addition and subtraction strategies

This partner activity exposes students to a variety of strategies while building their computation confidence! After discussing various addition and subtraction strategies, set up several stations for practicing the strategies shown. Place at each station a copy of the card on the bottom of page 293, labeled with a different strategy and problem to solve. Also place at the station any materials needed to implement the strategy. On your signal, have partners visit a station and use the strategy to solve the problem. Have each child record his work on a copy of page 294. When all pairs have completed their tasks, direct students to the next station. Continue in this manner until each duo has visited every station. Then follow up the activity with a discussion of the answers and which strategies students preferred.

Possible Strategies
Use known facts
Use doubles
Use a hundred chart
Use a number line
Make a model
Count forward or backward by tens

KEEP COUNTING
Multiplication strategy

To prepare this whole-class activity, give each student ten counters or cubes and invite students to sit in a circle with their manipulatives. Explain to students that they will take turns counting by multiples to reach the product of a problem. Next, write a problem on the board, such as 6 x 3, and remind students that the problem reads "six groups of three." Give a container to one student and direct him to place a group of three manipulatives in it. Then have the rest of the class say, "Three." Write the multiple on the board for reinforcement. Then direct the student to pass the container to the child on his right. Have her place three more manipulatives in the container and guide the class to respond, "Six." Students continue in this manner until six students have placed manipulatives in the container and the class has responded with the product. Review the completed number sentence, empty the container, and then present a new problem.

BAG OF TRICKS
Division strategy

Help students practice forming equal groups with this independent activity! Place in each of a supply of paper bags a different number of counters. Then label each bag with an appropriate divisor. Make the bags self-checking by writing the quotient on the bottom of each bag. To complete the activity, a child removes the counters from a bag and counts them. She writes the number of counters on her paper, adds a division sign, and then records the number from the bag. The student separates the counters into groups to find the answer and writes it on her paper. She turns the bag over to confirm her answer, returns the counters to the bag, and repeats the process with another bag.

Strategy and Problem Card
Use with "Exploring Options" on page 292.

Strategy _____

Problem _____

TEC43038

? ? ? ? ? ? **Searching for Answers** ? ? ? ? ? ?

Strategy	What I Did to Solve It	Answer	This worked well for me.
			☐ yes
Problem			☐ no
Strategy	What I Did to Solve It	Answer	This worked well for me.
			☐ yes
Problem			☐ no
Strategy	What I Did to Solve It	Answer	This worked well for me.
			☐ yes
Problem			☐ no
Strategy	What I Did to Solve It	Answer	This worked well for me.
			☐ yes
Problem			☐ no

Draw a ★ next to the strategy you like most.

Name_____

Finding the Right Product

Color the array on each can.
Write the product.

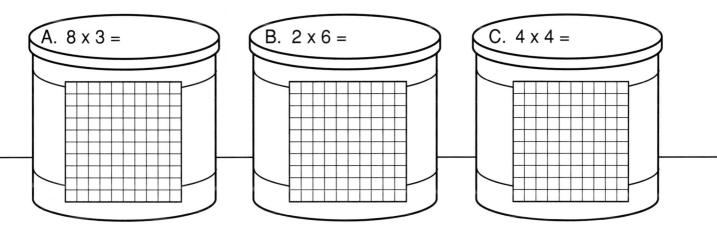

A. 8 x 3 =

B. 2 x 6 =

C. 4 x 4 =

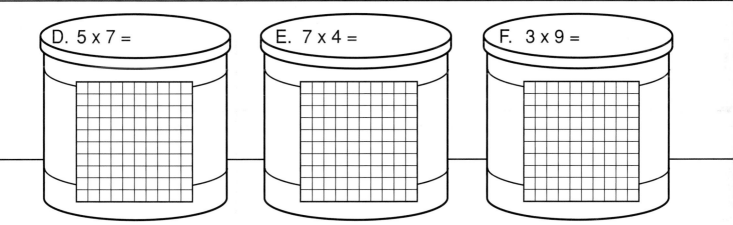

D. 5 x 7 =

E. 7 x 4 =

F. 3 x 9 =

G. 6 x 1 =

H. 10 x 8 =

Bonus Box: On the back of this paper, write a repeated addition sentence for each problem.

Addition and Subtraction

Stacie Wright, Millington School, Millington, NJ

COLLECTING SUMS
Two-digit addition with regrouping

To prepare this independent activity, a student cuts out the wheel patterns from a copy of page 297 and cuts out the garbage truck pattern from a copy of page 298. Next, he uses a brass fastener to attach wheel A atop its corresponding wheel on the garbage truck. To complete the activity, the child turns wheel A until Start is showing. He rotates the wheel one space and copies on the garbage truck an addition problem using the two numbers. After he solves the problem, the student continues with each space on wheel A. Then he attaches wheel B and repeats the steps for each space on wheel B.

COLORED COLUMNS
Multidigit addition and subtraction

Keep students focused on one column of numbers at a time with this easy viewfinder. To make one, cut a 1½" x ½" strip from discarded laminating film or plastic sheet dividers. Next, cut a strip of high-lighter tape about ⅛" wide and attach it to the right side of the plastic strip. To use the strip, a child holds the left side and places the highlighted portion atop the ones column. After she records the sum or difference, the student moves the strip to the left to highlight the tens column. She continues moving the strip to the left until the problem is solved.

Don't miss the addition practice sheet on page 299 and the subtraction practice sheet on page 300.

MYSTERY NUMBER
Two-digit addition and subtraction

The only materials needed for this partner game are a deck of cards (face cards removed), paper, and a pencil! Before play begins, explain to students that each ace equals one. To play:

1. Player 1 writes a two-digit number other than 50 on a piece of paper and then turns the paper face-down.
2. Player 2 asks, "Is the mystery number greater than or less than 50?" and Player 1 responds.
3. Player 2 takes a card from the deck and, based on Player 1's response, either adds the card's value to or subtracts it from 50.
4. Player 2 asks Player 1 if the resulting answer is the mystery number. If it is, the round ends and the students switch roles. If it is not, Player 2 continues taking cards from the deck and adding or subtracting the face values to each new sum or difference until she determines the mystery number.

Wheel Patterns
Use with "Collecting Sums" on page 296.

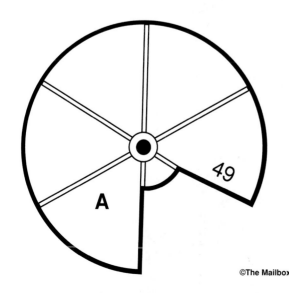

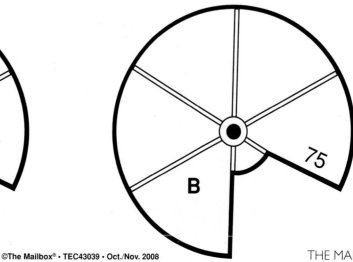

Garbage Truck Pattern

Use with "Collecting Sums" on page 296.

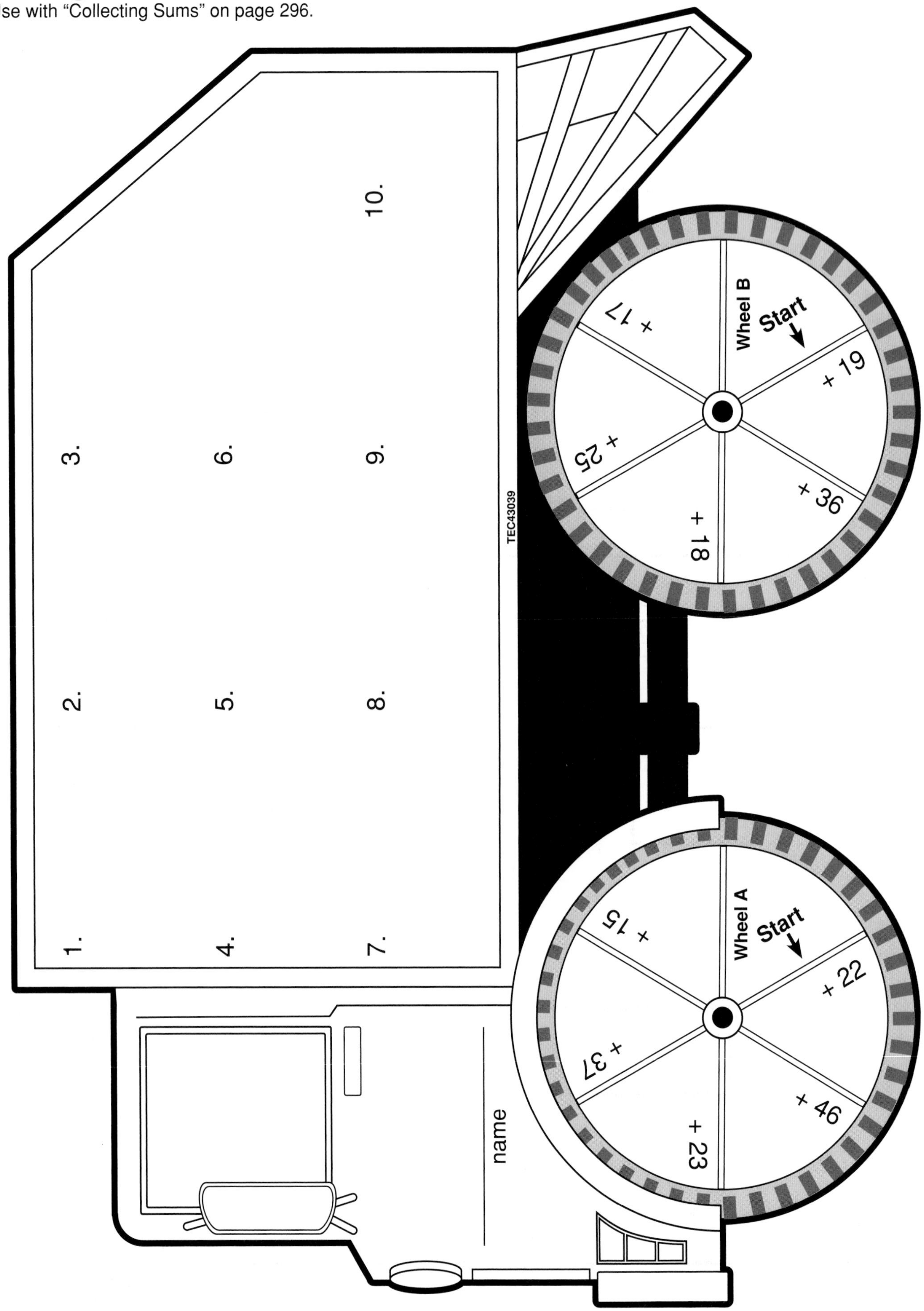

1.

2.

3.

4.

5.

6.

7.

8.

9.

10.

name

TEC43039

Wheel B

Start

+ 19

+ 36

+ 18

+ 25

+ 17

Wheel A

Start

+ 22

+ 46

+ 23

+ 37

+ 15

The Last Pickup

Add.
If you regroup, circle the problem.
Draw a line to connect the circled problems.

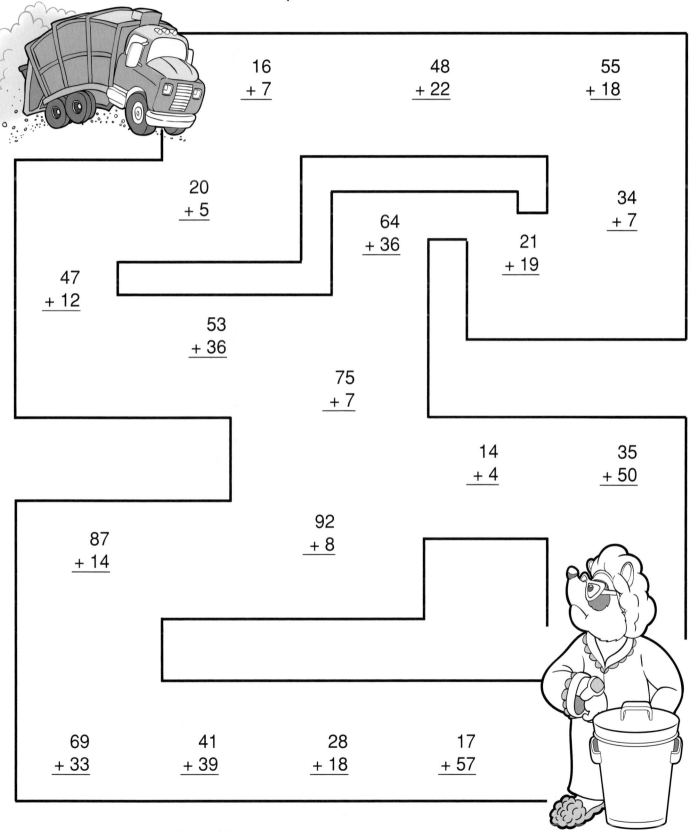

$$16$$
$$+\ 7$$

$$48$$
$$+\ 22$$

$$55$$
$$+\ 18$$

$$20$$
$$+\ 5$$

$$34$$
$$+\ 7$$

$$64$$
$$+\ 36$$

$$21$$
$$+\ 19$$

$$47$$
$$+\ 12$$

$$53$$
$$+\ 36$$

$$75$$
$$+\ 7$$

$$14$$
$$+\ 4$$

$$35$$
$$+\ 50$$

$$87$$
$$+\ 14$$

$$92$$
$$+\ 8$$

$$69$$
$$+\ 33$$

$$41$$
$$+\ 39$$

$$28$$
$$+\ 18$$

$$17$$
$$+\ 57$$

Name _____

Can-Do Attitude

On each can, write a subtraction problem that equals the difference shown.
Use the numbers on the can.

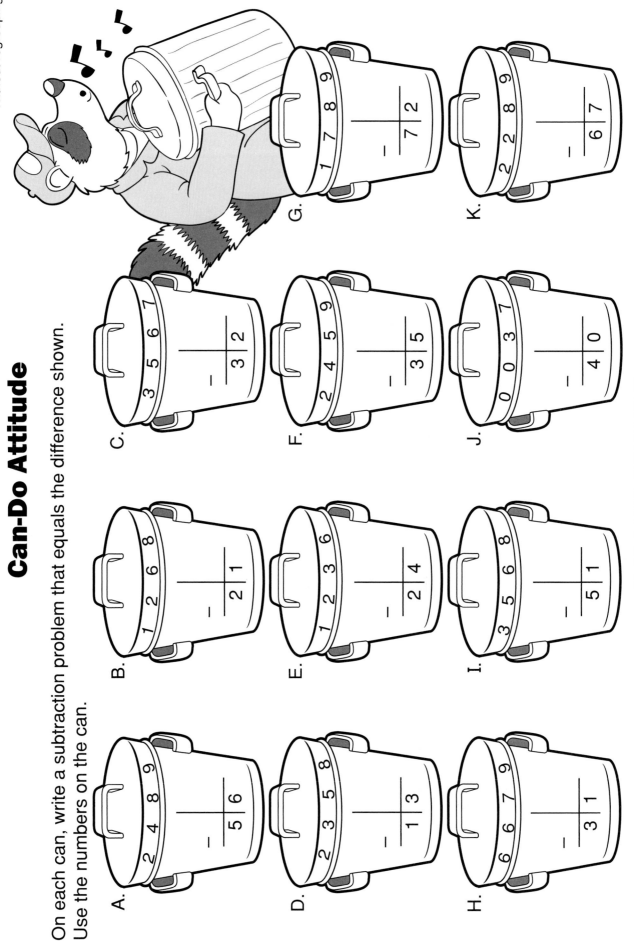

A. 2 4 8 9
    $$-\ \overline{}\ \begin{array}{c}5\\6\end{array}$$

B. 1 2 6 8
    $$-\ \overline{}\ \begin{array}{c}2\\1\end{array}$$

C. 3 5 6 7
    $$-\ \overline{}\ \begin{array}{c}3\\2\end{array}$$

D. 2 3 5 8
    $$-\ \overline{}\ \begin{array}{c}1\\3\end{array}$$

E. 1 2 3 6
    $$-\ \overline{}\ \begin{array}{c}2\\4\end{array}$$

F. 2 4 5 9
    $$-\ \overline{}\ \begin{array}{c}3\\5\end{array}$$

G. 1 7 8 9
    $$-\ \overline{}\ \begin{array}{c}7\\2\end{array}$$

H. 6 6 7 9
    $$-\ \overline{}\ \begin{array}{c}3\\1\end{array}$$

I. 3 5 6 8
    $$-\ \overline{}\ \begin{array}{c}5\\1\end{array}$$

J. 0 0 3 7
    $$-\ \overline{}\ \begin{array}{c}4\\0\end{array}$$

K. 2 2 8 9
    $$-\ \overline{}\ \begin{array}{c}6\\7\end{array}$$

©The Mailbox® • TEC43039 • Oct./Nov. 2008 • Key p. 313

Multiplication and Division

Jean Erickson, Grace Christian Academy, West Allis, WI

DUAL-PURPOSE PRODUCT LINE
Use tables to solve

Build a better understanding of multiplication and division facts with this handy reference booklet. First, give each child a copy of page 303 and point out that each page shows skip-counting with a different number. Show students that moving down each column of numbers reveals multiplication products. For example, refer to the page that shows skip-counting by two. Have students find the product to 2 x 8 by starting at 2 and counting down eight numbers. Next, show students that moving up the columns reveals the quotients to division problems. Have students find the answer to 16 ÷ 2 by starting at 16 and counting up the column until they reach 2. After providing time for students to explore other problems and their answers, direct each child to cut out both rows of booklet pages and glue them together to make one long strip. Then have each child accordion-fold the pages and keep the resulting booklet as a reference.

ROLLED INTO ONE
Associative property of multiplication

To complete this activity, each group of three needs three dice and a calculator. Direct each student to roll a die; then have the students use the numbers rolled to make and solve as many multiplication sentences as they can. After a few rounds, have groups review their results and identify any patterns that occur. Then lead students to an understanding that the order of the factors doesn't matter—the same multiples always equal the same product.

$2 \times 4 \times 5 = 40$	$4 \times 2 \times 5 = 40$
$5 \times 4 \times 2 = 40$	$2 \times 5 \times 4 = 40$
$4 \times 5 \times 2 = 40$	$5 \times 2 \times 4 = 40$
$1 \times 3 \times 6 = 18$	$1 \times 6 \times 3 = 18$
$3 \times 1 \times 6 = 18$	$3 \times 6 \times 1 = 18$
$6 \times 1 \times 3 = 18$	$6 \times 3 \times 1 = 18$
$2 \times 2 \times 5 = 20$	$2 \times 5 \times 2 = 20$
$5 \times 2 \times 2 = 20$	

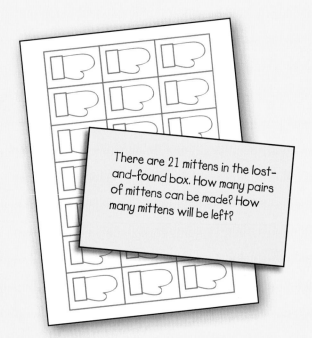

There are 21 mittens in the lost-and-found box. How many pairs of mittens can be made? How many mittens will be left?

SOLVING STUDENT WORK
Division

Each student writes a division word problem on an index card. Then he draws on a blank sheet of paper a grid that has the same number of boxes as the problem's dividend. He draws an image related to the problem in the first box and then repeats the image in the remaining boxes. Collect the problems and papers. Each day as a warm-up, write one problem on the board and have students use a copy of the corresponding manipulatives to solve it.

adapted from an idea by Jennifer Cripe
James Bilbray Elementary, Las Vegas, NV

NEW IDENTITIES
Multiplication facts

Here's an activity that works well as an introduction to multiplication or as a review! First, use a marker to write multiplication problems, each with a different product, on a supply of self-adhesive nametags. Give a tag to each student and tell her to find the product. Then announce that, for the rest of the day, each student will have a new name—the product of her multiplication problem. Refer to each student by her product and encourage students to do the same. For added fun, make and wear a nametag as well!

adapted from an idea by Amanda Gilmore
Beverly Woods Elementary, Charlotte, NC

HELLO
my name is
9 x 3

Turn to page 304 to check out the practice page for this unit!

On the Move

Name _____

©The Mailbox® • TEC43040 • Dec./Jan. 2008–9

1× → ÷1
1
2
3
4
5
6
7
8
9

2× → ÷2
2
4
6
8
10
12
14
16
18

3× → ÷3
3
6
9
12
15
18
21
24
27

4× → ÷4
4
8
12
16
20
24
28
32
36

5× → ÷5
5
10
15
20
25
30
35
40
45

6× → ÷6
6
12
18
24
30
36
42
48
54

7× → ÷7
7
14
21
28
35
42
49
56
63

8× → ÷8
8
16
24
32
40
48
56
64
72

9× → ÷9
9
18
27
36
45
54
63
72
81

Glue

Too Cool

Divide.
Multiply the quotient times the divisor to check your work.

(S)   Check.
 	
 8⟌56   →
 	
      x _____
	(A) Check.
	
	 9⟌72 →
	
	      x _____		

(M)   Check.
 	
 6⟌0   →
 	
      x _____
	(N) Check.
	
	 5⟌25 →
	
	      x _____		

(H)   Check.
 	
 3⟌6   →
 	
      x _____
	(Y) Check.
	
	 7⟌28 →
	
	      x _____
		(F) Check.
		
		 4⟌36 →
		
		      x _____

(E)   Check.
 	
 7⟌42   →
 	
      x _____
	(S) Check.
	
	 8⟌8 →
	
	      x _____
		(O) Check.
		
		 6⟌18 →
		
		      x _____

Why is the movie star so cool?
To solve the riddle, write each letter from above on the numbered
line with its matching quotient.

Because ___ ___ ___ ___ ___ ___ ___ ___ ___ ___ ___ ___ ___ ___ ___!
        7   2   6   2   8   7   1   3   0   8   5   4   9   8   5   7

©The Mailbox® · TEC43040 · Dec./Jan. 2008–9 · Key p. 313

Shapes, Lines, and Angles

Michelle H. Bayless, Harrison Road Elementary, Fredericksburg, VA, and
Carolyn M. Burant, St. John Vianney School, Brookfield, WI

A BALANCED FORM
Finding symmetry

To make this handy visual aid, cut a half-inch slit at the center top and bottom of a 4½" x 6" cardboard rectangle. Slide a 14-inch ribbon into the slits and then tie the ends of the ribbon together. Direct a student to choose a paper shape and slide it under the ribbon. Have him turn the shape to discover whether the shape is symmetrical and, if so, where lines of symmetry occur.

GET THE PICTURE
Identifying and classifying angles

Direct each child to label a large sheet of paper with the headings shown. Then have students cut from magazines or newspapers pictures of objects that have clearly defined angles. Have each child glue her pictures under the matching headings and then trace over the corresponding angles with glitter glue, puff paint, or permanent marker. Display the projects on a board titled "Picturing Angles."

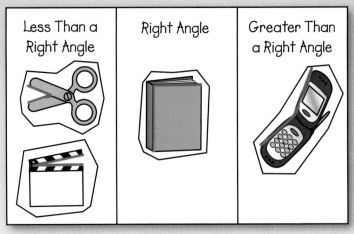

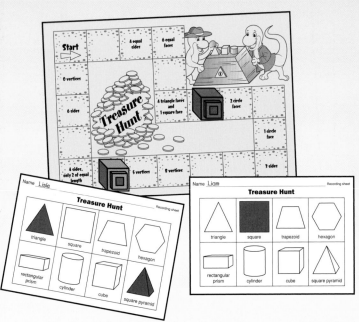

TREASURE HUNT
Identifying plane shapes and solid figures

To play this partner game, each pair needs a copy of the recording sheets on page 307, a copy of the gameboard on page 308, one die, and two game markers. To start, Player 1 rolls the die and moves his marker. If he lands on a space with a description, he reads the description and names the shape. If Player 2 agrees that Player 1 is correct, Player 1 colors the corresponding shape on his recording sheet. If Player 1 gives an incorrect response or lands on a blank space, his turn is over. Player 2 takes a turn in the same manner, and play continues until one student has colored all his shapes.

GEOMETRIC WEB
Identifying plane shapes, lines, and angles

Give each student a piece of masking tape with a different letter written on it, keeping a piece with the letter *A* for yourself. Direct students to sit in a circle; then use your tape piece to secure one end of a ball of yarn to the floor. Roll the yarn to a student and have her tape the yarn to the floor in front of her before she rolls the ball to another child. Continue until every child has placed her tape on the floor; then have students identify geometric shapes they see in the newly created web. Also have students use the letters to name visible lines and angles.

Jessica Catledge, Riverview Elementary, Fort Mill, SC

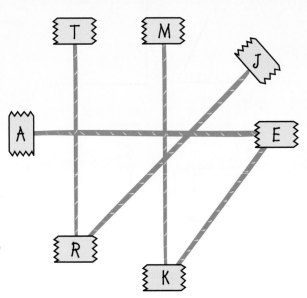

Name _____ Recording sheet

Treasure Hunt

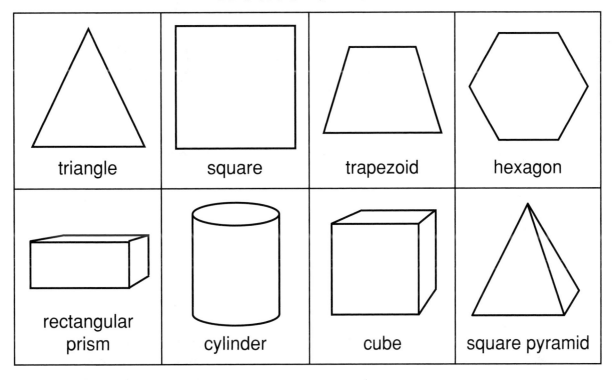

triangle	square	trapezoid	hexagon
rectangular prism	cylinder	cube	square pyramid

Name _____ Recording sheet

Treasure Hunt

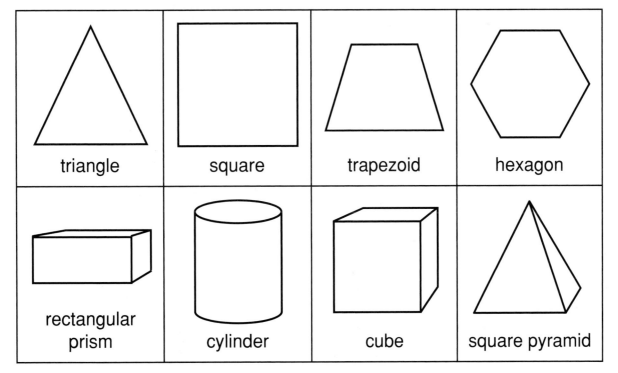

triangle	square	trapezoid	hexagon
rectangular prism	cylinder	cube	square pyramid

Note to the teacher: Use with "Treasure Hunt" on page 306.

THE MAILBOX **307**

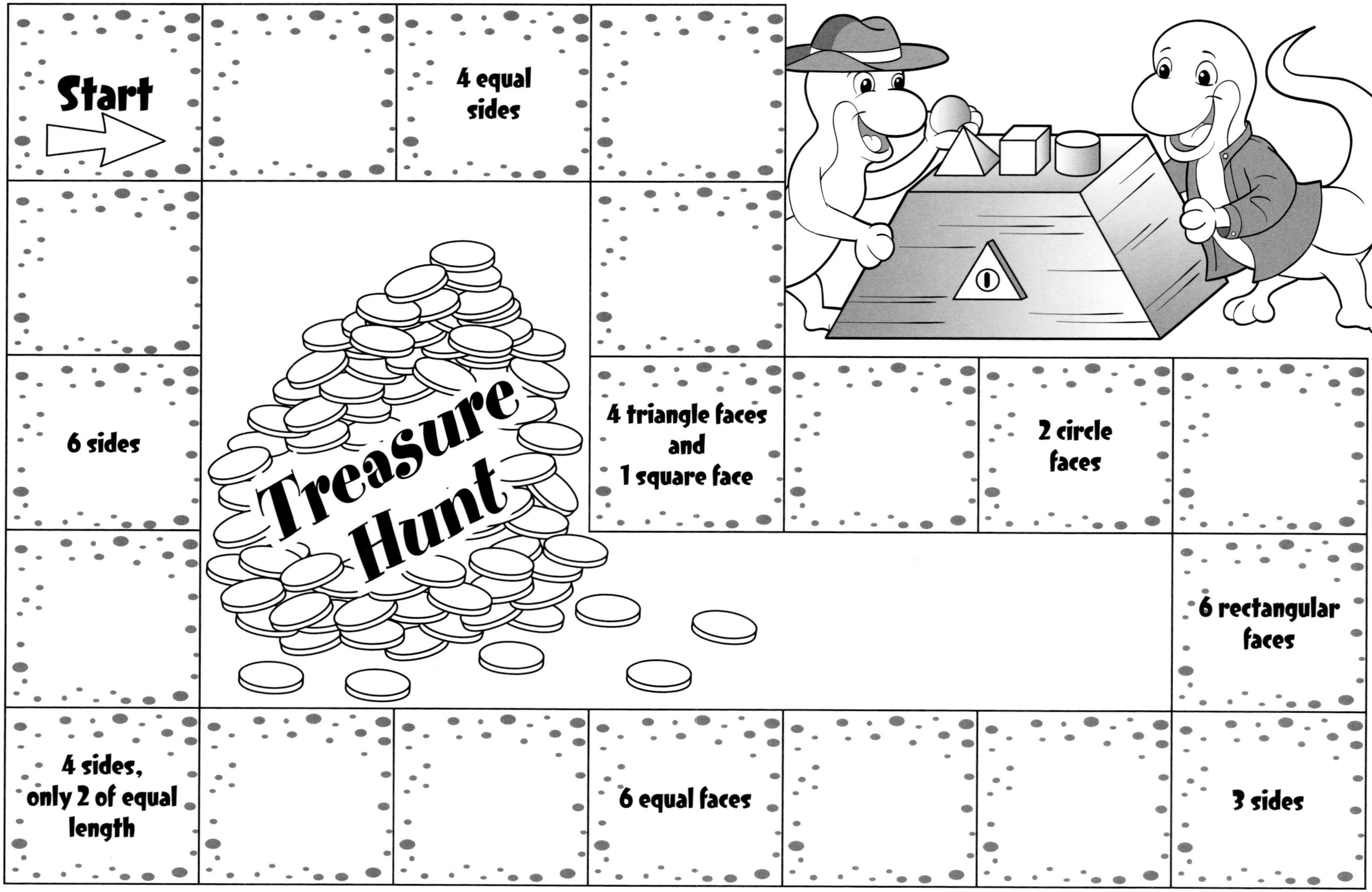

Start ↑

4 equal sides

6 sides

4 triangle faces and 1 square face

2 circle faces

6 rectangular faces

3 sides

6 equal faces

4 sides, only 2 of equal length

Treasure Hunt

©The Mailbox® • TEC43040 • Dec./Jan. 2008–9

Note to the teacher: Use with "Treasure Hunt" on page 306.

Answer Keys

Page 43
sunlight
lightweight
flashlight
lighthouse
doorknob
doorway
doorbell
indoor
housewife
birdhouse
houseboat or boathouse
doghouse

Page 47

1. Why do magicians do so well in school?

| Pencil 1 | 300 They're | 311 good | 325 at | 342 trick | 346 questions. |

2. Where do you go to learn how to make ice cream?

| Pencil 2 | 516 You | 531 go | 534 to | 535 "sundae" | 540 school. |

3. What should you do if you find a gorilla sitting in your desk?

| Pencil 3 | 636 Move | 674 to | 678 a | 682 different | 695 desk! |

4. Why did Sammy the snake have to stay after school?

| Pencil 4 | 825 Because | 846 he | 851 "hissed" | 858 the | 870 bus. |

Page 48

1. grow
2. plants
3. watch
4. buzz
5. begins
6. help
7. choose
8. cuts
9. bakes
10. loves

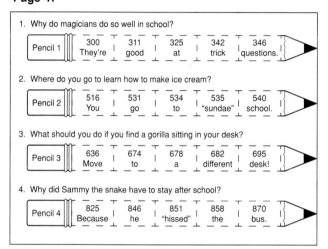

Page 49
1–4.

February 2009						
Sun.	Mon.	Tues.	Wed.	Thurs.	Fri.	Sat.
1	2 G	3	4	5	6	7
8	9	10	11	12	13	14 ♡
15	16 P	17	18	19	20	21
22	23	24	25	26	27	28

5. Friday, February 6
6. February 7
7. Tuesday
8. Sunday; The last day of February is Saturday.

Page 50

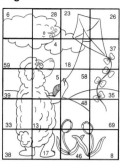

Page 51

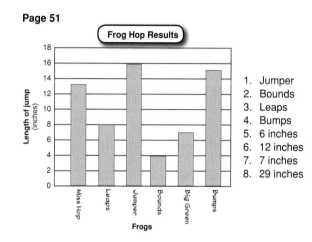

Frog Hop Results

1. Jumper
2. Bounds
3. Leaps
4. Bumps
5. 6 inches
6. 12 inches
7. 7 inches
8. 29 inches

Page 52

1. C	7. L
2. W	8. E
3. R	9. Y
4. E	10. A
5. Y	11. S
6. L	12. C

ALWAYS RECYCLE!

Bonus Box: Answers may vary.
1. Do you know how Earth Day began?
4. What would happen if no one started cleaning the earth?
7. People learned about things that hurt the earth.
8. They also learned how to help the earth.
10. Others planted trees and gardens.
12. What will you do to help?

Page 78

Page 79

1. s <u>c</u> a r c i t y
2. g <u>o</u> o d s
3. <u>n</u> e e d s
4. w a n t <u>s</u>
5. r e s o <u>u</u> r c e s
6. i n c <u>o</u> m e
7. s <u>e</u> r v i c e
8. p <u>r</u> o d u c e r

<u>consumer</u>

Page 81
1. how movies began
2. one
3. projection machine
4. 1905
5. *Steamboat Willie* was made.
6. 1877, 1929

Page 82
Answers may vary.

At the Farm
2. Products from the milk are sent by truck to a factory.

At the Factory
3. Then the ice cream is frozen.
4. The ice cream is put in cartons, and the cartons are put in a hardening room.

At the Store
1. The ice cream is placed in freezers.

Page 103
1. B 2. B
3. A 4. C

Page 109
A. 28 feet
B. 19 feet
C. 45 square feet
D. 36 square feet
E. 22 feet
F. 60 square feet

Page 110
Sentences will vary.

1. snap 2. bug
3. ruler 4. plan
5. tie 6. foot
7. stamp 8. sign
9. trip 10. bill
11. spring 12. wave
13. rock 14. safe

Page 153

			$3 + 4 = 11 - 4$	$12 - 6 \le 5 + 8$	$4 + 6 > 7 + 2$
$8 + 7 > 9 + 4$	$14 - 7 > 13 - 9$	$6 + 5 = 9 + 2$	$18 - 9 = 15 - 6$	$11 - 1 = 3 + 7$	
$15 - 5 \le 18 - 6$	$3 + 8 > 4 + 5$	$13 - 5 \le 9 + 9$	$6 - 5 > 4 - 4$	$2 + 6 = 16 - 8$	
$6 + 12 = 8 + 10$	$8 - 5 = 12 - 9$	$7 + 6 = 16 - 3$	$12 - 4 = 17 - 9$	$7 + 7 = 6 + 8$	
$11 - 5 = 10 - 4$	$9 - 6 \le 7 - 3$	$5 + 9 > 12 - 2$	$8 + 1 > 14 - 6$	$16 - 9 \le 5 + 3$	
$6 + 9 = 17 - 2$	$12 - 8 = 10 - 6$	$14 - 8 = 15 - 9$			

Page 154

Blizzard · Chilly · Frosty · Icy · Snowy

	striped	polka dot	white	plaid	black
Icy	X	X	X	✓	X
Chilly	X	X	✓	X	X
Frosty	X	X	X	X	✓
Blizzard	X	✓	X	X	X
Snowy	✓	X	X	X	X

Page 155

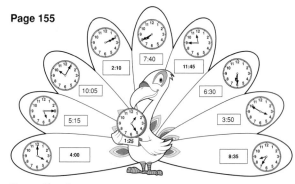

2:10 · 7:40 · 11:45
10:05 · 6:30
5:15 · 3:50
1:25
4:00 · 8:35

Bonus Box: Answers may vary.

Page 156

		butter	eyeglasses
boy	desk		
dog	pumpkin	envelope	paper clip
tree	television	shell	strawberry

pounds　　　　　**ounces**

Bonus Box: Answers may vary.

Page 157

A. 6
B. 12
C. 29
D. 25
E. 9
F. 33
G. 4
H. 3

Page 158

80 x 4 320	320	324	120	124
11 x 7 77	88	77	87	78
33 x 2 66	65	55	66	56
62 x 3 186	185	186	96	95
22 x 4 88	88	66	86	68
40 x 6 240	246	240	100	106
71 x 5 355	126	356	355	125
52 x 4 208	96	98	206	208
31 x 8 248	249	118	248	119
20 x 3 60	50	63	60	53

American　　Swiss　　Cheddar　　Mozzarella

Page 190

Order may vary.

Billy wanted to give his mother some candy for Valentine's Day; He bought some for her at the store.

Brad saw a candy wrapper on the ground; He picked it up and threw it in the trash.

Kelly ate a grape-flavored lollipop; It made her teeth purple.

Tim had some extra candy; He shared it with his brother.

Sarah left a chocolate bar in her backpack; The chocolate bar broke into pieces.

There was no more taffy in the store; Lily bought jelly beans instead.

Zack blew a large bubble, and it popped; The gum was stuck on his nose.

Tina lost the valentine she made for her teacher; She made a new one out of pink paper.

Ken and Susan both wanted the last cupcake; They cut it in half.

Page 198

1. straw
2. sprinkle
3. sprint
4. scratch
5. street
6. sprout
7. scream
8. strange
9. strong
10. scraps
11. spread
12. screen

Page 199

Order may vary.

-ful	-less
bellyful	bottomless
bowlful	endless
forgetful	flawless
frightful	priceless
spoonful	spotless
wishful	wireless

Page 200

Last week I had the flew/<u>flu</u>. My dad took me <u>to</u>/two the doctor. It felt like <u>hours</u>/ours before they were able to see me. When the nurse took me back, he had to way/<u>weigh</u> me. Then he said I had to <u>wear</u>/where a gown. I changed into the gown. Then the nurse had to ask me <u>some</u>/sum questions. I was glad my dad was their/<u>there</u> to help me answer them. Soon the doctor came <u>in</u>/inn. She told me I wood/<u>would</u> not need a shot. She <u>made</u>/maid me agree to drink a lot of juice. She said it would help me <u>heal</u>/he'll faster. The doctor also told my dad I would knead/<u>need</u> plenty of rest to get over the flu. I am happy to report that we followed the doctor's orders and I got better <u>right</u>/write away. Now I feel <u>great</u>/grate!

Bonus Box: Stories will vary. Words to include in the story are *flew, two, ours, way, where, sum, their, inn, wood, maid, he'll, knead, write,* and *grate.*

Page 201

1–4.

★
king (kĭng) *noun* (1.) A man who rules a country. *[George Washington did not want to be called our king.]* (2.) The person or thing thought to be the most powerful in a certain setting. *[The lion is known as the king of the jungle.]* (3.) A game piece in checkers and chess. *[It is important to protect the king when playing chess.] plural* **kings**

5. noun
6. three
7. kings
8. 3
9. 1
10. kingdom; The words are in ABC order, so *kind* would come before *king. Kingdom* would come after *king.*

Page 213

Drawings and descriptions may vary.

1. physical
2. wood to ashes caused by burning, chemical
3. [image] chemical
4. a baby to a child caused by growing, physical
5. [image] physical
6. ingredients to muffins caused by baking, chemical

Page 214

1. A cow has a pad of skin under its ~~lower~~ lip. top
2. A cow uses its ~~teeth~~ to pull on grass. tongue
3. The gap in a cow's mouth helps it ~~mow~~ grass. grab
4. The gap in a cow's mouth is found ~~below~~ the bottom teeth. above
5. A cow swings its ~~tail~~ to tear the grass. head

Page 216

1. An animal dies.
2. Animals like monkeys and toucans feed on the fruit.
3. The seeds are spread.
4. Animals open the pods to eat the pulp inside.

Pages 246 and 247

Rule 1
It can fly. We love summer! Do you want to eat?

Rule 2
Mr. Bug, Dr. Bright, Ms. Night, Airville, Pine City, Palm Beach

Rule 3
Friday, Tuesday, June, July, Flag Day, Father's Day

Rule 4
Dear Fred, Love, Sincerely

Rule 5
Bugville Parade, Wingtown Music Festival, Insectland Air Show

Rule 6
Stone Age, Space Age, Middle Ages

Page 248

Compound Subjects

1. Many men, women, and children play golf.
4. Woods and irons are two types of golf clubs.
5. Chris and Joy play golf every Friday.
8. Joy and Anna always have very good scores.
9. Chris and Ryan do not play so well.

Compound Predicates

2. A golf course is grassy and often has sand traps.
3. A golfer swings a club and hits the golf ball.
6. Sometimes they play with Anna and invite Ryan too.
7. These golfers spend hours talking and playing the course.
10. They all like the fresh air and enjoy the exercise.

Page 252

1. It
2. He
3. It
4. They
5. He
6. He
7. She
8. They
9. She
10. they
11. She
12. It

Page 253

1. (tongue) of a (frog)
   a frog's tongue
2. (rays) of the (sun)
   the sun's rays
3. (bill) of a (duck)
   a duck's bill
4. (edge) of the (water)
   the water's edge
5. (shell) of a (turtle)
   a turtle's shell
6. (egg) of a (tadpole)
   a tadpole's egg
7. (wings) of a (heron)
   a heron's wings
8. (leaves) of a (tree)
   a tree's leaves
9. (fins) of a (fish)
   a fish's fins
10. (stem) of a (plant)
    a plant's stem

Page 215

Answers may vary.

1. a kind of turtle that only lives on land and has a high, domed shell
2. newly hatched tortoises
3. to live

Bonus Box: Diagrams will vary.

Page 254

Did you know that the <u>first</u> time the Fourth of July was celebrated, back in 1777, fireworks were used? That's what my <u>good</u> friend Poppy told me. He knows all about these <u>exciting</u> displays. Poppy's <u>favorite</u> pastime is watching fireworks. He loves to hear the <u>loud</u> noises they make. He also enjoys their <u>colorful</u> sparks. Poppy told me that fireworks have <u>different</u> names, such as spider, cake, and willow. A willow has <u>silver</u> or <u>gold</u> sparks. The sparks fan out like a <u>willow</u> tree. Poppy always reminds me that fireworks are <u>fun</u> to watch but that they can be <u>unsafe</u>. He says they should only be used by experts.

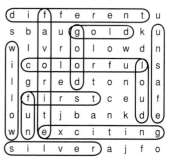

Page 259

1. His grandparents were visiting. He didn't see them very often.
2. Answers will vary. Possible answers include the following: he opens the box, his family walks in, and his family is disappointed in him; he peeks in the box and then reseals it; Devon waits for his family to come home, and his family lets him open the box.
3. Devon was sad because his grandparents were not there when he got home. Then Devon was happy because there was a box with his name on it.
4. Answers will vary. Possible answers include that the setting and character were named at the beginning, there is a problem, and the main character is an animal.

Page 264

1. place
2. quiet
3. kind
4. read
5. sink
6. equal
7. harm
8. heat
9. wash
10. sudden
11. plan
12. appear
13. flavor
14. look
15. view

Bonus Box: Sentences will vary.

Page 269

Sentences will vary. Possible sentences include the following:

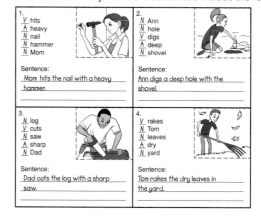

Page 282

Order may vary.

Listen to Learn
Joe gives a report about the moon.
Sue talks about jungle animals.
Cole tells about his trip to the zoo.

Listen to Follow Directions
Ben tells how to make a paper bird.
Jake tells how to build a castle out of blocks.
Ms. Lee explains how to line up quietly.

Listen to Be Entertained
Ty recites a poem.
Bart sings a song before the school play.
Claire tells jokes and riddles.

Page 287

A. 621
B. 166
C. 664
D. 901
E. 358
F. 790
G. 427
H. 149

(4 2 (7) (9 0) (1 (6 6 4) 4) 3 1 (3 5 8) (6 2 (1) 4 9)

Page 291

A. 3, 7, 11, 15, 19, 23, 27; 27 push-ups
B. 36, 34, 32, 30, 28, 26; 26 minutes
C. 18, 23, 28, 33; 33 minutes
D. 5, 10, 20, 40; 40 sit-ups
E. 74, 68, 62, 56, 50; 50 times

Page 295

Bonus Box:
A. 3 + 3 + 3 + 3 + 3 + 3 + 3 + 3 = 24
B. 6 + 6 = 12
C. 4 + 4 + 4 + 4 = 16
D. 7 + 7 + 7 + 7 + 7 = 35
E. 4 + 4 + 4 + 4 + 4 + 4 + 4 = 28
F. 9 + 9 + 9 = 27
G. 1 + 1 + 1 + 1 + 1 + 1 = 6
H. 8 + 8 + 8 + 8 + 8 + 8 + 8 + 8 + 8 + 8 = 80

Page 290

A. add 4, 24
B. subtract 2, 6
C. add 5, 33
D. add 6, 38
E. subtract 3, 7
F. add 10, 67
G. subtract 10, 39
H. add 9, 54

Page 299

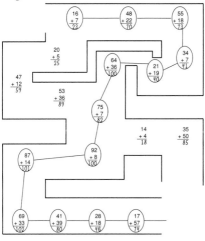

Page 300

Page 304

(S) 8)56 → 7	Check. 7 x 8 56	(A) 9)72 → 8	Check. 8 x 9 72	
(M) 6)0 → 0	Check. 0 x 6 0	(N) 5)25 → 5	Check. 5 x 5 25	
(H) 3)6 → 2	Check. 2 x 3 6	(Y) 7)28 → 4	Check. 4 x 7 28	(F) 4)36 → 9 Check. 9 x 4 36
(E) 7)42 → 6	Check. 6 x 7 42	(S) 8)8 → 1	Check. 1 x 8 8	(O) 6)18 → 3 Check. 3 x 6 18

Because <u>SHE HAS SO MANY FANS!</u>

ISBN-13: 978-156234923-3
ISBN-10: 156234923-6

9 781562 349233